THE REINCARNATION OF RUSSIA

THE REINCARNATION

OF RUSSIA ❋ *Struggling with the*

Legacy of Communism, 1990–1994

John Löwenhardt

DUKE UNIVERSITY PRESS   *Durham 1995*

Printed in the United States of America on acid-free paper ∞
Typeset in Trump Mediaeval by Tseng Information Systems, Inc.
Library of Congress Cataloging-in-Publication Data appear
on the last printed page of this book.

CONTENTS

PREFACE

Work on this book was started in July 1993 at the Slavic Research Center of Hokkaido University in Japan, which provided me with the luxury of nine months of uninterrupted research. Watching the NHK news broadcast on the evening of 9 August, I was struck by the symbolism of the confluence of two news items: the installation of the new coalition government and the commemoration in Nagasaki of the atomic bomb explosion that had destroyed the city forty-eight years earlier. Standing to the left of the emperor, outgoing prime minister Kiichi Miyazawa made a deep bow to the newly elected Morihiro Hosokawa, and with both hands he held the documents legalizing the transfer of power to the new government almost over his bent head. The orderly transfer of power after thirty-eight years of uninterrupted rule by the Liberal Democratic Party signaled a momentous event not only for Japan, but also in the history of democracy. The political system that had been forced on Japan by the occupying power had, since the departure of the Americans in 1952, been adapted to Japanese traditions. In the 1970s and 1980s many observers had started to ask whether in spite of the name of the ruling party, Japanese democracy, with its factions and powerful bureaucracy, state-steered economy, and corruption scandals, had much in common with "real" liberal democracy. But the elections of 1993, and the resulting transfer of power showed that Japanese democracy had withstood the test of time: the formative period was finally over when Hosokawa, representing a coalition of seven political parties and one parliamentary group, accepted the government documents from the hands of Miyazawa and could start political reform.

At the time, Russia was undergoing an extremely painful transition process, which, four months later, brought Russia's own (but very different) "Liberal Democratic Party" a major victory in free parliamentary elections. One might perhaps say that the transformation might have been easier had Russia been defeated by foreign powers, the way Germany and Japan had been. In a period of less than forty years after World War II, Germany and Japan had developed into two of the world's major powers; their demand for a permanent seat in the UN Security Council was not misplaced. In more than one respect, their miraculous recovery from total defeat had been due to the imposition of foreign stewardship and the fact that some of the principles of their postwar political and economic systems had been formulated for them. Russia, too, was guided by foreign constraints (as a precondition of financial help) and advice, but its domestic political forces had not been shattered the way they had been in Germany and Japan. Ever since Russia had proclaimed sovereignty on 12 June 1990, the reform-minded government of Yeltsin, Gaidar, and the Democratic Russia movement had been under increasing pressure from ultranationalists and communists determined not to allow a "Westernization" of the Russian state and society.

Studying Russia in Japan, one cannot help being struck by some of the analogies. At the time of this writing, both countries were plagued by corruption scandals characteristic of transition periods. Both countries adopted new electoral systems that showed striking similarities both in their aims and in the way these were translated into detailed rules. In both countries the essential problem was how to carry out a fundamental reform that would harm entrenched interests, with the exclusive use of constitutional means partly expressing such interests. Both countries, too, experienced the dilemma of trying to keep up with the rest of the world while redefining their identity.

But all these are side issues. This book is not about Russia and Japan. This book deals with the first four years of Russia's transformation from being the core (and founding) republic of the communist empire to that of a renewed and reduced state, desperately searching for its place in the world. Russian political history is presented here in the context of empirical findings on the transition from authoritarianism, and of the social changes underlying the reforms started by Gorbachev and continued by Yeltsin. The political history per se is condensed into two chapters in which—no question about it—I present only part of the multifaceted developments that in 1990–1994 transformed Russia with breakneck speed. Some aspects, such as the role of the media, the churches, and the courts, the details of economic legislation, and the wars on Russia's southern borders, will remain underexposed. But the main aim of this book is not to present an all-embracing history of "Russia after the Soviet Union." It is to test the alleged uniqueness of Russia against experiences with transition elsewhere in the world. Four years ago today, the Russian parliament declared its sovereignty. Now the Soviet Union is gone, and an impoverished Russia is its most important heir. But the country's transition from communist dictatorship to "something else" is not over yet, and we are well advised to keep in mind that the outcome of transitions is not necessarily a stable liberal democracy.

I would like to thank a few people. First: my wife Vera. Without her support and the irresistible smiles of our newborn daughter Hannah, this book would have been much more difficult to write. Then there are my Japanese, American, and Dutch colleagues, for their good fellowship and friendship. The book could not have been written but for the sound advice and frequent entertainments provided by my American colleague in Sapporo, the exuberant Sabrina Ramet, and it would not have been published by Duke University Press if it were not for her kind offices. The long dinner table discussions with Sabrina and her spouse Christine Hassenstab in our snowbound *gaijin* den brightened the long Hokkaido winter. I wish to express my sincere gratitude to Hokkaido University's Slavic Research Center for providing me with one of the 1993–1994 Foreign Visiting Fellowships and to its then director Shugo Minagawa and its former director Hiroshi Kimura for their fellowship and friendship; through them I thank all staff members of the Center for their kindness and support. Parts of the manuscript were read by Ger van den Berg, Erik Dirksen, Huib Hendrikse, Joke Hindriks-Stolker, Tetsuo Mochizuki, Shinichiro Tabata, and by my students; I greatly appreciated their comments; they are in no way responsible for mistakes or misinterpretations remaining in the text. I thank the Law Department of Leiden University for allowing me a leave of absence of an unusual nine months; and my colleagues at the Institute of East European Law and Russian Studies and the Political Science Department, who stood in for me during my absence from the effervescent academic scene of Leiden University. Valerie Millholland of Duke University Press bestowed help with almost Slavic verve, as did her colleague Jean Brady; and John Benson melded precision and perception in his copyediting. Finally, I should thank Leonard Peters and Maria van Ruiten for their excellent work as my home-based research assistants during the last two months in Japan;

Titia Bouma for being there when I needed her and for her e- and snail-mail communications; and last but not least my most faithful and trust-worthy companion in Sapporo, Van Dale's stout *Groot woordenboek Nederlands-Engels* (1986).

Leiden, 12 June 1994

ABBREVIATIONS

APSA	American Political Science Association
APSR	American Political Science Review
CBR	Central Bank of the Russian Federation
CC	Constitutional Commission
CEC	Central Electoral Commission
CIS	Commonwealth of Independent States
CPSU	Communist Party of the Soviet Union
CSCE	Conference on Security and Cooperation in Europe
DMR	Dniester Moldavian Republic
DPR	Democratic Party of Russia
DR	Democratic Russia
FNPR	Federation of Independent Trade Unions of Russia
GKCHP	State Committee for the State of Emergency in the USSR
LDP	Liberal Democratic Party
MID	Ministry of Foreign Affairs
NPG	Independent Union of Miners
NPSR	People's Party of Free Russia
PR	Proportional Representation
PRES	Party of Russian Unity and Harmony
RCPD	RSFSR / Russian Federation Congress of People's Deputies
RF	Russian Federation / Russia
RSFSR	Russian Soviet Federative Socialist Republic
RSPP	Russian Union of Industrialists and Entrepreneurs
RSS	RSFSR / Russian Federation Supreme Soviet
SIP	Soviet Interview Project

SOTSPROF	Association of Socialist (later: Social) Trade Unions
UCPD	USSR Congress of People's Deputies
UN	United Nations
USS	Union of Sovereign States (intended new name for USSR); in Chronology: USSR Supreme Soviet
USSR	Union of Soviet Socialist Republics
VR	Russia's Choice
VTSIOM	All-Union Center for Public Opinion Research

For abbreviations of journals and newspapers used in the notes, see the Bibliography.

A NOTE ON TRANSLITERATION

For the transliteration of Russian words and names the author has used an adaptation of the Library of Congress system. The ligature (⌒ in transliterating ц, ю, and я) has been neglected, resulting in ts, iu, and ia. In the case of Ю or Я, when these are the first letter of a name, they have been transliterated, respectively, as Yu or Ya, and the Е as Ye; thus Yazov and Yeltsin instead of Iazov and Eltsin. The newspaper Известия (*Izvestiia*) has been transliterated as *Izvestia*. In the text (not in notes and bibliography) the cyrillic "soft sign" (ь) has been neglected in transliteration— thus Yeltsin instead of Yel'tsin, and *glasnost* for *glasnost'*. The cyrillic ё (pronounced as yo) has been transliterated as e (Gorbachev instead of Gorbachov), but for personal names the correct pronunciation is given between brackets in the Index. In some cases Russian given names have not been transliterated, but the English equivalent has been used: Alexander instead of Aleksandr, Victor for Viktor. For almost all persons the Index lists the first name and father's name.

THE REINCARNATION OF RUSSIA

Anadyr

Chukchi AOk

Bering Sea

Koriak AOk

Palana

Magadan

Kamchatka

aimyr AOk

Sakha-Yakutia

Sea of Okhotsk

Evenkii AOk

Yakutsk

Kuril
Islands

Sakhalin

asnoiarsk

Amur

Yuzhno-Sakhalinsk

Krasnoiarsk

Buriatia

Blagoveshchensk

Khabarovsk

Hokkaido

17

bakan

Chita

Primorsk

Irkutsk

16

2

Sea of
Japan

Kyzyl

Ulan Ude

Vladivostok

Tuva

CHINA

Russian Federation

MONGOLIA

⭐ National Capital

Tomsk o City / Oblast or Krai Name

International Boundary

Republic, Oblast or Krai Boundary

Autonomous Area (AOk) Boundary

Komi Republic, Oblast or Krai Name

Oblasts or Krais have the same name as
their capital unless otherwise noted.

0   Kilometers   800

0   Miles   800

Key to Numbered Regions

1 Adygei
2 Aginsk Buriat AOk
3 Chechnia / Ingushetia
4 Chuvashia
5 Dagestan
6 Kabardino-Balkaria
7 Kalmykia
8 Karachaevo-
   Cherkessia
9 Khakassia
10 Komi-Permiatskii AOk
11 Krasnodarskii Krai
12 Mari-El
13 Mordova
14 Northern Ossetia
15 Udmurtia
16 Ust-Ordynskii Buriatskii AOk
17 Jewish Autonomous Oblast

INTRODUCTION

Today Eastern Europe is a bit like the description of the world in Genesis prior to the clear delineations between night and day, water and land. . . . The Eastern European environment is one of clots—political, social, ideological, economic—that have yet to coagulate into a coherent form (and of course there is no guarantee that coherence in any form will emerge). (Ken Jowitt, 1990) [1]

Russia does not have a face—and if she has one, it expresses not dignity but confusion and anguish. (Stanislav Kondrashov, November 1992) [2]

Political analysis presupposes the existence of a polity that is being studied—the word *polity* referring to a political community of which both the geographic and the conceptual borders are unambiguously clear. If one steps outside the border of the polity, its most important institution—the state—has no authority; if one steps inside the polity, the state can and will make laws, have them executed, collect taxes and distribute revenues over the population, stimulate economic development, and maintain law and order. Often, there is no question about the limitations of polities. No one will doubt that the United States is a clear-cut political community, although its federal nature will compel us to analyze political life in terms of several layers of polities, such as the country (federation) as a whole, and the fifty states of which it consists. Spain, Uruguay, Egypt, and Thailand are clear-cut polities, as was Chile under Pinochet—the fact that it was ruled by a dictatorship being of no significance here.

But polities change, and at times the citizens of countries may become thoroughly confused about the question of which polity they live in—or whether the country in which they live actually *is* a political community. The West German polity recently absorbed the German Democratic Republic. During 1989–1990, in the process that led up to unification, the West German government was forced to recognize existing German-Polish borders and to renounce explicitly any expansionist claims. The lands in the East were incorporated into the German Federal Republic and became subject to its effective state power. Serious economic problems and social tensions between *Ossies* and *Wessies* notwithstanding, both to the German population at large and to the outside observer, there can be no doubt that a new German polity exists and that its borders are clearly defined.

The same cannot be said for other countries that are going through the transition from communism to a free society. Poland, the Czech lands, Hungary, Romania, Albania, Slovenia, Ukraine, Belarus, and the Baltic states present relatively easy cases where a polity is seen to exist. Such polity exists in spite of occasional irredentist claims, the weakness of the state, or conflicts over the definition of citizenship. But post-Yugoslavia and Russia present serious cases of polity anemia.[*]

What is Russia? What defines Russia? And what defines its inhabitants? Where does Russia lie? Where are its borders? Are the Chechen and Tatar republics, successfully resisting rule from Moscow, part of the Russian Federation / Russia? And what about a thoroughly Russian province such as Volgograd, where the provincial soviet in the spring of 1993 declared that the area was a state? If the representative institutions of Russian and non-Russian territories inside the state borders of the Russian Federation decide, for reasons of political expediency, to declare their "independence," what is left of a basic feeling of community that should cement the polity?

The fall of empires will create long periods of uncertainty and instability during which new polities, and new alignments between them, come about. In some of the countries, the new or not-so-new elites that have taken over or inherited state power have a relatively easy time in defining their polity. Lithuania, for example, though only a fraction of the size it had once been in the fourteenth and fifteenth centuries, exited the collapse of the USSR as a clearly defined political community. This was due to several facts. First, the population of the country was homogeneous to a high degree, over 80 percent being Roman Catholic

---

[*] In this book the word Russia is used synonymously with the Russian Federation, unless otherwise indicated.

Lithuanians. Second, after the establishment of Soviet rule at the beginning of World War II, the Lithuanians had never fully given in to Russian domination. Guerrilla warfare against the occupying forces had lasted into the 1950s, and the next decade saw the rise of one of the strongest nationalist-religious dissident movements in the USSR. Finally, during the Gorbachev era the Lithuanian national elite had been among the first to demand liberation from Russian domination. By presenting party general secretary Gorbachev with impossible dilemmas, small Lithuania had made a significant contribution to the collapse of the USSR empire. In December 1989, Lithuanian communists led by Algirdas Brazauskas had been the first to sever relations with the CPSU's Moscow headquarters, and on 11 March 1990 the Lithuanian parliament had been the first to declare formal independence from the USSR. Small wonder that after their independence was consummated, the Lithuanians had no problem defining their polity.

The fifteen former republics of the USSR ended their cohabitation within the formal internal borders which separated them in late 1991. Some of them, such as Russia, Ukraine, and Lithuania, had by that time concluded treaties (implying that they were independent states before this was, in fact, the case) in which both parties had rejected claims to each other's territory. But all of them, with the possible exception of Armenia and Lithuania, inherited from the USSR a complicated ethnic situation and an administrative system that had been designed by Stalin with the exclusive aim to *divide et impera* (divide and rule). It was, as communists used to say, "no accident" that the Nagornyi Karabakh Autonomous Province, with its Armenian (Christian) population, was situated in Muslim Azerbaijan, subject to rule from Baku and separated by a corridor from Armenia, whereas the Azeri-populated Nakhichevan Autonomous Republic, subordinated to Baku as well, was situated between Armenia and the Iranian border. In the Abkhazian Autonomous Republic, situated in and subordinated to Georgia, only a minority of the population were of Abkhazian origin. Ossetia was divided into a North Ossetian Autonomous Republic located just inside the southern border of the RSFSR (the Soviet name of the Russian Federation), and a South Ossetian Autonomous Province on the Georgian side of the RSFSR-Georgian border. The first was ruled from Moscow, the second from Tbilisi.

The political elites of the fifteen newborn states had to face the challenge of accepting mixed populations within fixed borders and creating stable polities for them. In several of these states, particularly Latvia, Estonia, Azerbaijan, and Georgia, secessionist movements made it difficult for the new elites to resist the nationalist temptation, that is, policies aimed at reaching a nation-state with a homogeneous population. Many of them gave in to these pressures. As a result, the Caucasus has been plagued by war since 1989.

For Boris Yeltsin and the new Russian rulers, the task was even more forbidding than in the other successor states. In Armenia and Lithuania, in Uzbekistan and Georgia, it was at least obvious to the new elites what they had to prevent at all costs (renewed domination by Moscow) and on what nation their polities were to be based. The Russians were alone in facing a profound identity crisis after their empire had collapsed. They had internalized an image of themselves as a grand people that had created an empire stretching from Helmstedt in Germany to the Bering Strait, an empire in which they provided leadership to more than a hundred nations in their march to the radiant future of a communist society. With the exception of a handful of independent thinkers, Russians had come to believe not all, but some, of the grandiose claims of Soviet propaganda. At times, some of the subjects had been obstinate and quarrelsome—the Hungarians in 1956, the Czechs and Slovaks in 1968, the Poles forever—but ultimately, and after a little help from Soviet tanks, all of them had made the right decision and had yielded to Russia. To many Russians it was literally incomprehensible that within twenty-six months after the Berlin Wall fell on 9 November 1989, East Germany had become part of the German Federal Republic, and Hungary, Poland and Czechoslovakia, Uzbekistan and Estonia, and even Russia's "own" Ukraine had become independent states.

IDENTITY CRISIS

The loss of empire triggered a profound identity crisis. Political debates in journals and newspapers centered on the question of how to define Russia and the Russians. Old concepts, such as the uniqueness of *Rossiiane* (the people linking Asia with Europe, as compared to the ethnic Russians, *Russkie*), were resurrected. New bones of contention were easily found, such as the sometimes shaky position of Russians in the newly independent states. Political careers were made on the basis of the shameless politicization of ethnicity. Meanwhile, the Russian Federation itself continued to disintegrate as republics declared their sovereignty or independence and provincial soviets issued statements on the statehood of their territories. These developments were not of a declaratory nature only. They reflected a real breakdown of the executive powers of the center in Moscow. By the summer of 1993, Russia seemed to have become a collection of widely divergent regions, all more or less going their own way. The lands that had been "gathered" by the tsars of Russia were drifting apart.

To be sure, the central leadership in Moscow did try to hold the country together. But because of the lack of agreement on the definition of Russia, Yeltsin and his team seemed to be going around and around in a vicious circle. Until the dissolution of parliament in September 1993, they tried to make a revolution—a speedy transition from communism to democracy—using legal means, which of course was impossible. By definition, a revolution represents a break in the legal (constitutional) order, so that even a revolution which results in some form of democracy cannot be effected in a democratic way. Had Yeltsin used the confusion and momentum of the weeks following the failed August coup of 1991, he could probably have unleashed a real revolution with some real results. But he went on vacation to Sochi in order to reflect on the new situation. When he reappeared, the moment for revolution had passed. Two years later he regretted this "most important missed opportunity."[3]

This is not to say that nothing was accomplished at all. A confused beginning was made with economic transition. The conflict with Ukraine that erupted immediately upon independence was effectively de-escalated by Yeltsin, who worked more or less in tandem with Ukrainian president Leonid Kravchuk. In March 1992, representatives of over eighty republics and regions of the Russian Federation signed new federative agreements and gave an initial impetus to the process of creating real federative relationships. That same month, representatives of ten out of the eleven CIS member states signed an agreement on military observers and the collective peacekeeping forces of the CIS, and in May, Russia signed a collective security treaty with Armenia, Kazakhstan, Kyrgyzstan, Tajikistan, and Uzbekistan.

SHORTCUT TO DEMOCRACY?

But at the same time conflict erupted between the democratically elected president Yeltsin and the less democratically, but not wholly undemocratically, elected Russian federal parliament. Soon, the conflict was seen in the West as one between "democrats" and "excommunist nationalists," between good guys and bad guys, with Yeltsin and his team representing good democrats and parliamentary speaker Khasbulatov and the majority that he stood for representing the forces of the bad. But the conflict was too complicated and too fundamental to allow such easy stereotypes. Labeling the contending parties "democrats" and "ex-communists" implied that a new Russian polity with clear conceptual borders and with a vertical and horizontal delimitation of powers could be designed within a short span of time by reasonable people of good will. It denied the simple truth that a fundamental upheaval such as Russia was going through could not take place without political strife. Transition to democracy "is by no means a linear or a rational process."[4] Only in exceptional cases, such as the defeated Germany and Japan in 1945, could a new constitutional order be imposed on an old country; and such *démocratie octroyée* proved to be highly successful. Russia in 1992 was beaten, but not defeated; it had brought the collapse of its empire about and upon itself. Naturally, it had great difficulty in accepting the demands of the World Bank, the IMF, and Western governments and in accepting the well-meant advice of Western economists. For Third World elites, such a position was difficult; for the new Russian elite, accustomed as it was to seeing their country as a great power, it was all but impossible.

The Russian polity was to be reincarnated on its own, in a painful struggle that any people would have to undergo if they are to establish a political community. Political systems grow; they are the always incomplete outcome of a process where different social interests fight for dominance or for an equal place under the sun, for a constitutional order that protects minorities, separates powers, and guarantees the rights of individuals. Neither in France nor in the United States, Britain, or Brazil has such order come about without a fight. The sometimes maddening struggle between the Russian president and parliament, therefore, had an unmistakable historical function. Those who demanded a shortcut to democracy did Russia a disservice.

THE SOVIET SYNDROME . . .

The loss of empire was only one of two legacies that traumatized Russia in the 1990s and that impeded recovery from the shock.[5] The other legacy was that of the communist power system. This legacy, which I have earlier called the Soviet Syndrome, is a deadly mixture of symptoms that paralyzes normal political intercourse.[6] The Soviet system, after all, had been based on the negation of politics. It had banished free political strife with its inevitable uncertain outcome, and had replaced political parties by a select group of "seers" who claimed exclusive knowledge of scientific laws governing social development and who were, in their own view of course, in a unique position where they could decide what was best for society and for all of its segments. Nevertheless, the communists had been extremely resourceful in inventing all sorts of surrogate politics that served to simulate free political life. And their subjects had been equally creative at finding ways to simulate participation in a system many of them despised. These included "elections without choice" that demanded of the voters that they go through almost all the motions that voters in a democratic country go through; a parliament with separate chambers and standing committees that never in half a century voted other than unanimously; and public discussion of policy issues in newspapers and journals, stimulated by the Communist Party—but which never made more than a marginal difference to policies that were ultimately adopted by the wise men on the Politburo.

The role-playing of Soviet quasi-politics was supported from the wings by a communist director who provided watchful prompting. All participants in the play knew that improvising, spontaneous behavior, or independent thought were not appreciated. They were to stick to the script. If not, there were swift sanctions such as harassment, social isolation, dismissal, or a straight prison or camp term. Since Stalin, everybody knew that an inadvertent word or a careless act could destroy one's life. Sincerity was a quality not appreciated in the Soviet Union. Chicanery, intrigue, and hypocrisy were qualities that produced power and wealth. Those who preferred to stay sincere learned to keep their mouths closed—or prepared for prison.

No one was to be surprised when, in the 1990s, the Russians—like many other peoples in Central and Eastern Europe traumatized by Russian communism—proved incapable of quickly turning into reasonable, restrained, and retiring citizens. Too many traumas had to be overcome, too many old accounts had to be settled, too many vested interests were at stake, and too many misconceptions about normal politics had to be corrected. Inevitably, such a process was to take a long time.

Moreover, the transformation of Russia from a Soviet republic into a new polity was characterized by a set of impossibilities that could not be accepted for what they were. Trying to turn a quasi-federation into a real federation was an impossible mission with steerage from a discredited center, and Moscow was indeed discredited, since the place had been the center of both the USSR and the RSFSR, as well as a center that was seen as the locus of oppression and exploitation. Creating a law-governed state and a representative democracy for a society severely traumatized by centuries of autocracy and over seven decades of communist dictatorship was but to ask for trouble. Creating political parties and expecting a party system to develop in the absence of a developed civil society and of developed socioeconomic interests was an exercise in naïveté. Combining economic and political transformation was a Sisyphean struggle; one author referred to it as "the necessity and impossibility of simultaneous economic and political reform."[7] Trying to force a new constitution on a state and a society through the mediation of old politicians and institutions such as the Congress of People's Deputies amounted to a denial of the essence of the constitutional process.

And yet, the new elites of Russia had no choice but to engage in this losing battle. The Soviet Union was gone. The former Soviet republics were "lost." The Communist Party had peacefully disbanded. Its army of *apparatchiks* had gone into state administration and had quietly shifted their allegiances. The Soviet armed forces were no more, and the new Russian army lacked basic cohesion and morale. Inflation continued to soar, the rate of the ruble against the dollar continued to drop, and production dropped even more. By 1993 the country was struggling for its survival. There was no way back, even the road back to autocracy or dictatorship seemed to be cut off because of the weakness of the armed forces and the presidency. Ahead was an uphill struggle for the establishment of a minimum of order and cohesion.

But as the period covered in this book drew to a close, many in Russia and in the West had started to have serious doubts about whether postcommunism could evolve toward democracy. Perhaps a relapse into authoritarianism was, if not inevitable, at least very likely. Many authors were pessimistic, although some felt that an authoritarian relapse could not last for long. Leslie Holmes, for example, argued that the population would soon demand consumer goods in return for (temporary) dictatorship, that Western governments would hesitate to support such authoritarian regimes, and that the intellectuals had recently gained experience in how to overthrow them.[8] Others pointed to the West's overpowering interest in stability, even more so in the 1990s than in the period 1945–1948. They referred to President Roosevelt, who, for the sake of a "partnership in peace" following World War II, had closed his eyes (and ears) to the threat of Russian domination over Central Europe. They assumed that, for the same reason, Western governments were now prepared to support an authoritarian Russian government.[9]

Soon after the euphoria of 1989–1990, political scientists started to warn that a transition to democracy was not at all easy, because the problems of postcommunist states were much bigger than those of Latin American or Southern European countries that had recently "converted." Particularly after Yeltsin had disbanded parliament and after blood was shed in the "October events" of 1993, it came into fashion to speak of a return to dictatorship under "Tsar Boris." One of the main aims of this book is to bring more transparency to this issue by analyzing the Russian events from the perspective of experiences with transitions from autocracy elsewhere.

In their concluding volume to a series of studies on transitions from authoritarian rule, Guillermo O'Donnell and Philippe Schmitter comment on one of the central, but often neglected, principles of such transitions. This so-called "Stern Principle" is of relevance for Russia today. It states that the factors which were necessary and sufficient for provoking the collapse or self-transformation of these regimes may be neither necessary nor sufficient to ensure the installation of another regime, least of all a democracy.[10] In this book I hope to show the working of this principle in the context of the transition of Russia from communist dictatorship to . . . something else.

The book deals with a closely limited time period of three and a half years, between Russia's Declaration of State Sovereignty (12 June 1990) and its general elections and plebiscite of 12 December 1993. At the beginning of this period, Russia was still part of the USSR. On the last day of the period, its population, by plebiscite, adopted their first postcommunist constitution.

. . . AND THE TOTALITARIAN TEMPTATION

During the convulsive 1986–1990 period, the image of Gorbachev leading the Soviet Union from communist dictatorship to capitalist democracy descended upon the Western public through their journalists and politicians. Because of the nature of their craft, journalists have to report on, and respond quickly to, events; politicians are faced with demands to adapt their policies to changing circumstances while remaining responsive to the general mood of the public. Both were easily impressed by Gorbachev, and both responded with great, and often thoughtless, enthusiasm.

Specialists in the field of Soviet and Eastern European studies have in general been more guarded concerning the wisdom of Gorbachev's endeavors, his chances at success in reaching his stated objectives, and the malleability of Soviet society. Some Soviet specialists, carried away by the recognition they suddenly received from the Kremlin, displayed a noncritical attitude. But they were few and far between, and they were not generally supported by their colleagues.

When, after 1989, the Soviet empire fell apart, the Soviet Union ceased to exist, and the security situation throughout the world underwent fundamental change, politicians were the first to blame Soviet specialists for the difficult circumstances that they now suddenly found themselves in and for which they were unprepared. In their desire to cling to easy stereotypes, they had failed to listen to those whose job it had been to analyze the situation in Russia and its empire. In their enthusiasm for Gorbachev's "new thinking" and its prospective fruits for Western security, they had failed to back up their policy changes with sound advice on what a future world might look like. Their response to the disintegration of Yugoslavia and the Soviet Union was uninformed and erratic. Later, when the implementation of arms limitation treaties was in jeopardy, Western governments and international organizations panicked.

The reproaches of politicians have led some scholars in the field to look inward and to blame themselves and the community of area specialists for not preventing or at least predicting the breakdown of the communist empire. For example, Timothy Garton Ash stated in 1990 that no one had predicted the events of 1989; Leszek Kolakowski, Vladimir Shlapentokh, and Marcin Krol denounced the whole community of Sovietologists.[11] Such self-criticism is undeserved and is unnecessary. The precise date and place of Gorbachev's historic telephone conversation with Andrei Sakharov in Gorkii, the cutting of the iron curtain by Hungarian authorities, the breaching of the Berlin Wall, et cetera may not have been predicted, but the approaching end of communism definitely had been anticipated. As early as 1964, sociologist Talcott Parsons had predicted that "Communism will, from its own internal dynamics, evolve in the direction of the restoration—or where it has not yet existed, the institution of political democracy. . . . Political democracy is the *only* possible outcome—except for general destruction or breakdown."[12]

In 1969, the young Russian historian Andrei Amalrik wrote: "Will the Soviet Union Survive until 1984?"—in which he presented a forceful argument for the weak base of communist rule.[13] Between 1976 and 1987, Adam Bromke, J. F. Brown, Alexander Yanov, Ernst Kux, Pedro Ramet, George Schöpflin, and Ivan Volgyes predicted the collapse of communism and the resulting disorder in their various aspects.[14] And last but not least, the ethnic strife of the Gorbachev and post-Soviet periods has been anticipated, if not predicted, by many students of Soviet nationalities policy.[15]

In the past, politicians clung to concepts that allowed for an easy definition of the great divide between democracy and the "evil empire," a definition that was consistent with their preconceived ideas. Totalitarianism, a theoretical construct that heavily influenced policy makers in the West, tried to explain the system as it was *believed* to exist. It lacked a dynamic component and certainly made no predictions on what would happen *after* totalitarianism. Totalitarian elites were thought to be so powerful that they could only be brought down by intervention from the outside world. From the totalitarian perspective, many developments in Soviet society during and after the Gorbachev period could not be explained, for they were incompatible or inconsistent with the rigorous assumptions of the model. Only more refined and empirically based theories could yield such explanations.

Most Sovietologists had thrown the concept of totalitarianism overboard decades before Gorbachev came to power, and had adopted other models better suited for analyzing the internal contradictions of communist systems. Such approaches to communist rule were more dynamic; they took conflicting interests, changing attitudes and popular expectations, ethnic fermentation, quasi-political struggles, bureaucratic obstruction, patronage networks, and clan politics into consideration. These models and approaches were more successful at explaining Soviet developments than was the concept of totalitarianism. Given the limits set by the inaccessibility of Soviet society and politics, their proponents often engaged in innovative empirical research. This book is partly based on their findings.

The one thing that *has* surprised not only politicians but Sovietologists as well was the ease with which the Soviet *nomenklatura* and its vassals ultimately gave in to their defeat. They had expected that the demise of communist rule would be accompanied by a bloody battle— not just a few amateurish attempts at a coup. A battle is indeed taking place, but it comes in a form different from what was expected. The communist elites have, by and large, accepted the end of communism and are doing well in adapting to the new situation. They reap the benefits of their former positions by active participation in privatization schemes, and in some of the new states they simply remain in power under new colors. In contemporary Russia the political situation is characterized by conflicting and confusing tendencies. On the one hand, with free elections, a new constitution, and a new parliament, democratization is making slow progress. On the other hand, innate reflexes deform democracy into a peculiar Russian type. The criminalization of politics, the reassertion of expansionist appetites, and the revenge of the neofascists push Russia toward authoritarian rule. It is in this area of tension that this book is situated.

ONE *Toward Democracy?—Aspects of Transition*

In postcommunist Russia, we deal with a specific process for which the general regularities of transition do not fit. (Alexander Tsipko, January 1993)[1]

Democracy is more than just the absence of dictatorship. But what exactly is it, and how does it come about? When communist dictatorship collapsed in Eastern Europe, for the survivors of that dictatorship democracy was an "ill-defined objective with diverse associations," and it was uncertain whether there were sufficiently strong social forces to carry the process of democratization.[2] Several authors see the collapse of communism as a "double rejective revolution" against both the communist system of rule and imperial domination.[3] Communism collapsed because people could not bear it any longer, not so much because they had a clear idea of what else they wanted, or how they could reach that goal. Indeed, in many postcommunist countries, Russia not excluded, antidemocratic forces raised their heads. They threatened to arrest the transition process or to overturn weak democratic regimes. In the confusion of transition, the barriers to ongoing democratization often seemed formidable. In order to put this confusion into perspective, I will first deal with the question of what democracy and democratization are about.

Under what circumstances can or will a democratic regime come into being? And what are the requirements for it to sustain itself and to grow to full fruition? Which of the many possible arrangements for democratic rule is best suited for a particular society? Most authors on democratic theory agree that democracy is not an either/or concept; in other words, one can very well speak of more or less democracy—and thus of a process of democratization. They also agree that there is no single ideal type of democracy and that the actual forms that democracies take may differ widely. Representative democracy is seen as the most difficult type of rule to sustain, due to the paradoxes that arise from its basic formula: rule by the people for the people through their freely elected representatives.[4] Desiderata such as efficient and consistent rule or the protection of the long-term interests of society may conflict with the short-term interests of sections of society. An electoral basis for a majority government taking painful economic measures may therefore be difficult to find.

Let us first deal with the question of how a nondemocratic regime—a dictatorship or authoritarian system—may be replaced by a democratic one. As we do so, it should be stated from the outset that such a transformation does not take place at one single moment but is instead a drawn-out process that will start long before formal power is transferred and that will continue for quite some time under the new regime. This is partly so because democracy is the only type of rule where one can speak of real interaction between the political and the social spheres in the sense that developments in each of the two have a profound impact on each other. In a dictatorship or authoritarian system, society is largely subjected to the state; this can be stated differently by saying that there are only subjects—no citizens. Gradual changes in a society ruled by an authoritarian system may generate pressure on the current regime, a pressure that may result in the initiation of a transition process, and ultimately in institutional changes—a change of the regime. The political change away from dictatorship or authoritarianism will subsequently give rise to changes in society.

As far as Russia is concerned, it is clear that the social change that was at the root of later political change had started many years before the USSR came to an end. The emergence of a large social category of professionals over the decades of post–World War II Soviet rule laid the foundations for the transition from autocracy by creating a latent force for change. In this category of qualified specialists, representing about 25 percent of the workforce and 40 percent of CPSU membership, "society gained its first substantial group of people familiar with the rational norms and impersonal dealings of *Gesellschaft,* and hence capable of making political pluralism or a market economy work."[5] The democratic and nationalist movements (including, in particular, the literary movement of the village prose writers, *derevenshchiki*) during the long, drawn-out Brezhnev period created alternative value systems that were readily available at the moment when restrictions were lifted by Mikhail

Gorbachev, the great initiator of the transformation of his country. These undercurrents will be discussed at greater length in the next chapter.

Political scientists disagree on the preconditions and criteria for democracy, but this should be no reason for others to say that all generalizations on this subject are meaningless. The scholarly discussion on the subject is not taking place in an empirical void—that is to say that by now political scientists can draw from quite a large pool of historical examples of transitions to democracy. On the basis of these examples, they can formulate their generalizations.

WAVES OF DEMOCRATIZATION

Harvard political scientist Samuel Huntington has identified three long "waves of democratization" since the early nineteenth century, and two intermediate "reverse waves."[6] The first democratic wave, during which twenty-nine such systems came into being, started in the 1820s and lasted until the mid-1920s. By 1942, the first "reverse wave" had reduced the number of democracies to twelve. In Europe, fascism, Nazism, and Stalinism "came very close to obliterating democracy altogether."[7] The beginning of the second democratization wave coincided with the end of World War II; it peaked in 1962, when the world counted thirty-six democracies. The second "reverse wave," between 1960 and 1975, brought their number down to thirty. During the third wave (1974–1990), the number of democratic states doubled from thirty to sixty—providing for thirty recent transition processes from which to draw empirical data and theoretical generalizations. Since 1990, several more countries have adopted democratic systems or have reached more or less advanced stages in the transition to democracy. By the end of 1991, Freedom House counted between seventy-five and eighty-nine democracies—depending on the strictness with which the criteria for democracy were applied.[8] The growing number of independent countries in the world has been accompanied by a distinct growth in the share of democracies.

But there is no reason to believe that the third wave will not be followed by a reverse wave, and that wave in its turn by another democratization wave. The upsurge of nationalism in particular has made the outlook for young democracies in 1993 less good than it was in 1990. Nationalism and democracy certainly are not incompatible, the first being an ideology, the second a system of rule according to certain explicitly defined principles. But strong forms of nationalism which demand absolute loyalty to collective interests (those of the ethnic "nation" vis-à-vis other nations) are at loggerheads with the individualistic basis of democracy. Strong nationalist currents tend to come into conflict with human rights and to undermine some of the social conditions favoring democracy, such as tolerance, the protection of minorities, and the willingness to reach compromises.

One of the effects of the most recent wave of democratization has been to leave democracy, in the eyes of many—common people, political scientists, and political elites—as the one and only system capable of legitimizing political rule. This attitude was reflected in Francis Fukuyama's 1989 article "The End of History" and the discussion it provoked. Excluding Islamic fundamentalism, all systemic alternatives to democracy have in the twentieth century been discredited and have failed. As a result, even undemocratic or antidemocratic elites now often try to justify and legitimate their rule through a quasi-democratic constitution.[9] Some authors believe that democracy, being the most powerful instrument for legitimization, has the future; others such as Ken Jowitt, see no reason why competing systems should not come about in the future. From the present, extremely unstable "Genesis situation" in the postcommunist world, a "new way of life" characterized by a new militant ideology might arise, rejecting the democratic rules and institutions that have triumphed in this century and offering great appeal to broad sections of the population.[10] For the time being, however, Russia and other successor states of the Soviet Union are still in their "Genesis situation," and it is uncertain what it will bring. Transitions from authoritarian rule *may* result in democracy—and then they may not. The study of such transitions in other parts of the world may tell us something about the typical problems societies can expect in the process of changing their political regimes.

THE STUDY OF TRANSITIONS

As O'Donnell and Schmitter have stressed in the concluding volume to the study of transition processes in Latin American and Southern European countries, transition from authoritarian rule is characterized by extreme uncertainty.[11] To those involved in the transition, and to us observing it from outside, it is often unclear what is going on and what the result of momentous political events will be. Regime change—the transformation of an authoritarian system into "something else"—is typically a rapidly and unpredictably evolving situation in which established political rules break down and fierce battles are fought for the institution of new rules. The arenas in which such battles are fought may themselves lack established rules; a general feeling of disorder may drive

politicians to despair. After all, the way in which new rules and procedures are defined at the end of the struggle "will determine likely winners and losers in the future."[12] This dramatic political battle can be seen
as a fight over the new constitution—where "constitution" can be taken
to mean both the future shape of the polity and the rules and procedures
for institutions described in a written document. Thus, by definition,
regime change is accompanied by crisis symptoms, for regimes do not
change unless some of the major actors sense an oncoming crisis—most
often a legitimacy crisis. Large sections of the population may suddenly
become mobilized; members of the old political elite may make decisions with totally unforeseen consequences. The compression of time
in such revolutionary situations makes for hasty decisions or the promulgation of an unfounded new policy that is soon regretted by those
who promoted it. Information on the situation in society is often lacking. The study of transitions from autocracy, therefore, is not unlike the
study of crisis management. If it is to lead to empirical theory (theory
based on established historical facts), such a theory should be expected
to be a theory of abnormality in which "the unexpected and the possible
are as important as the usual and the probable."

At the end of their book, O'Donnell and Schmitter invite the reader to
visualize transitions as a multilayered chess game in which an indeter-
minate number of players has the ability on any move to shift from one
level to the other. The image conveys the extreme uncertainty surround-
ing political transition away from authoritarian rule, and its character
of a "tumultuous contest, with people challenging the rules on every
move, pushing and shoving to get to the board, shouting out advice
and threats from the sidelines, trying to cheat whenever they can—but,
nevertheless, becoming progressively mesmerized by the drama they
are participating in or watching, and gradually becoming committed to
playing more decorously and loyally to the rules they themselves have
elaborated."[13]

Transitions are wedged in between the stability and certainties of authoritarian politics on the one hand and the limited and manageable
uncertainties of a stable democratic regime on the other. This book
deals with such a confusing period of transition—the regime transition
of Russia from a communist dictatorship to "something else": hopefully (because usually they are less aggressive) a democracy, possibly not.
The intransigent political battles, the intrigues and the sly settling of
old scores, the dirty tricks and the failed attempts at breaking impasses
once and for all, the costly and painful mistakes of politicians with
good intentions, or, in short, the seemingly hopeless mess of the Rus-

sian political arena in the early 1990s—these confusing but unavoidable characteristics of regime transition demand a comparative framework that should allow us to understand them better and to place them in perspective.

Such a framework is available in the literature produced by those political scientists who have studied processes of transition in other parts of the globe. By the time, in the late 1980s, that the Eastern European glaciers started moving, an accumulated and aggregated knowledge of the mechanics and electronics of transition processes in twentieth-century countries had become available in empirical case studies. One of these studies has been the Woodrow Wilson International Center's research project on transitions from authoritarian rule in Latin America and Southern Europe—the areas where most of the transitions of Huntington's "third wave" took place. The project resulted in a scholarly volume with case studies of regime transformations during the second half of the twentieth century in Italy, Greece, Portugal, Spain, Turkey, Argentina, Bolivia, Brazil, Chile, Mexico, Peru, Uruguay, and Venezuela. From this wealth of empirical material, O'Donnell and Schmitter have painted a general picture of the processes, the dilemmas, and the paradoxes involved in the transition from authoritarianism to democracy. Another such study, involving twenty-six developing countries in Africa, Asia, and Latin America, has been undertaken by Larry Diamond, Juan J. Linz, and Seymour Martin Lipset.[14] The aggregated findings of both studies appeared in print in the mid-1980s. To these studies should be added one that was not so much concerned with the dynamics of democratization as with the explanation of variations in levels of democracy at a specific point in time, the year 1988. This study was undertaken by Axel Hadenius and involved 132 countries in Latin America, the Caribbean, Africa, Asia, and Oceania.[15]

Eastern Europe and Russia, of course, have their own political histories and cultures, which set them apart from countries in other continents. This precludes the possibility of mechanically applying the generalizations drawn by the authors of the studies mentioned above to regime change in Eastern Europe and Russia. On the other hand, it is obvious that the breaking up of authoritarian rule unleashes social forces that are basically the same everywhere on the globe, so that the recent experiences of mainly Catholic countries are not a priori irrelevant to the understanding of regime change in postcommunist countries. By relating to a conceptual framework and model developed on the basis of worldwide experience, we may better understand the dilemmas of transition in Eastern Europe and Russia, as long as we are aware of the specific circumstances in which such transitions have taken place, and of the histories of the countries and the peoples concerned.

THE CONFINES AND STAGES OF TRANSITION

As with so many subjects in social science, thinking about transition is made difficult by the many social, political, economic, and cultural variables involved. Choices have to be made on how to structure our thinking. The first such choice here is to determine what we mean by saying that a transition process has begun and by saying that it has ended—in other words to determine the confines of transition from authoritarian rule. Subsequently the process itself is to be described first in terms of the main characteristics of its stages. In the rest of this chapter the most important variables involved, and their interrelationship, will be analyzed.

In line with the project of O'Donnell, Schmitter, and Whitehead, "transition" is seen here as the interval between one political regime and another. That is to say that the consolidation of a political regime is not supposed to be part of the transition process. This is so because the main characteristic of the transition process is that during it, the rules of the political "game" are not defined. Unlike the periods before and after transition, at least some of the main rules will be hotly contested, and many participants in transition may be in a state of uncertainty concerning these rules. After all, what transition is about is the creation of a new, generally accepted (or imposed) set of rules. In reality, the application of concepts such as "transition" and "consolidation" is not so easy, for even new constitutions can be of a transitional nature. If the criterion is to be that transition is over once "abnormality" is no longer felt to be the central feature of political life, as O'Donnell and Schmitter have it, then the transition of the Russian polity extended far into the 1990s.

Transition is supposed to have begun "at the launching of the process of dissolution of an authoritarian regime." Historically, this has happened most frequently after the military defeat of an authoritarian regime in an international conflict. The typical sign that transition is beginning is seen to be the modification by authoritarian incumbents of their own rules concerning the rights of their subjects vis-à-vis the state; this is called "liberalization." It is necessary, however, that the rulers are believed and that their announcement of liberalizing measures is credible to the extent that others change their behavior and strategies. Transition is supposed to have ended with the installation of some form of democracy or the return to authoritarian rule.[16] The inevitable consequence of this definition is that we (and the people of the country undergoing transition) may for a long time be in a state of uncertainty concerning the question of whether transition has really come to an end.

In the many countries where it has occurred, the first phase of transition from autocracy was liberalization (but liberalization need not mean the beginning of transition, as the first years of the Khrushchev period in the Soviet Union testify). By liberalization is meant here a development in the direction of making human rights effective—with the exception of rights pertaining to government. Liberalization furthers the development of civil society and private economic initiative. Adam Przeworski has observed that an important effect of such development is that it lowers the real *and the anticipated* "costs" of individual expression and collective action.[17] Some people—often intellectuals—may suddenly become aware that there is a real possibility for their views of an alternative sociopolitical order to be realized. Liberalization is a period of rising civil expectations, a period in which the taking away of barriers by the authoritarian regime itself will have a multiplier effect in society. Longtime taboos are broken, things can be said and done that were severely punished only a few weeks or months previously, and seeing that courageous civil pioneers get away with it, more and more people start making use of their rights. The *discourse* of politics starts to change: new, formerly suppressed, concepts are introduced, new questions are being asked, and old words acquire new meaning.[18] During this period, the authoritarian regime remains in place and in possession of power, which may be used capriciously. Liberalization may be undone by the regime, bringing transition to an early halt. But if it does not do so, a critical stage is reached once the perceived costs of the annulment of liberalizing measures have become too high. Before they know what is happening, liberalizing authoritarian regimes may find themselves in a situation where they cannot recreate the status quo ante but cannot control further developments away from autocracy, either. They are trapped.

In order to understand how authoritarian regimes may trap themselves, we will have to be more specific on the makeup and internal dynamics of such regimes. On the basis of their empirical studies, O'Donnell and Schmitter have suggested the simple split of "hard-liners" (unconditional authoritarians) and "soft-liners." The soft-liners are the ones who take the initiative for liberalization and subsequent democratization, in the conviction that such measures have become inevitable for the preservation of the regime. Democratization is logically

the next stage of the transition process, although the stages are intertwined and may show considerable overlap; O'Donnell and Schmitter
visualize transition as a "double stream" in which the two subprocesses
of liberalization and democratization interact over time. Democratization involves processes whereby "the rules and procedures of citizenship
are either applied to political institutions previously governed by other
principles, . . . or expanded to include persons not previously enjoying
such rights and obligations, . . . or extended to cover issues and institutions not previously subject to citizen participation."[19] Democratization changes the structure of authority by making rulers accountable
to their subjects, thereby creating citizens. In all cases studied in the
Woodrow Wilson project, the installation of democracy was preceded
by significant, if unsteady, liberalization. Through the multiplier effect,
in combination with the human need for control over one's own life,
liberalization creates powerful pressures for democratization.

The aim of this book is not so much to explain the collapse of the
Soviet Union as to deal with the problems of the Russian phoenix that
rose out of its ashes. The collapse of the Soviet Union, and of communist rule in general, has been dealt with quite competently by others.[20]
Therefore in the rest of this chapter we will discuss aspects of the transition and its aftermath, selected on the basis of their relevance to the
problems of contemporary Russia.

IF SPAIN, WHY NOT RUSSIA?

One of the few authors optimistic about the prospects of transition from
autocracy in Eastern Europe is Giuseppe Di Palma of the University
of California. Writing in 1990, Di Palma claimed that democracy can
"emerge" from a regime crisis "as a simple matter of convenience or
compulsion": "Especially favorable conditions are not required."[21] If Di
Palma is correct, there may be hope for a democratic Russia with a
market economy. So let us investigate his arguments.

Di Palma's point of departure is that democracy may be adopted by
design or by default for lack of alternatives. For Russia, which has experienced the total collapse of its communist value system and a "devas-
tating failure of goals and will," there simply was no alternative: "What
is crucial is that they [the Eastern European countries] do move toward
democracy, not *why*."[22] Neither does it matter whether the new rulers
are genuine democrats and familiar with the rules of democracy: such
beliefs, attitudes, and skills can be learned with practice. The examples
of successful democracies and successful transitions abound, so that it

should not be too difficult for new rulers to copy the art. "If Spain," Di Palma asks, "why not Eastern Europe?" The vested interests of the old elite are not immutable, and most of that elite will make the best of the new situation. They may not desire democracy, "but may nonetheless back into it": "They may believe that a few liberalization measures will suffice, only to discover the truth of Tocqueville's observation that oppressive regimes are in greatest danger precisely when they begin to relax their grip."[23]

The likelihood of antidemocratic backlashes, Di Palma claims, has been exaggerated. In several countries there have of course been military and other coups that arrested democratization, but in many instances conservatives have opted for the safer way of expressing their views and interests through the new political channels of democratic institutions. The resulting mayhem—not unlike what we have seen in the Russian parliament in 1992–1993, may create the impression of serious instability and the risk of a backlash, but we should be able "to separate impression from substance." Save for Romania, Di Palma wrote in 1990, "the point of no return on the path to democratization is at hand in the region."[24]

But will not the economic disruption and hardships that accompany the transition to a market economy bring democracy down? Di Palma answers that during the Interbellum, disaffection from democracy "was not generally highest where its material performance was poorest." Instead, disaffection with democracy was high where "alternative totalitarian models had made great inroads." Now that democracy is on the rebound and no significant other models of rule are available, "democratic legitimacy need not be closely tied to what democracy can deliver in material goods."[25] The people of Eastern Europe, after all, did not take to the streets for bread, but for political dignity.

The dissenters of the past will have little difficulty in turning themselves into pragmatic politicians in a democratic system. Di Palma claims that precisely because the dissidents sought recognition for issues that "cut across conventional social cleavages" instead of the interests of specific classes or social categories, their lack of organizational prowess need not be a serious hindrance. The new political movements of "postmaterialist Western Europe" do not have a recognizable social or subcultural basis and do not suffer from this. A strong social base is apparently no longer necessary for a successful political movement, and Eastern European movements may benefit by "tapping into" a new style of Western European politics. The legacy of dissent "may help them to escape the dire prophesies of the theorists of backwardness."[26] Di Palma's optimism is buttressed by his high valuation of the legacy of dissent; he sees in Eastern Europe the "birth of a new structure of normative thought" as expressed in the centrality of civil society, unlike the transitions to democracy in Southern Europe or Latin America: "If placed in the context of a larger Europe, the new civic culture of Eastern Europe might even curb the threat of chauvinistic nationalism, which could otherwise be ignited by the political frictions to which backwardness gives rise."[27]

It is tempting for students of Eastern Europe to adopt Di Palma's line of reasoning. After all, who wants to be a "theorist of backwardness"? But it is difficult to escape the impression that Di Palma has confused the initiation of transition with its successful completion. His common sense on the circumstances of the initiation of transitions is borne out by the findings of O'Donnell and Schmitter. On the basis of much more empirical evidence than that provided by Di Palma, they have stated that the "players" of the game of transition from authoritarian rule "do not have to have attained a prior consensus on democratic values before muscling their way into the game" and can be made to respect "the rules that emerge from the game itself." It is certainly true that a transition may be set into motion by "stalemate and dissensus rather than by prior unity and consensus," but it is no foregone conclusion that the transition will result in democracy. O'Donnell and Schmitter allow for the possibility of democratization processes breaking down.[28] As against the paucity of solid arguments in Di Palma's article, students of transformation processes most of the time are much less optimistic. Why? I will return to that question later in this book when dealing with Russia specifically. For the time being, it is of greater interest to pursue the question of transition per se. Transitions do not have to result in democratic regimes; and political scientists are not necessarily interested in the outcome of such processes: they may study transitions just for the fun of discovering empirical generalizations. Still, the quiet understanding between this author and his audience is that a democratic outcome is desirable. Before dealing with selected aspects of transition processes, it is therefore not a bad idea to investigate this desired outcome: what precisely do we mean by democracy?

POLITICAL DEMOCRACY:
PRECONDITIONS OR CRITERIA?

Many authors on democratic theory list preconditions for the establishment of a democratic system, or criteria for naming the existing type of rule in a particular country democratic, which are, of course, two quite different things. Preconditions can be necessary, sufficient, or both; criteria can be of a "situational" or an instrumental character. Often the list of preconditions is very long, and as a result most authors tend to be rather pessimistic about the prospects for democracy in countries liberated from communist rule. It is less difficult to formulate criteria for naming a particular political system "democratic"—that is, criteria for speaking of "minimal democracy." This is what we mean when we use the term *democracy:* "a system of governance in which rulers are held accountable for their actions in the public realm by citizens, acting indirectly through the competition and cooperation of their elected representatives."[29] Still, such a simple criterion, even though it is considered crucial by most political scientists, may turn out to be no more than a bogus solution to one of the most complicated problems of our times.

If the central defining criterion is the free and periodic election of their officials by the citizens, this suggests that we can split the world's countries into two clearly distinct groups: the democracies (with periodic elections) and the nondemocracies. It also suggests that once a regime has given in to the institution of periodic elections, everything is OK from a democratic point of view. The suggestions, of course, are dubious. In reality we see wide variations among countries that are generally considered democratic, both within the central criterion of elections (i.e., in the different shades of electoral institutions and arrangements) and in the different combinations of other democratic attributes. We can also observe countries where free elections are more or less "undone" by nondemocratic institutional arrangements, and countries where elections are unfree or even absent, but where other attributes of democracy are found. Considering these variations, the search for a litmus test for democracy may be in vain. Indeed, some political scientists see no problem in rating political systems by their "level of democracy," with that level (in 1988) being, for example, 0.0 in Saudi Arabia, 0.8 in Cuba, 2.1 in Paraguay, 5.8 in Egypt, and 10.0 in Cyprus.[30]

If indeed democracy is not the univocal concept that many citizens think it to be, criteria for democracy should be considered as criteria for measuring the degree of democracy of existing political systems. A generally accepted list of criteria has been formulated by Robert Dahl. This set of "minimal rules" says that government policy is to be made by officials elected in frequent and fairly conducted elections in which coercion is "comparatively uncommon" and in which practically all adults have the right to vote and be elected; alternative sources of information (i.e., a free press) are protected by law, and citizens have a right to seek out the sources of information they want and to express themselves without fear of punishment; they also have the right to form "relatively independent" associations, including political parties and pressure groups. To this, Schmitter and Karl have added the conditions that the polity itself must be free from constraints imposed by outside powers, and that the officials must be able to exercise their constitutional powers "without being subjected to overriding (albeit informal) opposition from unelected officials"—that is, by the "fourth power" of the bureaucracy or by the military.[31] The use of such terms as "frequent," "fairly," "comparatively," "practically," and "relatively" in these definitions turns democracy into a relative instead of an absolute concept.

Democracy is thus a political regime with particular characteristics. The word "regime" or "system of governance" denotes that it is institutionalized and not "accidental," that is, that the patterns and rules of democratic behavior must be known, accepted, and practiced habitually by all actors in the system. For example, it must be unequivocally clear where the private sector ends and where the public sector starts. Democratic politics is about the public sector and, to a differing extent in differing democratic systems, the regulation of the private sector. In a democratic regime, political forces such as parties, movements, and pressure groups may try to move the border between the public and private sectors as long as they abide by the rules.

One of the central principles of democracy is majority rule. In direct or indirect democracy, the majority decides—one way or the other—even if that majority is slim. The rule was born out of necessity, out of the imperfectness of the human condition, and remains one of the less satisfying elements of democracy: situations can arise where elected officials representing half the population but one individual will have to accept the decision of the other half *plus one*. The amazement of subjects of communist regimes (who had been told that the party knew what was best for *the whole of society*) at the inequitability of majority rule was expressed by a Russian letter writer who in 1989 protested the unfairness of the fact that the character and policies of a popular representative elected with a slim majority were not necessarily better than his defeated opponent. Still, theorists of democracy generally acknowledge that we have no better rule.

It is also generally accepted, however, that in a democracy majority rule can conflict with individual interests. Political philosophers in the past and political scientists in the present have stressed the importance of minority rights and the obligation of democratic regimes to provide for institutional safeguards against their violation.

What methods are available for the protection of minorities from oppression by majorities? Constitutionalists would mention the inalienable rights of citizens that no regime, government, or fellow citizen may violate. Political scientists would tend to add other institutional mechanisms that may provide protection to minorities and may allow them a fair share of participation and decision making. Schmitter and Karl have provided a short list of the most common institutional arrangements of which the first three are usually fixed in written constitutions:

1. Bill of rights: constitutional provisions that place certain matters "beyond the reach of majorities";
2. Confederalism: the requirement of concurrent majorities in several different constituencies;
3. Federalism: guarantees for regional autonomy;
4. Consociationalism: the formation of grand coalition governments that incorporate all parties; and
5. Neocorporatism: the negotiation of pacts between major social groups.

These alternatives for the protection of minorities have, of course, special relevance for countries with ethnic minorities.

A characteristic of democracy that is often forgotten is cooperation. Indeed, this quality is of such importance that it has been termed a "central feature of democracy," for the actors in a democratic system "must cooperate in order to compete."[32] Democracy requires the ability of its citizens and their representatives to listen to each other; to engage in collective efforts; to organize a party, interest group, or association; to work with others; and to set aside minor differences in order to reach more important common goals. The same is required of those whose task it is to implement public policy. A government bureaucracy lacking in cooperative motivation and skills will undermine the democratic system.

The arena par excellence for the development of cooperative motivation and skills is civil society—the intermediate layer between citizens and government. It is here that interests organize themselves and clash; and it is here that conflicts are mitigated so that authoritative decision making by the government is not always necessary. The presence of a strong civil society is generally seen as beneficial to democratic government. Whether it is also a precondition will be discussed later.

LEGITIMACY AND CITIZENSHIP

Democracy is rule by the consent of citizens. The assumption of many authors on democracy is that populations, if allowed freely to express their demands, will not voluntarily opt for dictatorial rule. However true this may seem, both historical examples and the theoretical arguments of political scientists have shown that people need not always opt for democracy. Democracy is extremely difficult to sustain unless it provides those that it is supposed to benefit, the citizens, with at least a minimum of security and well-being. The democratic state is expected to deal more or less effectively with economic and social problems and clashes of interest—if not, people may, as Larry Diamond has written "prefer *not* to be governed through their own consent—they may choose not to put up with the pain of political choice any longer."[33] What Diamond refers to is that democratic rule requires consent, and consent requires legitimacy, whereas legitimacy requires effective performance.

But effective performance should not be considered the one and only basis for democratic legitimacy. A distinction is generally made between "performance (or eudaemonic) legitimacy" (based on the ability of regimes to "deliver the goods," that is, an acceptable distribution of income and wealth, basic social security, and public safety) and other types of legitimacy. Many political scientists, not only Francis Fukuyama, have pointed to the fact that the discreditation of nondemocratic sources of legitimacy at the end of the twentieth century has made democratic governments less dependent on "performance legitimacy" because democracy based on legal-rational legitimation has been widely accepted as the ideal political regime. And yet, as Samuel Huntington has stressed, sustained inability to perform can undermine the legitimacy even of democratic governments.[34] In such a situation, it is conceivable that people voluntarily give up their role as citizens by voting for nondemocratic rule, hoping that order will be established. If they do, they transform themselves from citizens into subjects.

The problem is particularly acute in aspiring democracies. This is so because a serious lack of legitimacy will usually accompany the transition from authoritarian rule. Such a situation will often result in a legitimacy crisis, and transition may have to take place in the circumstance of a "legitimacy vacuum," with the new rulers desperately struggling to obtain legitimation. Questions of legitimacy and legitimation are of particular importance for the transition from communist rule; it is therefore appropriate to deal with them before moving on to citizenship.

In analyzing legitimacy, several distinctions should be made. The first is between legality and legitimacy; the second between the different objects of legitimacy and legitimation; the third between legitimacy and legitimation, and between different "modes" of legitimation, to use the words of Holmes. Fourth, and finally, we should distinguish between different carriers of the legitimacy belief. For the sake of clarity, I will deal with these distinctions in a rather schematic way.

First, what *is* legitimacy, to begin with? Legitimacy is usually understood to be the belief that specific authorities in a specific political system have a right to rule, that their decisions should be respected, and that their orders should be executed. Shortly I will discuss *who* is to hold such a belief about *which* authorities and *which* political system; for now, it is important to note that legitimacy, although it derives from the Latin *legitimus* (legal), is not identical to legality. Legitimacy and legitimation are part of a political science (and political philosophy) vocabulary, subject to considerable disagreement among students of politics. Legality, however, is a legal (juridical) concept and refers only to the question of whether some action or rule is in agreement with formal law. Although some would expect that any legal government is legitimate, this is not always so. In the Soviet Union of the late 1960s, the Kosygin government was legal, having been installed in accordance with the rules of the 1936 Constitution. So was the rule of the Communist Party led by General Secretary Brezhnev, for it pulled the strings of government legally (on the basis of Article 126 of the Constitution).[35] But many inside and outside the country questioned the party's legitimacy. After all, it had seized power in October 1917 and had willingly destroyed the opposition. President Yeltsin's dissolution of parliament in September 1993 was illegal (being in conflict with the Constitution), but for many it was a legitimate act aimed at solving the constitutional crisis. As these examples indicate, it is easier to establish the legality of a ruler, a government, or their acts, than to establish their legitimacy.

With this we come to the second distinction, concerning the objects of legitimacy and legitimation—in other words, *what* is being legitimized? Both Max Weber, whose work on legitimacy is considered classical, and contemporary authors such as Rigby and Holmes distinguish between the legitimacy of a regime (the political-social order) and that of its current rulers, implying that one may have more legitimacy than the other. In the mind of an orthodox Stalinist living in the Soviet Union of Nikita Khrushchev (1953–1964), system legitimacy will have been high, but the legitimacy of the reform-minded (experimentally inclined and accident-prone) Khrushchev low. In the minds of liberal writers and other intellectuals, however, system legitimacy will have been low, whereas the legitimacy they ascribed to Khrushchev, who eased their lives, will have been much higher.

Third, I have up to now referred both to legitimacy (a quality) and to legitimation. Legitimation is seen as the way in which legitimacy is acquired, its dynamic aspect. Modifying Weber's scheme, and using Rigby's work, Holmes has identified seven different "modes" (or types) of legitimation that are of importance in understanding questions of legitimation in communist and postcommunist societies.[36] They are:

1. "Old" traditional legitimation such as the "divine right of monarchs": the belief that tradition justifies particular rulers;
2. Charismatic legitimation, based on the belief that a particular ruler has exceptional qualities;
3. Goal-rational or teleological legitimation, in which the ultimate goal (e.g., communist or Islamic society, the *telos*) justifies rule;
4. Social eudaemonic legitimation: the system and/or rulers receive legitimation because they provide the population with economic stability and reasonably satisfying socioeconomic conditions;
5. Official nationalist legitimation, in which nationalist (ethnic) feelings translate into the belief that the rulers represent a nation;
6. "New" traditional legitimation, invoking recent "traditions" (such as the longtime "performance" of the CPSU); and, last but not least,
7. Legal-rational legitimation, which brings us back to legality. Under legal-rational legitimation as it was seen by Weber in 1947, a political order and/or its rulers are believed to be legitimate because they and their rule are legal and in conformity with impersonal rules that apply indiscriminately. Allegiance under such legitimacy is not to individuals (such as in "old" traditional or charismatic legitimation) but to the norms that govern their behavior: to the *rule of law*.

The waves of democratization identified by Huntington have washed the legal-rational mode of legitimation onto the shores of more and more countries. However, in modern times, legitimacy is rarely if ever based on one exclusive mode of legitimation. Although the leaderships of many postcommunist societies try to gain legitimacy stressing this mode, it is seldom enough.

Finally, there is the question of the "carriers" of legitimacy. Usually legitimacy is interpreted as the beliefs among the wider population concerning their system and their rulers. This explains why many students of communist systems have been particularly intrigued by questions of legitimacy: they had to explain why a system and regime that was seen as illegitimate by many was nevertheless able to survive for four (in some countries) to seven decades, even after (with the death of Stalin in 1953) terror was abolished. The answer they found was that the beliefs of the *rulers themselves* are of far more importance for the legitimacy of the regime. Generally they distinguish three types of groups that should be analyzed for their legitimacy beliefs: the ruling group, their staffs (bureaucracies), and the mass of the population. Reverting to Max Weber, they found that legitimacy should above all exist in the minds of the rulers and their staffs, that is to say that they should be convinced to have (by whatever mode of legitimation) a right to rule. Mass-based and legal-rational oriented legitimacy may greatly support their rule in the case of temporary failures (such as a severe economic recession affecting eudaemonic legitimation), but it is not necessary for prolonged rule.

Let us now turn to citizens and subjects. The point I want to make is that citizens and subjects should not be seen as opposing absolutes, but as roles. Democracy requires adults to play both roles. All regimes have rulers and a public realm, write Schmitter and Karl, "but only to the extent that they are democratic do they have citizens."[37] The concept of citizenship, democracy's key attribute, flows from the individualist assumptions of classical liberal theory: "It is the individual rather than the family, the clan, the city, the nation or humankind, that is the 'legal subject' of the state. A citizen is an individual with rights within the political system, in contrast to the subject."[38] Democratic citizenship, therefore, should be considered a pleonasm, communist citizenship a contradiction in terms.

Nowadays, the criteria for political citizenship are simple and unambiguous: all adult (i.e., over eighteen years of age) inhabitants of a country enjoying membership in the polity (to be called here: "constitutional citizenship") are eligible to vote their representatives into institutions such as parliaments and local councils, and thereby have a voice in politics. In different democracies there may still be different restrictions on aliens not (yet) enjoying constitutional citizenship, on detainees, and on psychiatric patients, but the general norm has been accepted more or less worldwide. In the past, of course, as democracy came to fruition in Western Europe and the United States, a long struggle had to be waged for the criterion of citizenship to be widened to all inhabitants over eighteen years old. Recent converts to democracy around the world have accepted this age threshold as the one and only criterion. But in some countries majorities have tried to manipulate "constitutional citizenship" in such a way as to exclude certain ethnic minorities both from political citizenship and from distinct economic rights.

Citizens can vote fellow citizens in or out of office, and almost all of them can present themselves as candidates for representative offices—usually the age threshold for the right to be elected is somewhat higher. As such, they transfer authority to duly elected officials and are participants in politics. Democracy requires that citizens care about politics—but, as has often been stressed, not too much. Democracy demands that citizens assert themselves and participate actively in the public realm, "but also that they accept the government's authority."[39] Democracy is generally seen to be sustained by what Almond and Verba have termed a "civic culture," of which a balanced mix of the citizen and subject roles is an essential ingredient.

Often during a transition, people will turn into citizens overnight. They may have been raised in a political system that allowed them only the role of subject while the dominant political culture tried to make them believe that they were citizens. Their recovery of the personal dignity of citizenship may entail unwarranted expectations. They may not be aware of the fact that citizenship confers both rights and obligations on both the citizens themselves and the officers of the state. Citizens have the right to be treated as equal in the making of collective choices, but they also have the obligation to respect and implement the choices of their freely elected representatives and, alas, to pay taxes. The officers of the state have the right to apply coercion when necessary in order to promote the effectiveness of their choices and to protect the polity from threats to its persistence, but they in turn have the obligation to be equally accountable and accessible to all citizens.[40] For newborn citizens and democratic rulers it may be extremely difficult to get used to this complexity of rules and obligations. During the transition process, the rights of citizens and of their organizations are the focus of attention and provide for hope and expectation. Disappointment may come once freshman citizens realize that democracy does not run on rights alone.

The general paradox of the development of democracy and citizenship, as formulated by T. H. Marshall, may pose particular problems. This paradox consists of the fact that citizenship implies equality, whereas capitalism is a system of inequality.[41] The development of democracy with citizenship rights cannot be separated from the development of capitalism, but the two systems are based on conflicting principles—democracy on equality, capitalism on inequality. In socialist countries, where history has left a legacy of surrogate citizenship in the political sphere and quasi-equality in the economic sphere, it will be extremely difficult to bring about a concurrent political and economic transformation. The project of developing both democracy *and* capitalism at the same time is ridden with a basic internal conflict: that between fostering equality in the political sphere and inequality in the economic sphere.

POLITICAL DEMOCRACY, CIVIL SOCIETY, AND THE CAPITALIST MARKET

Analysis of the relationships between political democracy and social-cultural variables has shown that the democratic form of rule is *statistically* most likely in countries dominated by a Christian religion, with a relatively homogeneous and well-educated population, a capitalist economy, and a small military.[42] But statistical likelihood itself is of course no guarantee for the establishment of democracy in a particular country, for it does not provide a clue to the dynamics of the processes of transition and democratization.

One of the first and foremost tasks in a transition from *communist* rule is to separate the private from the public sphere. All democratic governments adopt legislation for the regulation of the private sphere, but one of their essential characteristics is a basic respect for the independence of social and economic life. The road to such respect makes hard going, for a fragile infant democracy is asked to take firm measures with far-reaching implications for different group interests and for the well-being of the general population. Most theorists agree that, at least in Western-type societies, there is a close link between the presence of a free civil society, a capitalist economic system, and political democracy. This is considered to be so because the citizens in a democracy will not be prepared to accept the restrictive measures of a centrally planned and owned economy.[43] What theorists do not agree on is the question of the chicken and the egg.

What comes first? Is it necessary to have a more-or-less developed civil society before the capitalist market can take root? Or, is it perhaps necessary to have a developed capitalism before it makes sense to start building democracy? Can democracy work while the transition from state socialism to market capitalism is taking place? Will a young democratic regime be able to withstand the pressures generated by such a transition? The answers differ.

We have seen above that Di Palma rejects the notion that there cannot be democracy until after a civil society, based on a market economy, has come into bloom, or that the coinciding economic and political transformations should make democratization in Eastern Europe especially difficult. He argues that the simultaneous processes of political and economic transition "may help the latter ride piggyback on the former." Market-oriented interests may be weakly developed, but Eastern Europe "does not have to reinvent the wheel, for today everyone knows how the market works."[44] A "process" should be "chosen" such that the losers will be few and will not be able to arrest the process.

On the relationship between the market and civil society—the much discussed question of what comes first—Di Palma agrees that in the long run there cannot be a viable civil society without a market economy. But the market need not precede the development of civil society— the latter "may be instrumental in preparing the cultural and associational terrain for a market." There is, after all, the beginning of a civil society, thanks to the dissenters and the democratic movements of the communist era who "strove to build a fairly open and visible parallel society."

Jon Elster of the University of Chicago is not convinced by the "piggyback" argument. In his article "The Necessity and Impossibility of Simultaneous Economic and Political Reform," he has sketched an "impossibility theorem" on the basis of the assumption that essential on the economic side are price reform and ownership reform, and on the political side democracy and constitutional guarantees for individual rights.[45] The problem is that the interdependence of these reform processes forbids their being obtained simultaneously. For example, to be efficient, ownership reform presupposes price reform, but political democracy excludes price reforms that would lead to massive poverty and unemployment: the discontented citizens would not allow it; neither would they allow a class of nouveaux riches to benefit from ownership reform. Ownership reform demands legal stability and credible constitutional guarantees, and thus presupposes democracy. Within the assumptions of the theorem, therefore, full-scale reform is impossible. It may just be that Di Palma's piggy will have to muddle through mud.

Di Palma and Elster represent two extreme positions in a controversy that has caught the attention of many political scientists, historians, and philosophers. Their theorizing, however, has not provided workable answers for those who are supposed to provide leadership to the transitions in Eastern Europe. The complications of simultaneous political, economic, and social reform are such that one can only say: the proof of the pudding is in the eating. In chapters 3 to 5 we will taste Russian pudding.

LEADERSHIP AND PACTS

Concluding an article on the paradoxes of democracy, based on the comparative study of democratic transition processes in twenty-six developing countries, Larry Diamond has pointed to the pivotal role to be played by political leaders in the transition of Eastern Europe. His call for restraint was echoed by Julio Maria Sanguinetti, president of Uruguay from 1985 to 1990, during its transition from twelve years of military dictatorship to democratic rule. A process of transition to democracy faces so many difficulties and paradoxes that the exemplary behavior and the leadership of elites is essential in preventing a premature breakdown of the process. Leaders representing opposing political forces must show restraint in their political demands, a willingness to overcome resentments of the past, adherence to the rules of the game, and the establishment of working relationships with each other, and, above all, "they must manifest a faith in the democratic process and a commitment to its rules that supersedes the pursuit of power or other substantive goals." For political leaders to join hands for taking such a "leap of faith" requires that they will "believe that whatever results from the democratic process will, in the long run, serve their interests better than an intransigence that risks the breakdown of democracy."[46]

A transition to democracy, Sanguinetti wrote, "requires the constant management of two emotions: fear and impatience." Those who have lost power fear retaliation, whereas the elites that have gained power often impatiently demand immediate results. But for a transition to succeed, everyone, including former opponents and enemies, "must somehow be made to feel like a part of the new democratic process; no one must be denied the right to speak out, to compete politically, and to have influence."[47] In the economic sphere as well, leadership should aim at limiting the number of "losers" and softening the impact of the transition to the market on those who, in the old systems, held economic power. Powerful elites such as the former economic *nomenklatura* should be "interested in joining the very market they now disdain."[48] To exclude them from privatization would mean the spoiling of valuable human capital and unnecessarily making enemies in the process.

The demands for a leap of faith, for reconciliation, and for former dictators and their victims to engage in a joint project of building a democratic polity are truly formidable. They may be managed and steered by wise leaders in a country with limited problems of economic transition and limited ethnic and socioeconomic cleavages, but they may be forbidding in a situation where different types of crises pile upon each other.

One of the important tasks of leadership in transitions is the initiation, negotiation, and renegotiation of pacts among different established group interests in which the pacting groups agree "to forgo or underutilize their capacity to harm each other by extending guarantees not to threaten each other's corporate autonomies or vital interests."[49] The significance of such explicit deals lies in their capacity to prevent cataclysmic developments that might be destructive to the transformation process. The forging of pacts, an exercise in compromise and accommodation, is thus the business of moderates, not of extremists or maximalists. Pacts may be meant to be of limited duration, to overcome a particularly difficult stage in the transition, with the understanding that the pact is to be dissolved or renegotiated once that stage has been overcome. To newly emancipated citizens in particular it may be a shock to learn that such pacts "move the polity toward democracy by undemocratic means."[50]

Pacts are not seen to be necessary elements in all transitions from authoritarian rule, for in some of them the political situation may be such that one particular group can dictate its rules to others, or that the leaders of the outgoing authoritarian regime do not care any longer. But often pacts can be highly beneficial to the process of democratization. In fact, as early as 1970, Dankwart Rustow conceptualized democratization as a process that advances "on the installment plan," as actors preferring differing models of democratic rule, none of them sufficiently dominant to be able to impose his will, enter into a series of enduring compromises.[51]

Related to pacts is the concept of "contingent consent," considered to be one of the main principles of modern democracy. It refers to the understanding between political elites on the procedural norm of contingency. In conrast to the theory of liberal democracy (which stresses the dependence of political elites on the electorate), contingent consent stresses the links between elites, subject only periodically to electoral approval. O'Donnell and Schmitter have formulated the principle concisely, so that they may be quoted in full:

> [T]he actors agree to compete in such a way that those who win greater electoral support will exercise their temporary political superiority in such a way as not to impede those who may win greater support in the future from taking office; and those who lose in the present agree to respect the contingent authority of the winners to

make binding decisions, in exchange for being allowed to take office and make decisions in the future. In their turn, citizens will presumably accept a democracy based on such a competition, provided its outcome remains contingent upon their collective preferences as expressed through fair and regular elections of uncertain outcome.[52]

The coming about of such an agreement between the main political actors is no easy affair, for it demands more-or-less gentlemanly behavior. Such behavior presupposes that all actors are aware of what Robert Axelrod has called a "shadow of the future."[53] This is to say that cooperative behavior is unlikely as long as the actors do not feel that they will have to deal with each other in the future as well as in the present. Cooperation can be expected if parties are more or less convinced that losing now does not preclude winning in the future, and vice versa. But during the process of transition, the interests of possible "winners" and "losers" in the battle over a new constitution (written or otherwise) may clash to such an extent that they start to behave based on the assumption that their political struggle is a zero-sum game in which the winner takes all. Once that happens, the atmosphere will be poisoned for a long time afterwards.

On the basis of their study of recent transitions in Latin America and Southern Europe, O'Donnell and Schmitter have presumed to formulate two specific generalizations of which we will later see the relevance for explaining the difficult transition of Russia. The first generalization, formulated in terms of their "multilayered chess game" metaphor, says that "it is forbidden to take, or even to checkmate, the king of one of the players"—the king symbolizing the property rights of the bourgeoisie. This player may be forced to make broad concessions, but its property rights must be treated as inviolable. Players who would seriously threaten such rights, risk "being eliminated, pushed to the margins, or reduced to the status of kibitzers."[54] The second generalization says that it is forbidden to threaten the transitional regime's queen: the military. Should the military feel their existence threatened, "they may simply sweep their opponents off the board or kick it over and start playing solitaire." Particularly in situations where opposition and the drive for democratization comes from the "Left," these restrictions allow for little play and demand a great deal of patience from those who want to institute full democracy. Although the situational parameters of transition in Russia have shown similarities to those in the Latin world, there are a great many differences as well.

INSTITUTIONAL CHOICES

The first questions demanding answers at the end of the transition period are those concerning the best institutional arrangements for governing the country.[55] Is it to be ruled by a presidential or a parliamentary system; and are elections to be structured by proportional representation or by the majority (first-past-the-post) rule? Often in these matters, the choice is not completely open because the young democracy may inherit a particular system from the authoritarian (and possibly the preauthoritarian) period, and none of the major political actors may have problems with the system. But if political forces or groups want to change the governing system, they may have to face an uphill battle against the inertia of the historical legacy and against vested interests. Such vested interests may invoke traditions with the aim of preventing institutional arrangements that would undermine their position. Muddy compromises may have to be made for the sake of temporary political peace.

For a clear perspective of what the choice between different types of democratic government involves, and what the consequences of different alternatives may be, the discussion on the pages of the *Journal of Democracy* in 1990–1992 will be illuminating.[56] The main concern of the participants in this intellectual sparring match was what combination of institutional arrangements to recommend for adoption by aspiring democratic countries. Almost all of their arguments and sometimes biting counterarguments were based on different interpretations of theoretical reasoning and historical and empirical evidence. Here the main arguments for and against the different combinations of institutional arrangements will be reproduced, and our main concern will be to find broad areas of agreement and to identify the consequences of different choices.

A useful point of departure is Arend Lijphart's classification of four basic types of democracy on the basis of two criteria: presidentialism versus parliamentarianism, and plurality elections versus proportional representation (PR). The first indicates whether the country's executive (government) is selected by an independently elected president or by parliament. In a parliamentary system, governmental power is based on a majority in the legislature, and depends on it for survival. In a presidential system, this is not so. The second criterion indicates the way in which the president and members of parliament are elected: either according to the "first-past-the-post" system (the majoritarian, or Westminster model) or on the basis of proportional representation, possibly mitigated by an electoral threshold. Political scientists generally agree that these two yardsticks are the main determinants of different types of rule. Most contemporary democracies can be accommodated in Lijphart's model of four different combinations of these criteria.[57]

First come presidential systems with plurality elections, such as the United States (the inventor of the presidency), the Philippines, and Puerto Rico. Presidential systems with PR are found in Latin America. Third are parliamentary-plurality systems, that is, the Westminster model, adopted in many former colonies of Great Britain: Canada, Australia, New Zealand, India, Malaysia, and Jamaica. Fourth and finally are the parliamentary systems in which members of parliament are elected on the basis of some form of PR, and after elections the political parties form a coalition government: they are concentrated in Western Europe. The structured regional distribution of countries over these four combinations suggests that the adoption—by choice or otherwise—of one of the combinations depends mainly on "prepolitical" factors, such as culture, religion, geography, and history. Two of the historical factors worth mentioning are imitation (particularly of the Westminster and U.S. presidential models) and the way in which hereditary monarchical power has been democratized. In some countries (Western Europe) this was done by "taking away most of the monarch's personal political prerogatives and making his cabinet responsible to the popularly elected legislature"; of no little importance for the stability of democracy was that in many such countries the monarch remained on his throne. Elsewhere he was "simply" substituted by a democratically elected "king": the president.[58]

This difference implies a fundamental difference between parliamentary and presidential systems, namely that in the first, the head of the executive branch of government is, for the time he enjoys the confidence of a majority in parliament, merely that, and no more; whereas in the second system he or she is head of state at the same time, a surrogate king elected by popular vote for a fixed term and symbolizing national unity. The consequence of this difference in the positions of prime minister (P.M.) and president have made some political scientists into opponents of presidential rule.[59] They argue that presidents may come into office with a small proportion of the vote, nevertheless claiming democratic legitimacy for the period of their fixed term in office. The president may be seen by his supporters, and by himself, as representing the whole nation, whereas he nevertheless stands for particular partisan political interests and views. He is thus asked to combine two roles, the demands of which may easily come into conflict. Presidents may govern effectively—and may abuse their power easily—if they enjoy the company of a parliamentary majority consisting of followers or sympathizers. However, in the event that parliament is dominated by the opposition (i.e., if both the president and parliament can claim democratic legitimacy, but their ideological "profile" is different), a democracy can provide no rules to resolve the many disputes and the possible deadlock that may result.

Another objection to the presidential system is that it tends to make the political process inflexible. Presidents are extremely difficult to remove from office without creating a regime crisis. On the other hand, the breakdown of coalitions or the occurrence of crises in majoritarian parties may make parliamentary systems *seem* unstable, whereas they can in fact be highly flexible mechanisms for dealing with profound political conflict. In contrast to a president, a P.M. can easily be removed by a parliamentary majority, and deep crises may be prevented by asking for votes of confidence, or by new elections. Presidential elections are a zero-sum game where the winner takes all, and thereby contribute to polarization in society and in politics. For the duration of his fixed term, the "winners" and "losers" are sharply defined. This situation may induce a president to neglect the interests of minorities and to see his own policies as "reflections of the popular will and those of his opponents as the selfish designs of narrow interests."[60] Presidents, especially those who have come to power after a populist campaign, may soon find that the power they possess is utterly insufficient for satisfying the expectations they have generated. This unhappy situation may cause them to demand the broadening of their powers to the detriment of the legislature.

A final indictment concerns the quality of a presidential cabinet as compared to the governing team headed by a P.M. Ministers in a presidential cabinet are said to be less likely than those in a parliamentary cabinet to be experienced, strong, and independent-minded. Presidential ministers are dependent on the whims of their chief and can easily be shielded against parliamentary criticism. Parliamentary ministers, on the other hand, make for future (and therefore experienced) prime ministers. Nevertheless, considering the counterarguments of proponents of presidential systems, their most vocal opponent has formulated his conclusion cautiously, stating that "certain parliamentary systems are more likely than most of their presidential counterparts to solve certain knotty problems of multiparty politics."[61]

A crucial question, discussion of which is long overdue, is what the effect of the two alternative forms of rule might be in profoundly heterogeneous societies. Donald Horowitz, a student of divided societies in

Africa, has claimed that in such societies, parliamentary systems based on the Westminster model have often been sources of instability. They have made interethnic conflict worse and have favored the exclusion of minorities from power. Sir Arthur Lewis, an economic advisor to West African governments during the 1960s, has condemned the introduction of the Anglo-American plurality system in divided societies as "the surest way to kill the idea of democracy."[62] Presidential systems, its proponents claim, can ensure stability, provided the president is not elected by plurality rule. Horowitz has given the examples of the Nigerian Second Republic since 1979 and Sri Lanka since 1978; both countries adopted electoral systems that promoted centrist candidates and encouraged compromise.

With this, the focus has shifted from the question of parliamentarianism versus presidentialism to that of the electoral system, "the most specific manipulative instrument of politics" in the words of Giovanni Sartori.[63] The central issue that runs like a cleavage through the community of political scientists is whether it is better to have an electoral system that stimulates political parties to make deals *before* elections, or one that allows them to make deals (while forming a coalition) *after* the elections. Proponents of the first often characterize the second as "secretive wheeling-dealing" on which the voter has no influence; they deplore the tendency of such systems to allow extremist minorities a voice in parliament. They greatly value the tendency of the Westminster plurality model to generate a two-party system with broad centrist parties. Proponents of the second (PR) list the many disadvantages of the winner-take-all character of plurality elections. A party that may not even have received a majority of the votes may in fact effectively exclude minorities from a voice in government. In the cradle of the Westminster model, for example, "none of postwar Britain's governing parties was put in power by a majority of the voters; all of these parties gained power in spite of the fact that most of the voters voted against them."[64] Moreover, when coalition cabinets are replaced, their ideological-political profile usually does not change as much as that of radically alternating cabinets in parliamentary plurality countries; radical government changes are thought to be detrimental to steady economic development.

Of course, the suggestion of an exclusive dichotomy between the plurality and PR systems is misleading. Different shades of intermediate voting systems are possible and are in fact applied in several countries. It may be useful here to describe what solutions have been adopted in the presidential systems designed for the multiethnic societies of Nigeria and Sri Lanka. In the Nigerian federation, to be elected president, a candidate needed a plurality *plus* at least 25 percent of the vote in no fewer than two-thirds of the states. Sri Lanka, where the candidates were unlikely to gain a majority, adopted a majority requirement with alternative voting; that is, each voter could vote for several candidates by ranking them in order of preference. If no candidate attained a majority on first preference, the second preferences of voters for all but the top two candidates would be counted and added to those of the top two, until one of them gained a majority.[65] Both systems were inclusive in the sense of giving many ethnopolitical groups some influence. They have produced moderate centrist presidents.

Nevertheless, the system of proportional representation has been promoted, particularly by Arend Lijphart, as the electoral system for stimulating political consensus in divided societies. This system's major purpose is to facilitate minority representation and to further broad consultation and bargaining. In theory, it meets the demand of power sharing in divided and multiethnic societies. The earliest moves toward PR are said to have come in the most ethnically heterogeneous countries. Lijphart claims that especially in countries "where there are deep ethnic cleavages or where new democratic forces need to be reconciled with the old antidemocratic groups," the engineers of new constitutions should consider the adoption of a PR electoral system. Lijphart rejects the conventional wisdom that the economic development of a democracy would require the unified leadership of either a strong president or a Westminster-style cabinet. One of his arguments is that if this were so, the economic record of authoritarian governments (free from opposition or internal dissent) would have to be much better than that of democratic governments. But with the exception of the few "economic miracles" in Asia, this is disproved by the sorry economic performance of dictatorships and communist governments the world over.

Comparing the performance of fourteen democratic states on such indicators as representation, protection of minority interests, voter participation, and control of unemployment, Lijphart has concluded that parliamentary-PR governments have "almost invariably" performed better than presidential-plurality or parliamentary-plurality governments.[66] But Lijphart's plea in favor of PR for ethnically divided societies is based mainly on theoretical arguments and on empirical evidence from societies that may hardly be called ethnically divided. The theoretical arguments are sound enough and tend to urge democratizing states at least to consider this electoral system seriously. But the problems of "ethnically divided" countries such as Belgium, Canada, and Britain pale in comparison to those of the successor states of the Soviet Union and Yugoslavia. In opposition to Lijphart, it has been claimed that PR can be outright dangerous for countries faced with ethnic-cultural divisions.

Presidentialism, parliamentarianism, plurality rule, and PR in their various possible combinations continue to draw diverse proponents and opponents from the scholarly community. Historical examples, such as the Weimar Republic and the French Third and Fourth Republics on the one hand and the record of British majority government and American presidential rule on the other, have been used and misused to bolster conflicting arguments. Basic differences, such as on the desirability of consociational pacts and agreements *before* or *after* elections, are interpreted in conflicting ways. Some hail the coalesced clarity of the alternatives presented to the voter in the first (Westminster-type) case and the moderation that this entails in the parties; other authors implicitly value the making of such consociational deals "after the people have spoken." Agreement and certainty exist only for limited generalizations, namely the by now almost truist statements that PR tends to stimulate a multiparty system while plurality voting encourages two-party arrangements, and that coalition governments are more often subject to stress and dissolution than single-party governments.[67] The profound lack of consensus among political scientists, due mainly to the multitude of variables involved and their differing "weight," would seem to call for extreme restraint in advising particular systems of rule to countries in transition from autocracy. Political forces in such countries are ill advised to base their new systems on the fancies of individual Western consultants, who will often further one particular solution while neglecting or understating its drawbacks. They should be aware of Seymour Martin Lipset's warning that because constitutional arrangements can be changed relatively easily, political scientists, consultants, and politicians concerned with furthering stable democratic government tend to focus on such constitutional arrangements. Cultural factors, however, are at least as important and may explain stable democracy even better than electoral systems or constitutional provisions. Unfortunately, such cultural factors are extraordinarily difficult to manipulate.[68]

CLEAVAGES AND PARTY SYSTEMS

Cleavages in cultural, social, economic, religious, or ethnic spheres may be wide and deep; their patterns in different societies may vary from crisscrossing to parallel. The electoral system adopted is not the only determinant of the party system's structure: cleavage patterns are at least as important in the formation of party systems. The type of cleavage pattern dominating a country is therefore of no small importance to the prospects for democracy. Often the main cleavage in society is assumed to be the socioeconomic one, on which income, wealth, economic (in)dependence, ownership, and job security are the main dividing criteria. But what if this cleavage is put in the shade by another, more powerful one: that of ethnicity or religion?

An important question concerning cleavages, party systems, and their contribution to the development of democracy has been dealth with by Ottorino Cappelli.[69] It concerns the question of why territorial (i.e., ethnic) and socioeconomic cleavages usually generate different kinds of political alignments that are not equally conducive to the development of pluralist party systems. The question is of importance because the development of democracy in Western Europe had been based on the preponderance of socioeconomic cleavages over territorial cleavages, as symbolized in Karl Marx and Friedrich Engels's call to the proletarians *of all countries* to unite. The answer Cappelli has given, on the basis of the work of S. M. Lipset and S. Rokkan, is that if the territorial dimension is stressed, communities tend to unite against the outside environment. Territorial cleavages stress differences in values, while socioeconomic cleavages stress differences in interests. In societies characterized by dominant territorial cleavages, differences and conflicts of interest tend to be pushed from the political arena by the strong urge to unite against a common enemy. Socioeconomic cleavages, on the other hand, force people to align according to their conflicting economic interests even if this brings them into conflict with members of their own community. Western democracy came about through the "domestication" of such class struggles and their institutionalization in parliaments, parties, and electoral emancipation.

But *why* have territorial cleavages come to dominate the Soviet political arena during *perestroika* and after? Lucian Pye has observed that transformations from authoritarianism—or the process of modernization—involve a constant battle between two forces. One is that of "the impersonal and universalistic requirements of the world culture," that is, economic development, rationalization, education, and the spread of modern technology and information. The other is that of the "particularistic passions of politics and of group identity," for nationalism inevitably accompanies political development.[70] Thus, the process of transformation involves both the opening up of society and politics to the outside world, and an urge to huddle together in defense of what are felt to be traditional national values threatened by modernization.

GOVERNABILITY

The institutionalization of the new regime is to be reflected in a new constitution outlining the organs of the state and their interdependence, and providing for the protection of society, minorities, and individuals against the arbitrariness of the state's agents. Thus the rules of democracy may at some moment in the transition process "be packaged together into a single handbook—the constitution," but informal rules and norms of prudence are likely to supplement the written constitution, and may occasionally circumvent it.[71] A constitution patterns the political system, but it is not necessarily a written document; and if it is, it is not necessarily a long and comprehensive text. On the contrary, probably the best constitutions are short and concise. Constitutions are to be completed anyway by constitutional legislation providing for the details of the operation of state institutions.[72]

The significance of written constitutions is, of course, that they are usually more difficult to change than normal legislation. In trying to protect their constitutional setup from malevolent change by chance majorities, most societies write qualified majorities for amendments into their constitutions. Another characteristic of written constitutions is that they usually do not provide rules for their own abolition. They assume their own permanence and imply that they can only be abolished by unconstitutional means. In times of transition, this feature can create particularly painful dilemmas for those who want to move ahead in the direction of a democratic constitution. They may have to act in ways that are not considered democratic at all.

Assuming the successful completion of a transition process by the installation of a minimal democratic constitution, the consolidation of such a democracy is no easy matter. The new citizens have been raised as subjects in conditions of high certainty about the behavior of the authoritarian rulers and about the possible consequences of their own behavior. Democracy suddenly institutionalizes a degree of uncertainty that most citizens will find difficult to accept and to live with. Often the installation of democracy is accompanied by an outburst of rising expectations among the populace.[73] They expect that now that they have a voice in public decision making, economic and social wrongs will be corrected overnight. They tend to identify democracy with the good life and to expect that long-overdue grievances will be met promptly. Few are aware of the instrumental character of democracy and the uncertainty it entails on the outcomes of the democratic process. As long as democracy is young and inexperienced, this natural attitude of its citizens makes for serious problems in the consolidation of the system.

One of these problems is that the political agenda may be overloaded with issues demanding authoritative decisions while the economy may be in ruins. The political elites face the dilemma of fighting their battles over the division of power while at the same time having to answer public demands for basic redistributions of income and wealth. They will not be able to do first what comes first, so that the two struggles become intertwined. In order to bolster their power position, elite groups may promise and, at least temporarily, deliver benefits that undermine economic stabilization and the reorganization of public finance.

These problems raise the question of *governability:* the ability of rulers to govern. By this I mean not so much their personal political skills but the situational arrangement in which they find themselves and the limits that such an arrangement may pose on the effectiveness of their rule. Sabrina Ramet has distinguished between "weak" and "strong" society and "weak" and "strong" government to highlight the problems involved. By "strong society" she means "a society capable of defending itself against tyranny in whatever form it might take" (a weak society obviously not being capable of doing so), or more specifically a society with (1) an educated public and independent intellectuals, in which individuals and groups (2) have access to accurate information about their sociopolitical environment, (3) can organize autonomous organizations, (4) have access to the channels of mass communication not controlled by the government, and (5) are mobilized in the sense of being aware of the issues on the political agenda and engage in public debate.[74]

A strong government is one with (1) the ability to obtain accurate information about developments in society; (2) the capacity to reach a consensus about appropriate actions and to assure that its decrees and laws are carried out and enforced; (3) a developed infrastructure, financial and coercive resources, and instruments of propaganda and socialization; (4) the conviction, on the part of the governing elite, that their governance is legitimate; and (5) either the clear legitimacy of the system and the regime in the eyes of the population, or the ability of the government to terrorize, intimidate, and crush any hint of criticism or opposition.

One can easily see why the traditional Western democracies have such wide appeal: they combine strong government (of the legitimate type) with strong society and thus tend to be stable. Modern authoritarian systems have generally been characterized by the combination of a relatively strong government (with oppression instead of legitimacy) with a weak society. Such systems, too, can be stable for a long time, although pressures for change will build up under the superficial illusion of social peace and political consensus. Two other possible combinations are (1) weak government with a weak society and (2) weak government with a strong society. The first, typical for traditional societies, can be stable for a long time; the second is potentially explosive.

Concerning communist systems, there is no question that their societies were weak. But were their governments weak as well, or were they strong? The answer depends, of course, on the status of the indicators listed above. Are these to be considered necessary and sufficient conditions—or merely criteria of which it can be said that the more a government "obtains," the stronger it is? Some consider the lack of popular legitimacy of communist governments to be an indication of their weakness; others have located the beginning of failure where the communist elites themselves started to have doubts about their own legitimacy and began experimenting with different modes of legitimation. Of course, their having been socialized in Marxism-Leninism gave them a basis for feeling confident of their right to decide what was good for society—but to what extent was confidence eroded by the popular revolts in Berlin (1953), Poland and Hungary (1956), Novocherkassk (1962), Czechoslovakia (1968), and, again, Poland (1980–1981)? Probably full conviction in this sense existed only during the reign of Lenin and Stalin (1917–1953).

On the first three indicators, communist systems clearly scored stronger, although even here questions can be raised. Through their police and other organizations, the elites were able to collect information about the "state of society," but in the process of gathering and aggregating information, the ideological (and bureaucratic) filters of those reporting information upward often distorted such information. Statistical information on the economy and on demographic-ethnic questions was especially vulnerable. The elites usually could reach a consensus in decision making, but often their ability to have decisions implemented was limited by the self-serving behavior of regional and sectoral elites and bureaucracies. In contrast to the ideal-typical democracy, communist systems lacked a civil service convinced of their serving the general interests of society and the state. Finally, the systems could dispose of massive infrastructures, resources, and propaganda machines, but the lack of popular legitimacy restricted the impact of their functioning. So were these governments strong? The least we can say is that in spite (or because) of their suppressive capacity, they were not nearly as strong as established democratic governments. Their lack of popular legitimacy tended to corrode all remaining indicators, including the self-confidence of the self-appointed elites.

TWO *The Soviet Bequest*
to Russia

Only people in power care about politics; everyone else is only concerned about their lives. (Konstantin Michelev (32), veterinarian in Tula, September 1993)[1]

We are new, we are different. We direct our appeal to those who are weary, those who are bored, those who do not believe in anybody anymore and who feel they just don't want to go to the polls. (Vladimir Mironov of "Russia's Future–New Names" party in a campaign broadcast on Russian television, November 1993)[2]

Political scientists with an interest in the problem of transition generally show a limited awareness of the specific dilemmas of postcommunist societies. On the other hand, communist-area specialists tend to emphasize the specificity of their field of study and to reject the application of general "transition theories" to the countries of Central and Eastern Europe. It is argued that one cannot compare countries as different in their history and political culture as Uruguay and Ukraine. This book would not have been written if its author did not think that one can in principle compare a lady's garter belt to a country's constitution (both being there to uphold something, and both being, for some people at least, exciting objects of study). To the objection that a comparison has to make sense and serve a reasonable purpose, he would reply that comparing the Russian transition with those in the rest of the world serves the purpose of gaining insight not only into the specificities of *la condition Russe*, but also into the ways in which the Russians are not-so-different from the rest of us. Comparison involves the investigation of similarities and differences; it is a tool in tracing the way in which differences in geography, tradition, and trauma modify the working of general regularities. It is also a device for gaining a deeper insight into the problems of a specific country.

So let me deal first with the question of in what way Russia-in-transition is set apart from the rest of the world. Upon reflection, the obstacles to normalization of Russian society, if compared to other countries, are huge indeed. They can be summarized in four sections. In doing so, I will use the terms "noncommunist" for the countries of the transition studies referred to in the previous chapter, "outer empire" for the (post)communist countries of Eastern and Central Europe, and "inner empire" for those (post)communist countries that used to be part of the USSR. I should stress that the four sections show some overlap: they are separated here for analytical reasons only.

THE RUSSIAN CONDITION

The first reason why transition is exceptionally difficult in Russia is the very long duration of abnormality in that country. In contrast to most noncommunist countries and the outer empire, and even to such inner-empire countries as the Baltic states and Moldova, communist rule in Russia has had seven decades to thoroughly poison human minds and relations. In contrast to these other countries, by 1990 in Russia no people were alive who could remember the relative normality of the first decade of the century. The simple fact that in countries such as Poland and Estonia communist rule had been a post-1945 phenomenon gave them a head start over Russia in the transition. And it was not only a matter of memory. The communists had had seven decades to shape the Russians into *Soviet men,* with very distinct value and behavior patterns that set them apart from Hungarians or Lithuanians.

Second is a complex of circumstances resulting from the fact that the Soviet Union was not an average authoritarian state, but a special sub-type: a communist state (some would say a totalitarian state). It had a state-ruled economy in which private property (of everything but objects for personal use) was outlawed, and an official ideology that functioned to give the ruling elite an inflated self-confidence and legitimacy. As a result, when Russia started out in its transition, it had no category of people trained in dealing with accumulated wealth for their own interest and (indirectly) that of society (one could use the terms bourgeoisie and entrepreneurial class); it had many farmhands, but no people used to the risk taking of independent farming; and its elite and population had been brainwashed into thinking that individual property was reprehensible. Igor Kliamkin has summarized this condition in stating that the Russian population had unlearned to think and behave according to their "productive interests" and were thinking and behaving exclusively in terms of "consumerist interests." In such a society, he wrote in 1993, "people see and understand each other as competitors exclusively in the field of consumption, not in production."[3]

Such sweeping characterizations, of course, tend to exaggerate. There had indeed been signs during the long, drawn-out Brezhnev period that private initiative, even in the productive sphere, was not dead but in a state of suspended animation.[4] It could not have been otherwise, given the explosion of producer cooperatives once the Gorbachev regime changed the law (in 1988). One should also keep in mind that Soviet man ("homo sovieticus") had developed skills at taking initiatives in manipulating the rules of the system for his or her own benefit, while reducing risks to a minimum. The many nonofficial ("black" and otherwise colored) markets of the Brezhnev period testified to this. Such skills were not always harmful to the late-communist system, and they showed that Russians had not completely unlearned how to reduce risks while taking initiatives.

Another part of this complex of circumstances is the structure of the Soviet economy. Transition was not only made difficult by the legacy of central planning and the absence of sound economic indicators for production and distribution decisions, but also by the fact that the economy was heavily dominated by the military-industrial complex, to a far greater extent than in the noncommunist countries that underwent transition. The introduction of market mechanisms and the privatization of industries and farmland had to be complemented by a thorough restructuring of the economy away from military domination. It was no surprise that military-industrial interests turned into one of the strongest political forces putting the brake to transition.

Then there is the fact that Russia, as part of the Soviet Union, had suffered from the imposition of an ideology that allowed no argument. Although very few people by the late twentieth century believed the postulates of Marxism-Leninism, the ideology had had ample time to poison their minds. This was because Marxism-Leninism was forced upon them in very specific (and varying) interpretations, justifying the rulers and their policies of a particular period. This left the Russians with seriously maimed minds, in stark contrast to the Chileans during the rule of Pinochet, or the Hungarians during Kadar. The Russians of the second half of the twentieth century knew little about their own history *or* about their present, and had almost no opportunity to learn if they wanted to do so.[5] The imposition of Marxism-Leninism left them with distorted views of what politics, democracy, and capitalism were like. The force of the ideology in combination with the long duration of its rule explain why, in contrast to the noncommunist and outer empire countries, so very few independent thinkers were left in Russia. Even in some countries of the inner empire (such as the Baltic states or Ukraine), far more independent thinkers survived communist rule and were able to present an alternative vision of the future once such an alternative became (in the Gorbachev period) a realistic possibility. Apart from Andrei Sakharov, whose role in presenting such a vision during the twenty years between 1968 and 1989 can hardly be overestimated, Russia had only a very small group of "dissidents." Lacking in numbers and organization, they were in no position to present a counterforce to the communists, either in the streets or at the negotiation table.

One other aspect of the combination of single ideology with state-run economy should be mentioned: the unprecedented degree of "social engineering" that Russia (in addition to at least the countries of the inner empire) suffered. By this I mean the purposive and pitiless creation of a "new-type society" by the communists, at least up to the Brezhnev period. Most of the authoritarian regimes did not try to do this, or at least to a far less threatening or destructive degree. The traumas left behind by social engineering are deep and extremely painful.

Finally, in this complex of socioeconomic circumstances that sets Russia apart from other countries, we should not fail to notice the enormous scale of the mess that communist rule has left behind, and the social tensions and pressures that it may generate. To most of us in the West, this scale is beyond imagination. Pollution of the environment has seriously undermined the health of the population in many regions of the country, to the extent that infant mortality is rising and the percentage of healthy newborns is sometimes very low. One could also mention the soaring crime rate, the social disruption that will result from bankruptcies and rising unemployment, the ethnic tensions, and the increasing risk of uncontrollable disasters affecting the lives of many people. The citizens of Russia do not differ from us in that they consider such daily problems to be of far greater urgency than the installation of democratic structures in faraway capitals. This complex of dislocations will thus draw heavily on the nerves of rulers and legislators, and on their abilities to steer the transition process.

A third circumstance setting Russia apart from most of the other countries experiencing transition is its multinational character in combination with the fact that, from the border of Ukraine, the Russian Federation extends eleven time zones eastward to the Bering Straits, and between the forbidding tundra of the North to the mild climate of the Black Sea. The only (but much smaller) country in a similar situation is the former Yugoslavia, which, during the early phase of transition, erupted into civil war. Yugoslavia, however, had a tradition of handling disputes on the distribution of resources and subsidies between different nations that was very different from the Soviet tradition.[6] In contrast to Yugoslavia, Russia was unfamiliar with a process of bargaining between the communist elites of different ethnic groups over the distribution of such resources. The populations of most of the other countries are relatively homogeneous, or show manageable diversity. In Czechoslovakia, the greater part of the problem was defused by the "elegant divorce" between Slovakia and the Czech lands. Although the percentage of Russians in the Russian Federation (approximately 82 percent) is considerably higher than it was in the Soviet Union (about 52 percent), tendencies similar to those that drove the Soviet nations apart are visible in Russia. Such tendencies are of the utmost concern for the Russian leadership: they affect the preservation of the "integrity of the Russian state." The situation is confusing indeed. In the Soviet Union intermarriage between people of different nations was widespread. Children of mixed origin could choose their "passport identity" from among those of their parents; a "passport Russian" could have, for example, a Russian father and a Jewish mother or two Russian parents. Differences between a "pure Russian" and a person of mixed Russian-Mari or Russian-Ukrainian descent are not at all obvious. The Russians, therefore, have a real problem in determining who they are and what they stand for. The formation of their national consciousness coincided with colonialist expansion, the "gathering of the lands" adjacent to those of the Muscovite *Rus* and farther away. This concurrence had two consequences. It "blurred the ethnic and cultural definition of Russian nationality and made Russia's political identity heavily dependent on the tsarist state's imperial exploits."[7]

Russians can be (and are) often blamed for the bad handling of interethnic relations by the communists. The lack of an accepted mechanism for economic distribution between different republics and regions in the Russian Federation (taxation, subsidies, investments, support of particular industries) has required such a mechanism to be created in the course of transition. In addition, the multinational makeup of the population facilitated the use of nationalist symbols by republican leaderships, in order to strengthen their hand vis-à-vis the leaders in Moscow. After all, percentagewise, the numbers of Tatars in Tatarstan and Yakuts in Sakha-

Yakutia may dwarf in comparison to the number of Russians (Tatars, the "second" nation of the Russian Federation, are less than 4 percent of the population), but they do have considerable natural resources in their territories. Disputes erupted about which elites were to control these resources and for whose benefit. As if all this were not enough, the Russian political agenda of the transition period is burdened by the issues of protecting Russians in the "near abroad" (the new states of the inner empire) and of absorbing large numbers of destitute Russian immigrants.

Fourth and finally comes a set of two related conditions that set Russia apart from the other countries: Russia originally created the Soviet empire and is now heir to its (nuclear) great-power status. This situation, unique to Russia, has various implications. It strengthens the distrust of Russian intentions among the populations and elites of the former outer and inner empires, and thus hampers the normalization of relations between Russia and its neighbors in Eastern and Central Europe. It sharpens international conflicts, such as with Ukraine, by the presence of nuclear arms as objects over which such conflicts are fought. It leaves a series of unresolved problems behind for politicians who should rather concentrate on managing the transition of Russia proper: problems such as the withdrawal of troops, the redistribution of assets, and the ratification of multilateral treaties. It has resulted in a country that is potentially rich and strong but is actually in dismal straits, which can voice a veto over decision making in the UN Security Council, whereas Germany and Japan cannot. It has brought about an attitude on the part of Western leaders whereby they tend to overprotect the Russian leadership out of fear for the worse. As a result, the Russian political elite tend toward an "imperial mentality" and tend to overestimate their role on the international scene. Their major struggle of the 1990s is either to give in to the historical reflex toward expansion as the essence of Russian national identity, or to redefine that identity in more modest terms. Russia, unfortunately for the Russians, lacks the psychology of total ruin that so greatly helped the Germans and the Japanese to regain their economic footing after 1945 and build a democratic polity in the process.

RUSSIAN HISTORY

In fixing the specific position of the Russian body politic among countries that have experienced or are still undergoing transition, it seems that we cannot escape from the conclusion that the problems of Russia are insurmountable. Is there nothing to be said for Russian society that would offer some hope? There is. In the analysis of the problems of transition, one factor has often been overlooked, and that is the cultural and social changes that have occurred in Russian and Soviet history. In estimating the possibilities of a successful transition, it would be foolish to ignore them.

It is misleading to say that Russia has an exclusively autocratic tradition. The country has experienced long periods of repressive rule, and several false starts. But if we take a bird's-eye view of its political development, we cannot fail to note the representative bodies that came to play a role in state affairs. These institutions were not so different from the advisory councils and representative assemblies that in Western and Central Europe had accompanied the transition from feudalism to centralized monarchies. Such councils and assemblies of the nobility, clergy, and townsmen gave parts of the population a voice vis-à-vis the monarch and allowed him to keep in touch with those social forces that were of importance to his rule. England had its Parliament, Holland and France their Estates General, Sweden its Riksdag, and Poland its Sejm. In Russia they were called the *Boiarskaia Duma* (Barons' Council, from the tenth to the early eighteenth centuries) and the *Zemskii Sobor* (Assembly of the Land, from the mid-sixteenth to the mid-seventeenth centuries).[8] Like their counterparts elsewhere, these institutions injected ideas and traditions of representation, power sharing, consultation, and even joint decision making into the minds of the political elite.

The degree of institutionalization of the *Zemskii Sobor* was limited in that it was not subject to fixed rules for its calling or for its procedure, and also in that it met, on and off, at the whim of the monarch. Nevertheless, the Assembly of 1613, called to elect a new tsar, adopted the principle that some of the Assembly's members should be elected from their constituencies instead of appointed from above; and for the Assembly of 1648–1649 some of these elections were indeed sharply contested. The different social interests represented in the Assembly of 1648–1649 succeeded in forcing a number of concessions from the government in the drafting of the *Sobornoe Ulozhenie* (Assembly Law Code). Although the Assembly had initially been created by the government to gather information on society, the government soon discovered

> that delegates to a Zemskii Sobor legitimized what it wanted to do anyway. Thus the Zemskii Sobor proved to be a useful instrument for deciding whether the country could fight wars and pay for them and for legitimizing new monarchs. But when the elected delegates discovered that they could force the government to enact new laws

that the oligarchs running the government did not want, the government tired of the institution and may even have become fearful of it.[9]

Both the Barons' Council and the Assembly succumbed to autocratic-bureaucratic rule. It should be noted, however, that so did some of the parallel institutions to the west of Russia. The ideas that the Duma and the Assembly had fostered lingered on. One of these ideas was that of a largely representative parliament that would have its say in the country's legislation. Such ideas, and that of the rule of law as the supreme principle for the organization of the state, were laid down in the plan for a new political system that Mikhail Speranskii wrote in 1809–1810 for Tsar Alexander I. Although it was not adopted, and the full plan was published only at the end of the century, Speranskii's plan was one more sign indicating that ideas about representative and responsible government were not at all foreign to Russia.

If seen in long-term perspective, Russia moves slowly, but it does move. One century after Speranskii's plan, the revolution of 1905, triggered by Russia's defeat in the war with Japan, resulted in the Constitutional Manifesto in which the tsar promised universal suffrage and true legislative responsibility (but not governmental dependence upon parliament) for the lower house of parliament, the State Duma.[10] In terms of representation, stability, and governmental responsibility, the four Dumas that convened between 1906 and 1917 compared unfavorably to parliaments in Western Europe. Nevertheless, they provided a new arena for the expression and aggregation of the interests of different sectors of society, for training in the political struggle with autocracy, and for the institutionalization of parliamentary procedure and parliamentary parties. A wide range of political parties, from rightist to the Kadets, Social Democrats, and *Trudoviks*, formed their factions in parliament.

By 1917, it could be said that, compared to the rest of Europe, Russian development toward democracy had been slow and uneven, but that development was nevertheless unmistakable. As Rigby has observed, Russia had a parliament, although it did not yet have parliamentary government:

> Seen in the European context, Russian political development was certainly retarded, but it was headed in the same general direction and gradually narrowing the gap. So when the monarchy was overthrown in February–March 1917, opening the way to a true parliamentary democracy, this was not something out of the blue.[11]

But the Bolsheviks seized power in October, and held onto it. What followed was a period of roughly thirty-five years of unprecedented terror and arbitrariness (1917–1953), and another thirty-five years (1953–1988) of limited repression accompanied by unchecked, though not always unresponsive, rule. With memories of the long Brezhnev period (1964–1982) quickly fading, it may seem odd to many, particularly in Russia, to claim that part of the legacy of Soviet rule is positive to the institutionalization of democracy. And yet there are two points to be made. They flow from the fact that in the 1936 (Stalin) Constitution, the communists had adjusted their initial ideas about the sovereignty of the proletariat to the discourse of democracy. The 1936 Constitution (and its follow-up, the 1977 Brezhnev Constitution) adopted a new approach, which copied the institutional structure of Western European democracies. Of course, the communist party firmly held the strings of power, but from the 1930s the formal organization of the Soviet state was similar to that of a modern liberal democracy. The main principle that was lacking was the separation of powers between parliament, the executive, and the judiciary. Full sovereignty was supposed to reside in parliament. And yet, there was a perceived need for some mimicry of the separation of powers. Parliament (the two-chamber Supreme Soviet) was elected directly by the population, and it confirmed the prime minister. The government resigned when a new parliament was elected, and bills were adopted by that parliament.

This had two important consequences for postcommunism. First, it was of no small significance, both to Gorbachev's *perestroika* and to postcommunism, that a formal structure for democratic rule had been in place for more than half a century. Communist rule had been implemented through soviets (elected representative councils) that were subject to a plethora of rules and regulations. People's deputies had been trained in a long-established process for the adoption of legislation. If set against the criteria of democratic rules and procedures, the balance of this process was, of course, negative. At times, during the Khrushchev and Brezhnev periods in particular, there had been opportunities for organized social and political interests to exert a limited influence on legislation.[12] But such opportunities had been undermined by the tendency of the parliament's Presidium to accumulate more and more unchecked power by legislating in the form of decrees. Mikhail Gorbachev's constitutional experiments of 1988–1990 were essentially (unhappy) modifications of the existing structure; and when in late 1991 Soviet rule collapsed, there were institutions in place in the successor states.

Now it may be objected that these institutions had been completely discredited—but that is not the point I want to make here. Even though the structures of the Supreme Soviet and the government had been misused by the communists, they were nevertheless in place when democratization came. The fact that Soviet politics was under a cloud because of its inherent hypocrisy had another consequence that positively affected postcommunism. Several authors, including Harry Rigby and Michael Urban, have focused on the self-destructive spin-offs of this hypocrisy. Rigby has observed that traces of a democratic consciousness were preserved thanks to what he termed the "institutionalized hypocrisy" of the regime. These traces were the result of the sometimes stark discrepancy between the formal rules of the communist regime concerning political democracy and human rights (in, for example, the USSR Constitution and the Communist Party Rules' *Moral Code of the Builder of Communism*) and their day-to-day implementation.

The Leninist concept of council (soviet) democracy, practiced in the Soviet Union from 1917, was presented as the highest form of democracy, superior by far to the perverted capitalist "democracy" in quotation marks. This had a double effect. On the one hand, as Urban wrote in 1990, "the hypocrisy displayed by the regime towards the soviets corrupted the very identity that the regime claimed for itself."[13] On the other hand, since hypocrisy is a discrepancy between deeds and professed ideals, the ideals were preserved by the continued hypocrisy: the hypocrisy of the communists contributed to the preservation, and maybe even the strengthening, of democratic norms and values in the minds of the Russian people. Moreover, their social engineering resulted in the creation of a new generation of professionals that came to dominate Russian society in the latter part of the century. This generation came to be a powerful social undercurrent, and the hidden engine of transition. To a high degree it embodied the very values of democracy that the communists were unable to exterminate. It showed that Russia's greatest asset is its people. Let us now turn to them.

SOCIAL CHANGE

Several authors have called attention to the often underestimated role of social change in the Soviet Union since World War II. They have been quite correct in stating that during the 1970s and 1980s the community of Soviet specialists in the West had well-nigh neglected sociological studies of the Soviet Union. In the mid-1980s they focused mainly on questions of power (re-)distribution, foreign policy, security, and nationalities policy, but they often failed to see and to investigate the profound changes that the population of the USSR had undergone as a result of social engineering by the communists. Among the first to set the record straight was the historian Moshe Lewin, who in 1988 published *The Gorbachev Phenomenon*.[14] American Political Science Association president Lucian Pye highlighted the issue in his 1989 presidential address and referred to the work of both Lewin and Seweryn Bialer.[15] Later, in a well-balanced assessment of the Gorbachev record, John Miller again pointed to the crucial role of social forces.[16]

The focus on social change falls within modernization theory, which seeks to explain changes in the political system in terms of the underlying and peremptory changes in the structure of society, such as the elimination of illiteracy; urbanization; changes in professional structure; and the spread of education and information. The theory claims that such social changes create strong pressure for changes in the political system in the direction of democracy. Here I will not deal with all aspects of modernization theory as applied to the Soviet Union and Russia.[17] I merely want to characterize the society that communist rule has left behind, and to show in what ways it can be expected to be more receptive to democratic values than Russian society was half a century ago.

The essence of social change during the four decades following the end of the war was the formation of a new generation of professionals within a comparatively short span of time. For the time being I will refrain from designating these professionals as a "new middle class," the label used by several authors on the Gorbachev period. One of the crucial questions of the Russian transition is whether the new professionals did indeed constitute the core of a new middle class that could provide for the social integration and stabilization that Russia needed so badly. That question will be taken up in chapter 5. In the current chapter, I will try to reveal more about their views on society and politics. This concerns the crucial concept of political culture: the knowledge, beliefs, perceptions, expectations, and values of individuals concerning political life and their place in it. Finally, the question of their role in the transformation of Russia is to be dealt with, in particular their importance for the revitalization of civil society and for the democratization of politics.

Basically, what had happened after the war was that in a very short span of time—much shorter than for similar social changes in Western societies—Soviet society had become highly urbanized and its population highly educated. At the time of the 1917 revolution, Russia had been a profoundly agrarian country with 80 percent of its population living in villages or small towns. Illiteracy was widespread. Three decades later, half the population were still peasants, albeit peasants in collective or state farms, who were quickly unlearning the skills of independent farming or peasantry. But by the late 1980s only one out of every eight people was a peasant. The USSR had become an urban country in which the mass of the population had come to adopt urban values and had become estranged from rural life.

Simultaneously, education levels rose dramatically. In 1959, nine out of ten workers and ninety-eight out of every one hundred *kolkhoz* members had no more than an elementary school education. Twenty-five years later, over 80 percent of all manual workers had more than an elementary school education, and the proportion of the population that had a secondary school education was similar to that in the United States.[18] By the late 1980s, the professionals came to dominate Soviet society—and Mikhail Gorbachev was their most vocal political exponent. These highly trained employees, called "suppies" (Soviet urban professionals) by Thomas Remington, comprised about one quarter of the workforce and 40 percent of the urban population and of CPSU membership.[19] Many of them were sent to help develop industries, agriculture, and administration in the rim republics of the USSR. Between 1959 and 1989, five million Russians left the RSFSR, mainly for the developing cities in Ukraine, Belorussia, and Kazakhstan.[20] Both the Baltic states and the republics of Central Asia experienced an influx of Russian-speaking professionals and skilled workers as well; in many cities they came to dominate public life.

The new professionals were one of the strongest social forces contributing to the collapse of communist rule. This new generation of highly educated people had been kept from articulating and expressing its distinct interests for a long time. As John Miller has observed, "They remained second-class auxiliaries to the (party's) *apparat*, never strong or confident enough to compel entry into the ruling class, whilst the latter became too stupid to save itself by co-optation and evolution."[21]

One indication of their breakthrough during the Gorbachev period was their representation in parliament. The share of people with jobs in "middle management," such as directors of farms and factories, headmasters, and heads of hospitals or laboratories, rose from 7 percent in the 1984 USSR Supreme Soviet to 35 percent in the new Supreme Soviet elected (by the new Congress of People's Deputies) in 1989. Most of them had been trained as engineers. Just over half of the deputies of the 1984 parliament had had tertiary qualifications; in the USSR Congress of People's Deputies, 76 percent had such qualifications, and in 1990 in the newly elected parliaments of the RSFSR and Ukraine, over 90 percent of the legislators had such qualifications.[22] Moreover, the members of parliament were new and comparatively young. In the Congress of People's Deputies of the RSFSR elected in March 1990, 94 percent of the deputies were elected for the first time, and 80 percent were between thirty-six and fifty-five years old.[23] They had been born between 1935 and 1954. A new generation had come to power, a generation that had received its political education and training during the postwar period.

GENERATION CHANGE

Gorbachev's misjudgment of the interests and demands of the suppies was one of the reasons for his partly failed revolution. What exactly did these professionals think? How did they evaluate the political system; what did they expect of politics and of personal involvement? It is often thought that such questions could not be answered as long as the Communist Party kept the country closed to independent social research, and social statistics were unreliable. And yet, since the war, several research projects have been undertaken which altogether have yielded a considerable amount of hard data on the psychological profile of the Soviet population and of specific substrata.[24]

One first such endeavor was the Harvard Refugee Interview Project in the late 1940s, in the course of which a great many refugees and displaced persons were interviewed. The project resulted in the first empirically based sociological study, The Soviet Citizen, by Alex Inkeles and Raymond Bauer, a book that had a profound impact on the field of Soviet studies.[25] Between 1968 and 1985, some 375,000 Soviet citizens were allowed to leave the country; they again provided raw material for Western researchers. In Israel and the United States, emigrants were interviewed by Zvi Gitelman.[26] Further, in 1983 a random sample of 2,793 respondents was interviewed in the Soviet Interview Project (SIP), sponsored by the U.S. National Council for Soviet and East European Research.[27] They were asked about their experiences and feelings during their "last normal period" in the USSR, that is, the five years prior to their decision to emigrate. For almost all respondents this period had ended between 1978 and 1981, so that the outcomes of the project refer to Soviet attitudes during the late 1970s. The results of the Soviet Interview Project are of particular significance because they have fixed the state of mind and political behavior of a particular segment of the Soviet population on the eve of the deep changes introduced by Gorbachev.

Only by the early 1990s was the compromise solution of interviewing emigrants no longer necessary: Western investigators were allowed access to Soviet society. One of the first studies was undertaken by a team from the University of Houston, who arranged for the interviewing of a random sample of 504 citizens of Moscow *oblast* (44 percent of them living outside the city of Moscow) in late February to early March 1990.[28] Of course, before and during the Gorbachev period, opinion polling and sociological research had been undertaken by Soviet scholars as well, but their studies had lacked fundamental methodological rigor and were of little value.[29] It is on the Western studies that my generalizations concerning sociopsychological change will be based. I should stress here that for the sake of readability I will refrain from providing precise statistical demonstrations in each and every case; they can be found in the works to which I am referring.

The most significant general finding of the Soviet Interview Project has been that between the late 1940s and the late 1970s a profound transformation in the structure of support for the regime had taken place. The Harvard Project had shown that right after the war the young and the well educated had been the most supportive of the Soviet regime, and that the older and less well educated were far more critical. The SIP, however, showed the opposite result: in the late 1970s, the younger and better educated were the most alienated from the system, despite the fact that they were disproportionately reaping the benefits of the Soviet system—as they admitted themselves.[30]

Perhaps this dissatisfaction was simply a matter of changing views during a person's life cycle; perhaps it will go away as the new professionals age? It will not. Donna Bahry has argued that to speak of a generation gap is indeed no exaggeration.[31] In the SIP data she has found a clear-cut break between the views of successive generations, with the generation born between 1941 and 1960 showing significantly more interest in politics and more willingness to participate in both regime-supporting and unconventional or nonconformist activities. The new generation showed less fear than earlier generations who lived through the Stalin years, and it expected more; they judged the Brezhnev regime on its current performance, not (as did their parents) on its performance in comparison with the past. Since in all probability the SIP sample was representative of adult Europeans from large and medium-sized cities in the Soviet Union, these are indeed the people that now matter to Russian society and politics, being in their thirties, forties, and fifties.[32]

The "best and the brightest" in contemporary Russian society have enjoyed significantly more and better education than earlier generations. Moreover, their material well-being before the collapse of the USSR was also much better than before. They have benefited greatly from the communist system; and the regime has employed several means (including education and satisfaction of material wants) to enlist their enduring support in return for these benefits. Yet, as Brian Silver has shown, on the basis of the same SIP data, education worked to weaken support for the regime both directly and indirectly (by reducing the subjective material satisfaction of people in similar objective material conditions). Writing in the early Gorbachev period, Silver summarized his statistical analysis by stating that "the apparent disaffection of the educated class as a whole presents a challenge for Soviet leaders. This is the middle class for whom the Big Deal was arranged. This class is growing in size and importance to the Soviet economy, but with its increasing political sophistication comes increasing disaffection."[33]

We should keep in mind, however, that it is still undecided whether it is justified to term the "educated class" a new middle class. There is no doubt that up to the early 1990s the category was quite distinct from the middle class in Western societies. As John Miller has observed, its origins did not lie in trade or industry; it had no history of independence of the state; it had hardly developed a sense of identity, and it lacked organization; and it was "easily distracted by populism or nationalism."[34] It was indeed dubious whether the term "middle class" could rightfully be used.

POLITICAL CULTURE

From these general findings we should move to the level of specific views and expectations concerning politics and political activity, that is to say the specific political culture of the professionals. The concept is of some importance in evaluating the possible success or failure of transition from authoritarianism. For it is generally understood (on the basis of empirical findings) that political democracy will have a very difficult time in a society lacking a so-called "civic culture."[35] The question that remains unsolved concerns the precise relationship between political structure and political culture. Is a democratic political culture a necessary precondition for the installation of a democratic regime? Or can the norms and values of such a culture grow after such a regime has been installed—in the way that Giuseppe Di Palma has suggested? The question bears on Russia in particular, and the contemporary Russian experience in its turn is of some importance for the general discussion in political science on the link between structural and cultural change. Russian political culture is notoriously undemocratic; many observers

have claimed that it makes democracy impossible. It is indeed not difficult to find historical arguments for the proposition that democracy can
never succeed in Russia. Yet, such arguments often assume an uncritical
extrapolation of historical experiences to the present, and they pass by
the profound changes that Russian society has undergone. The answer
can only come from painstaking empirical research or from real developments—such as a democratic government that has been stable for at
least two decades.

Before Mikhail Gorbachev started tampering with the Soviet system,
the general wisdom in the West was that Soviet citizens had no influence
over politics, were not interested in politics (and therefore had extremely
limited "political self-confidence" or political efficacy), and only took
part in political life on a massive scale (in elections, in political meetings) because it was demanded of them and because the costs of such
ritualistic political behavior were significantly lower than those of ab-
stention or deviant behavior. People were thought to have no trust in
their fellow citizens—let alone in members of the *nomenklatura*. In the
hostile environment of the communist state, such absence of trust (and
the accompanying "social atomization") was thought to block the rise
of independent social and political associations for the promotion and
protection of collective interests.

However, within three years after Gorbachev came to power, social,
economic and political associations shot up like mushrooms after an
autumn downpour. What did this say about the structure of the Russian "earth," the political attitudes of the population, and in particular about the new professionals who dominated these associations? If
"Soviet men" had indeed been only passive, untrusting collaborators,
what is the explanation for the sudden outburst of political activity (and
trust in fellow citizens) once barriers were removed by Gorbachev? If
in the political culture of Soviet citizens their interest in politics, their
trust of fellow citizens, and their sense of political efficacy had been
almost nil, how could they suddenly rise in spontaneous political behavior?

The simplistic picture of the Soviet population, originating in the
totalitarian model, was misleading. Long before 1985, several Sovietologists had tried to correct it, using limited hard data in combination
with creative research techniques. Its main defect turned out to be that
it failed to distinguish between the Stalin-to-Brezhnev generations on
the one hand, and the postwar generation that was growing up during
the times of Khrushchev and Brezhnev. The older generations were indeed to a great extent intimidated into obedient ritualistic participation.

Many decades after the death of the tyrant, the fear they had experienced during their formative years still dictated their behavior, whereas the gradual improvement in living conditions (including less severe penalties for deviant behavior) mellowed their views concerning the system and its leaders. The young, however, were cast in a different mould.

In 1990, reporting on SIP-based research concerning the late-Brezhnev period, Bahry and Silver grouped the different forms of political participation of Soviet citizens (i.e., Europeans living in medium to large cities) along four dimensions: (1) *unconventional political activism* such as distributing *samizdat* (unauthorized publications), participation in public protests, involvement in unsanctioned study or discussion groups, and avoidance of voting; (2) *compliant political activism* such as serving on a committee at work or in a political organization, or in a comrades' court; (3) *social activism* such as membership in parents' committees and housing commissions; and (4) *contacting*, that is, individual efforts to contact officials in the party, in government, or in the mass media with the aim of either solving personal problems (housing repairs and pension benefits, for example) or of filing a complaint about the behavior of officials.[36] The categories are not mutually exclusive, and indeed the investigators found that the younger generation in particular engaged in both compliant *and* unconventional participation. They also found a positive correlation between such activism and individual motivations and attitudes, signifying that contrary to the simple picture of Soviet society as a nation of sheep, "people made choices whether to participate in most types of activity, choices that reflected their attitudes as well as their social position."[37]

Moreover, the assumption that activists in conventional political organizations supported all aspects of communist rule proved wrong. For example, people who occupied leadership positions in such organizations usually favored free, state-provided medical care and state ownership of heavy industry. However, they were usually not happy at all with the state's restrictions on individual freedom. Thus, they believed in the right to strike and in private agriculture, and strongly disliked the system of permits restricting residence in the bigger cities.

Variables such as the attitude toward free, state-provided medical care or the residence permit system are intermediate instruments for measuring the political culture of the population. If we want to draw a more precise picture, we should gauge the individual citizens' tolerance for the views and activities of groups they dislike; their support of the value of individual liberty and of democratic norms such as equal legal rights for everyone independent of their political views; and their willingness to assert basic citizenship rights for themselves, being active and self-conscious citizens. The idea that citizens should have the right to disagree with the policies of their government and should be able to express such disagreement freely should also be endorsed, as should the need for independent media that provide trustworthy information on the government's actions and on social and political developments generally. Finally, in a democratic political culture, people are expected to support the idea of competitive elections for political offices.

Precisely these seven elements of political culture have been at the heart of the study conducted by the University of Houston research group in 1990.[38] On the basis of interviews with a representative sample of Moscow Province residents, the researchers found that, in this province at least, early in 1990 (when the Soviet Union still existed and the power of the Communist Party was not yet fully broken) the support for democratic values was quite high. For example, almost 70 percent of the respondents agreed with the statement that competition between the communists and other parties (which were not yet allowed to participate in political life) would improve the way in which the authorities worked, and almost 85 percent disagreed with the statement that "it is necessary to ban elections and allow the CPSU to rule the country."[39] Almost nine out of ten respondents agreed that "it is necessary that everyone, regardless of their views, can express themselves freely," and 73 percent disagreed with the statement that "if someone is suspected of treason or other serious crimes, he can be sent to prison without trial." Seventy percent disagreed with the claim that "society should not have to put up with political views that are fundamentally different from the views of the majority," yet only 28 percent disagreed that "it is better to live in an orderly society than to allow people so much freedom that they can become disruptive."[40] In a factor analysis of the seven subdimensions of democratic political culture, the research group found that those who tended to support one democratic value also supported other values. Thus, they concluded, there was a "remarkable level of support for democracy"—with only one exception: political tolerance.

The low tolerance found in the 1990 study is of sufficient significance for later developments to warrant more detailed analysis. Tolerance of opponents is considered to be of crucial importance for the stability of a democratic system; tolerance is thought to be an extremely precious political attribute, and tolerance is particularly difficult to instill in a population traumatized by authoritarian rule. Russians have been viewed as an intolerant nation—and that view is certainly supported by the study. This finding, however, leaves a question that demands explanation: the incongruence between general support for democratic values on the one hand and a lack of tolerance on the other. In order to understand this incongruence, we have to take a closer look at how individual tolerance was measured.

The problem is that in measuring tolerance one cannot simply ask people whether or not they are tolerant. The strategy adopted by the research group was first to ask the respondents which two political groups (of their own choice or from a list) they disliked most. Subsequently each of the respondents was asked whether the groups they had mentioned, or members of them, should be allowed to make speeches, hold public rallies, should be outlawed, and/or should be banned from running for public office. The results were interesting, with differences in answers concerning the most and the second most disliked group being minimal. Only 27 percent felt that members of the group they disliked most should be allowed to make speeches, and 15.5 percent that they should be allowed to run for public office. No more than six out of every one hundred respondents felt that members of their "disliked groups" should be allowed all of the activities mentioned.[41] Gibson, Duch, and Tedlin, who reported the Houston study, provided an explanation for the incongruence between high support for democratic values and low tolerance. They believe that tolerance is unique among the seven subdimensions of a democratic political culture that they measured, in that it has a more "applied" character than the other subdimensions. In other words, it is comparatively easy in an interview to declare that individual rights should be respected in all situations; it is less easy to say that your most hated opponent should be allowed to exercise such political rights freely.

The types of strongly disliked groups and their ranking by the Moscow respondents were striking, and served to remind one of a dialogue in a German movie long ago. When confronted with an anti-Semitic remark blaming Jews for all the troubles of German society, German movie actor Heinz Rühmann responded that "Yes," the Jews were to blame, "and the cyclists." "Why the cyclists?" was the puzzled response, to which Rühmann replied: "Why the Jews?" People obviously need negative labels, even if their general ideas are of a democratic nature.

Jews, communists, and "right-wing, pro-Slavic groups" such as Pamiat were not at the top of the list of most disliked groups in Moscow *oblast*. They were mentioned as most or second most disliked by only 4.6, 4.6, and 8.1 percent of the respondents, respectively. The most disliked groups by far were "Neo-Nazis" (56.2 percent as most or second most disliked) and "nationalists" (32.8 percent), trailed by "homosexuals" (26.2 percent) and "Stalinists" (25.2 percent). What are we to make of this?

The labels, of course, refer to stereotypes; still, we should try to achieve a rational understanding of the irrational. The divergence between the feelings toward Stalinists and communists is the easiest to explain, for by 1990 an increasing number of communists had distanced themselves from the Stalinist past, and many ordinary people had set their hopes on Gorbachev and the relatively progressive communists of his entourage, expecting that they would free the country from the Stalinist legacy. The Communist Party was split between progressive factions such as the "Democratic Platform" and the centrist "Communists for Russia" bloc in the Russian parliament, and the reactionary (Stalinist) faction that organized their own Communist Party of Russia. Many people felt that there were "good" (progressive, flexible, competent but frustrated, and tolerant?) communists and "bad" (conservative, reactionary, arrogant) communists, and they naturally despised the latter. But why did they mention "nationalists" four times as often as (nationalist) "right-wing groups" such as Pamiat? Why was the totally unpolitical category of homosexuals at the top of the list, and that of Jews at the bottom?

A final answer to such questions is impossible, partly because of the limitations of the research project of which these data are the result. But considering the moment when these questions were asked (early 1990), it seems likely that by "nationalists" the respondents of Moscow Province did not mean *Russian* nationalists or nationalists in general, but the non-Russian nationalists in the republics that were still part of the Soviet Union. At the time of the interviews, Nagornyi Karabakh, Georgia, and Azerbaijan were in turmoil, and the national independence movements in the Baltic republics were putting heavy pressure on the authorities in Moscow. Russian ("pro-Slavic") nationalists were apparently disliked by far fewer people in the Russian heartland. In 1990, after all, these people were going through a process of redefinition of their own identity; they quickly came to replace their identification with the *Soviet* state by an identification with the *Russian* nation.

The high listing of "Neo-Nazis" is surprising because, in 1990, life in Moscow Province was still quite safe, and such groups, if they existed, were of marginal significance. Moscow City and Province residents could not possibly feel threatened by neo-nazis, and certainly not by homosexuals. Apparently "Neo-Nazis" and homosexuals served as labels for an abhorrence that was unrelated to reality. Still, it is a significant finding that so many Russians would deny homosexuals the right to participate in political life. Even if one appreciates the Russians' irrational hatred for homosexuals, such intolerance bodes ill for the future of democracy.

On the other hand, the high listing of "Neo-Nazis" and "Stalinists" may be interpreted as indicating that people feel that there should be limits to tolerance. The Russians are not alone in feeling that for neo-nazis access to the political arena should be restricted. Many people in democratic countries feel that the democratic state should protect itself from antidemocratic movements. As a result, in many democracies the precise mix of political rights that should be allowed to antidemocratic parties and movements is controversial. There is no easy fix for the dilemma of allowing democratic space to antidemocratic movements. If interpreted in this way, the Moscow results are much less depressing— excluding, again, the high listing of homosexuals.

We should also take into account that, particularly in unstable situations such as in the Soviet Union and Russia, there obviously is a socio-psychological need for strong negative "labels" symbolizing evil and capable of receiving the (irrational) projection of the fears of the population. Inconsistent and irrational behavior was visible in the 1990 election of the Moscow City Soviet, when the electorate chose to provide "Democratic Russia" candidates with a clear victory. For the movement stood for the speedy introduction of a market economy and the promotion of private sector initiatives such as the cooperatives, but many Muscovites who voted for its candidates concurrently disliked cooperatives and their managers.[42] Negative labels will be manipulated by political elites to boost their support among an uncertain population. Later this process was clearly visible when both during the "October Events" and after the December elections of 1993, the neo-Nazi label surfaced; it was manipulated by President Yeltsin and his supporters to blacken the leadership of the Supreme Soviet, and by "Russia's Choice" leader Gaidar in an effort to reconstitute the alliance of radicals that had broken down in the course of 1993. Obviously, in Russian society the label of homosexuality serves a similar function—but it requires the expertise of psychoanalysts to explain it.

Although the Moscow *oblast* sample included both urban (56 percent) and rural (44 percent) residents, we cannot generalize these findings to the whole of the population outside Moscow Province.[43] However, it seems unlikely that non-Muscovites in the Russian Federation are significantly more tolerant. If this is so, and if tolerance is indeed a crucial element in a democratic political culture, the important question is in what way the tolerance of the population can be raised. Obviously, sequencing (in the sense of waiting with the installation of democratic structures until tolerance is sufficiently high) makes no sense. The development of tolerance and of democratic structures and procedures should go hand in hand. In this process, the political elite sets the norm by showing mutual respect and restraint. Ideally, there should be a process of mutual influence between elite and society that would lay a strong fundament for stabilization of the democratic system.

This is the ideal situation. Later we will see in what way the post-communist Russian elite furthered or hindered the consolidation of tolerance in society. Now it is of some importance to look for stratification in the findings on political tolerance. Up to now I have presented only the general results of the University of Houston research group, considered to reflect the basic political psychology of a regionally delimited section of the Soviet population. But in this chapter we are dealing specifically with the attitudes and views of a category delimited in another way: the new professionals that came to dominate Soviet social life during the late-Brezhnev era, a social category that to a large extent is the recruitment base for the new political elite. Do their political values and norms or their expectations and beliefs differ from those of the rest of the population?

As we have seen above, it has been found that education—one of the major defining characteristics of the new professionals—was both in a direct and in an indirect way (through diminishing satisfaction of material well-being) negatively related to the support for regime norms in the late-Soviet period. This was so in spite of the effort of Soviet authorities to use the instrument of education for instilling compliance and regime support in its population and particularly in potential members of the nomenklatura and of the bureaucracy. The University of Houston team has indeed found in their statistical analysis that "the strongest predictor of democratic attitudes is level of education: those who are better educated tend to be more supportive of democratic rights, liberties, and institutions," so that "the more highly educated, and typically more influential, elements of Soviet society are likely to be a positive force in the democratization process."[44] Further, it was found that support for democratic values was more prevalent among the younger generation and among men. Thus, those most likely to influence political change were the most committed to democratic values.[45]

THE PROFESSIONALS AND CIVIL SOCIETY

As Lewin, Pye, Miller, and several other authors have argued, during the four decades between the end of the war and the assumption of office by Gorbachev, Soviet society gradually developed the characteristics conducive to democratization. Only during the late-Gorbachev period, using the holes Gorbachev had drilled, did social change burst through the reinforced concrete crust of the Stalinist political system, quickly creating a volcanic landscape with shattering eruptions that destroyed the fabric of Soviet quasi-politics.

Still, the mighty social force that lay behind the demise of the Soviet system—the professionals who were fed up with being treated as halfwits by almost senile leaders—need not at the same time be conducive to stabilization of the post-Soviet landscape. We should keep in mind that according to the "Stern principle" (see Introduction), the conditions that made for the collapse of the Soviet system are not necessarily the same as those that promote the coming about of a democratic successor regime. In the mid-1990s, the professionals are still traumatized—even more so than at the end of the 1980s. To the trauma of the Soviet period have been added those of the difficult first years of transition: the unemployment, poverty, and frustration at seeing that improvements would take much more time than expected. Would the general democratic attitude of this important social category withstand the strain of social, political, and personal disorder? Would it be able to resist the sweet-smelling bait of populism and nationalism? Would their values and attitudes, as measured in the late-Brezhnev and Gorbachev periods, remain unaltered by the shocks of 1990–1993? Would the new professionals be a guarantee against a relapse into authoritarian rule?

Many authors on postcommunism have pointed to the disenchantment and disappointment of the populations involved at the slow pace and high cost of reform. That disappointment was only natural. Most if not all new professionals had unrealistic expectations of the future. Their lack of experience with the irrationalities, frustrations, and disappointing compromises of "normal politics," their ignorance of the problems of transition from autocracy, and their distorted views of life in Western-type societies caused them to underestimate the problems and duration of transition to at least some sort of stability, not to mention the introduction of democracy. Moreover, in the perception of many, the success of popular movements such as Solidarity (Poland) and Civic Forum (Czechoslovakia) in toppling an empire that had been thought to be all-powerful implied a rosy future in which, after a short transition, normal politics would take over. If a revolution could be "velvet," as in Czechoslovakia and in other countries where the "passing of the torch" went relatively smoothly and without bloodshed, why not the installation of normal, democratic politics in Russia? Few at the time (1989–1990) were fully aware of the explosive potential of nationalism and of the painful dilemmas of transition to a market economy, or of the potential social havoc created by both. Few were aware of the long period of time that democracy had taken to develop in Western Europe, or of the prolonged struggles that it had involved. People tended to take an optimistic view, assuming that political democracy and a social market economy could be introduced mechanically.[46]

When faced with the chaos of the early 1990s, withdrawal from political life, disinterest, low voter turnout, and even anomie were the result. During the power struggle between president and parliament in 1992–1993, for example, many Russians turned away from politics in disgust. After Yeltsin, in September 1993, had disbanded the parliament they had elected in 1990, seven to eight out of every ten Muscovites were not prepared to take part in a meeting or in a strike in support of either of the sides to the conflict.[47] Few have placed such phenomena in the context of patterns of democratization and political development elsewhere. Often, and particularly among Russian commentators, a special status is claimed for the postcommunist countries, and for *Rus* in particular.

However, disappointment and withdrawal are not only normal, but even useful and thus positive phenomena. To a large extent, regime change and transformation from authoritarian rule involves learning processes in the broadest sense. During authoritarian rule, people may have developed democratic attitudes and values, but they often have very little idea of how they apply to real life. Their political expectations and skills will be inadequate for handling the turmoil of the transition period. Typically, they expect results too soon and have too low an estimate of the social and personal costs. Particularly in the case when an authoritarian period has lasted for a long time, they are inexperienced in competitive politics, whereas the dilemmas of the transition period demand an elite highly skilled in the techniques of bargaining, compromise, and restraint. In case of the Soviet professionals, both in their education and in their early political experience, the principle of rationality reigned supreme. Later they tended to apply the same principle to their expectations of postcommunist politics, not knowing that in competitive politics rational choices are seldom made. The learning that comes out of disappointment is useful. In his study on democratization in the late twentieth century, Samuel Huntington has made an argument for disillusionment and the lowering of expectations as being "the foundation of democratic stability." In his words, "democracies become consolidated when people learn that democracy is a solution to the problem of tyranny, but not necessarily to anything else."[48] To his arguments, we can add findings which show that the population of Russia now has a more sober view (or that more people have a sober view) of transition than we would expect.

In the March to June 1992 period Jeffrey Hahn found considerable support for market and democratic reforms among deputies in the *oblast* and city soviets of five provinces in central Russia. The 1,280 deputies who answered his survey questions (60 percent of whom were "freshman deputies") belonged to precisely that category of people that was thought to be the most obstructive of change. Both President Yeltsin and the Western press depicted the provincial capitals where these deputies worked as strongholds of reactionary forces. Hahn's results showed not only that it was misleading to put all local deputies in one box; they also confirmed earlier findings that the support for free-market and democratic values was "consistently higher among younger, better-educated, professionally employed deputies holding office for the first time."[49] For the population at large, the picture is equally diverse. In August of the same year, when Russians were experiencing rapidly rising prices and increasing unemployment, the opinion research institute VTSIOM conducted a poll among a sample of 1,600 people in cities and rural areas. They were asked whether they thought that economic reforms should continue or whether they should be stopped. Twenty percent expressed a desire for reform to be stopped; 53 percent wanted economic reform to continue. Eight months later, in April 1993, Russians were asked a similar question in their national referendum. The second of the four referendum questions asked whether the voters approved of the social-economic policy of President Yeltsin and Prime Minister Gaidar during 1992; 53.05 percent answered in the affirmative.[50] This outcome was all the more surprising given the fact that a poll taken at the same time found that 58 percent of the population of European Russia believed that their economic situation had worsened over the previous year.[51] Of course, behind these national arithmetic means were significant differences between sections of the population and regions of the country. In twenty-six referendum districts (with 22 percent of the eligible voters), a majority rejected the reforms.

There is thus basic support for painful economic reform, and at the same time disillusionment with competitive politics. Perhaps the uncommitting responses to survey and referendum questions show only what people think is appropriate? Gibson and his coauthors have questioned the profundity of the changes in political culture. "Like Levi jeans and religion," they wrote in 1991, "democracy is quite fashionable in the USSR today."[52] The question in particular is whether the population values democracy in itself, or as a means to economic change; they found that the persons with the strongest democratic values were also the ones most dissatisfied with the regime, but were unable to ascertain whether this dissatisfaction was primarily political or economic.

Can a civil society develop in a situation of both a state-in-retreat (de-étatization) and considerable disenchantment with politics? Can the new professionals be its new avant-garde? Does the bickering between Moscow politicians hamper the development of independent cultural and sports associations and economic interest groups that are to form the core of a civil society? It does, in that the protracted disputes over the profile of the Russian polity have delayed the coming about of a stable state. Sovereign state power is an indispensable condition for the development of civil society.[53] The unhindered crystallization of social and economic interests into organizations that interact with each other and (as interest and pressure groups) with the political arena, requires a state that sets limits and protects human rights both in word and in deed. In the Russian context this means that the state both has to withdraw from social and economic life, and has to provide legal criteria and safeguards for civil society to organize itself.

But all this in a situation where the state itself has been in great turmoil and, at least up to late 1993, remained essentially undefined. The conflicts over the future political profile of Russia perpetuated uncertainty and a tendency for the regions to shield themselves from the chaos in Moscow, and thereby to create their own civil societies and economies. The development of a healthy civil society on which democracy could grow called for basic political stability, unambiguous legislation, a strong executive, and an efficient police force. These desirables could be reached only once the political forces in the capital had agreed on the main lines of the Constitution: the profile of the federation; the relationship between legislative, executive, and judiciary powers; citizenship; ownership; and the role of the state in economic transition. It was precisely over these issues that fierce battles were fought, slowing down the modeling of civil society.

Civil society thus developed slowly, and in adverse circumstances. It was not the disillusionment with politics that was to blame, for a shifting of energies from the political arena to the social, cultural, and economic spheres was in itself beneficial for the development of a civil society. In Russia, people had to learn the basic skills of social organization. During the seven decades of communist rule they had been considered incapable of independent organization. The Communist Party, the Komsomol, and their "transmission belts" (the Stalinist designation for social organizations that transmitted the energy coming from the Communist Party, their source, to society) had done so for them. They also had to learn that in a free society, rights often have to be fought for, even if they are protected by law; that tenacity and perseverance are required for the defense of interests; and that, excluding rare periods of economic abundance, each social group is well advised to organize itself for receiving its "share of the cake."

The development of civil society in Russia was impeded by the continuing uncertainty and the social dislocations resulting from economic transformation. Exploding crime rates and insecurity; corruption; poverty; mass unemployment—such phenomena led to a mutilated civil society, a civil society that seemed to have degenerated into a battlefield.[54] Of equal importance were the processes of elite formation and accommodation, for it is through their elites that societies translate their changes into political accomplishments. We have seen that in 1990 the composition of Russia's soviets underwent considerable change in that a high percentage of its elected members were relatively young professionals who had not served on a soviet before. However, with the exception of the handful of former dissidents and dropouts, they came from *within* the system, and very many of them at the time were members of the Communist Party. Compared to several lands in the outer and inner empires, in Russia the pool of untarnished politicians was extremely small. For as long as the first postcommunist generations have not yet come to maturity, Russia will have to make do with reformed ex-communists, who are the only people with experience in public administration.

But reformed communists are of many kinds, and it is an exaggeration to state that all of them tend to undermine the democratization of Russia. We should remember that in the Soviet Union, Communist Party membership was a prerequisite to upward mobility, and that many of the new professionals were indeed members of the party. Those who stress the sheer hopelessness of a transition with ex-communist elites tend to underestimate the degree to which many postwar communists were opportunists and the degree to which people can adapt to changing circumstances. Mikhail Gorbachev was a communist, and this did not prevent him from setting the transition into motion; the misconceptions originating in his communist background provided much of the explanation for his initiative. Boris Yeltsin, like Gorbachev, was a former regional party boss, but changing circumstances in combination with his personality turned him into one of the main actors in the breakup of communist rule. To the extent that communism, and Communist Party membership, had been indispensable to one's career, once that party had been removed from the scene people had to find new allegiances. Only a limited number of former party members turned into the hard-core fundamentalists who insisted on a recreation of the lost empire and who undermined democratization and the transition to a market economy.

It was these ex-communist elites who negotiated the final breakup of the Soviet Union and who later fought the battles both in Moscow and between Moscow and the regions. At the initial stage in Russia, as compared to Hungary, Poland, and Czechoslovakia, there was little to no accommodation between elites speaking for conflicting socioeconomic interests. Only later, when the issues of tax generation and the distribution of benefits in the new Russian state arose, regional elites started to behave as representatives of their regional interests.

But having dealt with what the Soviet experience left behind for Russian society and politics, I suggest that we now move to the real men and women who were faced with the seemingly impossible task of creating a political order out of chaos. The drama of the emancipation of Russia from Soviet rule is the subject of the next two chapters.

THREE   *Between Sovereignty*
and Independence

We no longer have time for a transition period. We have to jump into the water and float. (Liliia Shevtsova, May 1990)[1]

Postcommunist democracy carries a powerful internal potential for anti-democratism. (Igor Kliamkin, January 1993)[2]

The new Russia was born in anger and frustration. Some of this it shared with other regions of the USSR. But the shock to the Russian self-image and confidence was much more unsettling than in the other republics. Unanticipated by the Russians themselves, the disestablishment of the USSR, to which they had contributed, made Russia lose its mooring and its identity. If this chapter focuses on Russia's role in the demise of the USSR and its recovery from communism, it necessarily abstracts from events elsewhere. Our prime concern is Russia and its difficult voyage transiting the uncharted waters between Soviet communism and the shores of an unknown land of freedom.

As we have seen, the values of democratic rule were not foreign to Russia and its inhabitants. But they had been released only by Gorbachev's policies of *perestroika* and *glasnost*. During 1986–1989, *glasnost* had led to a tremendous consciousness-raising among the citizens and especially the intellectuals of Russia. With it came feelings of anger and frustration at the fate of Russia while in communist hands and, perhaps, at the Russian's own collaboration with the communist regime.

And so we are reminded of the fact that, with the exception of "accidents of history," historical changes never come unannounced. They are the outcome of changes in society that may need a long time to reach fruition and that often are difficult to observe, particularly in the country that the Soviet Union was. Russia's Declaration of State Sovereignty, the starting point for this chapter, did not come out of the blue. During the preceding decades, Russian intellectuals had shown a gradually increasing assertiveness in formulating, defining, and defending the interests of Russia and its population vis-à-vis the Soviet system.

FRUSTRATED RUSSIA

In politics, facts play a minor role. Politics is about perceptions, about the concepts that people entertain concerning factual situations. Such perceptions may, of course, be correct—or they may be totally wrong; but most of the time, citizens' perceptions of social, economic, and political realities are somewhere in between. Thus, the question of the *objective* relationship between the RSFSR and its citizens on the one hand and the USSR on the other is of little importance. In the non-Russian republics of the USSR, the latter was perceived as an instrument for domination by the Russian hegemon, although many republics did in fact benefit considerably from Soviet rule. An objective cost-benefit analysis of the effects of Soviet rule for the different republics (for example in terms of personal sacrifices, the exploitation of natural resources, economic development, the raising of educational levels, health programs, and welfare) would require agreed-upon standards that will be difficult to achieve. What is important here is the perception that the Russian population and its elite had of their own condition under Soviet rule, and the ways in which they acted upon that perception.

During the 1970s and 1980s, the Soviet literary scene had become increasingly dominated by the so-called village prose writers (*derevenshchiki*). In their works, writers such as Abramov, Astafev, Belov, Mozhaev, and Rasputin had glorified the values of Russian rural life in contrast to the perverted life in the contemporary Soviet city. Their writings—and their popularity among the Russian population and among sections of the communist establishment—could be seen as a spiritual revolt against the consequences of the social changes that have been analyzed in the previous chapter. Alcohol abuse, cruelty toward women, women's liberation, moral degradation, the perversion of youth, prostitution, decadence, divorce, industrial development, the unlimited exploitation of natural resources, and environmental pollution were all implicitly blamed on the Soviet system and, more explicitly, on the Western influences it had undergone. The message of many of their works was that only a return to the unspoiled Russian (rural) past could save Russia from moral and physical ruin.[3]

During the same period, public manifestations of non-Russian nationalism had occasionally flared up and had quickly been suppressed. They threatened the indigenous ruling groups in the rim republics of the Union. The tacit understanding between the communist rulers in Moscow and those in the non-Russian republics was that the indigenous rulers (selected by the Moscow leadership) would have some leeway in return for executing the most important demands from Moscow. But while non-Russian nationalism was suppressed, Russian nationalism was often protected and at times even stimulated by factions in the communist leadership. On the pages of one official journal (*Molodaia Gvardia*), in the late 1960s and early 1970s, Brezhnev's détente policy of accommodation with the West was criticized in a vicious anti-Western campaign. The new Soviet professionals—the "diplomaed masses" that had been created by communist education policy—were presented as a class leading Russia on a "ruinous Western path" that would end with "the bourgeoisification of Russia."[4] Communist rule over Russia was presented by some as the result of a worldwide Judeo-Masonic conspiracy. Some high-ranking communist leaders such as Alexander Yakovlev (later Gorbachev's comrade-in-arms) tasted defeat at the hands of nationalists in the Communist Party. Small Russian-nationalist dissident groups led an intermittent existence, flourishing at times when their protectors at the top of the Communist Party felt strong. They circulated old ideas, adapted to modern times, about the uniqueness of Russians and the Russian Spirit and their moral superiority over a degenerate Western liberal democracy and capitalism.[5] Mellow and nostalgic nationalists found a home in the Russian Society for the Protection of Historical and Cultural Monuments, a mass organization popularly known as the Russkii Klub and since 1980 in Pamiat, a society for the promotion of the study of Russia's past. From his American exile, and with the help of Western radio stations, Alexander Solzhenitsyn influenced the Russian population in the direction of anticommunism, antimodernism, anti-Westernism, and a rejection of the democracy he despised, for the benefit of a restoration of the Russian Spirit. It was a complicated but powerful cocktail of emotions.

By 1978, Alexander Yanov, an emigrant from the Soviet Union, could observe the mutual adaptation of the "dissident right" (Russian-nationalist dissidents) and the "establishment right" (Russian-nationalist communist leaders who were hard pressed by the bankruptcy of their ideology).[6] Almost a decade before the Gorbachev period, he showed that Russian nationalist and anti-Soviet feelings had metastased in the Soviet body politic and were waiting for an opportunity to attack the core of the system.

That opportunity was provided by Communist Party leader Gorbachev during 1986–1989, the period of *glasnost*. *Glasnost* worked in three ways to intensify Russian frustration: more became known, more could be expressed, and more had to be swallowed. Soon the Russians were at the receiving end of most of the complaints against communist rule. The easing of censorship was accompanied by revelations on the past and present of Russia and its population; disclosures that confirmed the sorry state they were in. Now the literary works of the village prose writers and the emotional ravings of nationalists were sustained by official statistics on increasing infant mortality, shortening life expectancy, poor public health, environmental pollution, divorce rates, and crime that painted a gloomy picture of the Russian condition. The disaster at the Chernobyl nuclear power plant in April 1986 and the irresponsible behavior of most of the communist leadership reinforced feelings of despair at being at the mercy of rulers who cared first and foremost about themselves.

The opening-up of Soviet and Russian history to public scrutiny, the disavowal of Stalin and his henchmen, the rehabilitation of his victims, and the publication of studies on Russia's long-forgotten past, raised people's awareness and made them ponder the question what had *not* gone wrong. Books that had been kept in special sections of libraries closed to the public (the *spetskhranilishche*), were made available. Honest controversy among historians on the significance of personalities and events in the Soviet and Russian past suddenly became possible. Communist crimes such as the purges of the early Soviet period and after World War II; the 1932–1933 famine that Stalin had brought about, trying to bring Ukrainian farmers to their knees; the Molotov-Ribbentrop Pact of 1939; the mass murder of Polish officers and intellectuals at Katyn (April–May 1940) and of Soviet citizens by the NKVD were no longer flatly denied, but investigated. Andrei Sakharov, exiled to Gorki in 1980 for criticizing the intervention in Afghanistan, was brought back to center stage and allowed to take up a political career. Alexander Solzhenitsyn, exiled from the country in 1974 for the publication abroad of his *Gulag Arkhipelago*, was invited to "come home." In 1989 his most famous book was finally published in his home country. It shocked the Russians.[7]

The impact of all this on the Russians came both directly and in a roundabout way. Many of the disclosures of the Soviet leaders were incomplete and insincere, out of fear of the repercussions. Crucial documents on the gruesome events of Soviet history were held back, or their existence was denied until it was too late. Fact-finding committees were kept dangling. The inconsistent behavior of Gorbachev and his entourage infuriated independent-thinking Russians and the elites of the non-Russian peoples. It raised more questions than it answered, and set people to thinking.

The first explicit manifestations of nationalist activism were among the Baltic peoples; among the Tatars, who had been exiled from the Crimea by Stalin (and not allowed to return by Khrushchev); and among the Armenians in Nagornyi Karabakh and in their home republic. They voiced long-suppressed demands for redress of injustices inflicted upon them by Russian communists. Soon nationalist movements radicalized. Crimean Tatars demonstrated in Red Square until the government agreed to deal with their grievances; in December 1986 the replacement of the party leader of Kazakhstan, Kunaev, by the Russian Kolbin triggered riots in Alma-Ata; the indigenous peoples of the Baltic states demanded autonomy and their communist parties disengaged from the CPSU; the uncompromising Armenians rejected the party leader that "Moscow" tried to force upon them, and fought the Azerbaijanis.

Among some Russians, these developments raised feelings of indignation at so much ingratitude. Soviet propaganda had led them to believe that, being the big brother of the other Soviet nations, they had sacrificed for the benefit of the welfare of the Balts and the Armenians, the Kazakhs, and the Uzbekis. Other Russians, the radical intellectuals in particular, felt sympathy toward the Baltic demands. Still others showed genuine surprise at what in their view was irrational behavior among people with whom they had coexisted in a harmoneous way. It had been one thing for the Jews (in the 1970s) to demand the right to leave the country and to emigrate to Israel and the United States. Jews were different. From the perspective of many Russians, they were in the enviable condition of having a homeland elsewhere and enjoying international protection for their demand to exercise their human rights. But why should Latvians or Georgians—not to speak of Ukrainians—want to separate from Russia? The non-Russian nations had so many things of which the Russians felt deprived: a pleasant and beneficial climate, well-being and a relatively high standard of living, limited cultural freedom, and their own cultural organizations such as academies of science and writers' unions.

The double (direct and indirect) impact of developments on the Russian consciousness contributed to the radicalization of Russian nationalism. Anti-Semitism had never been far below the surface and had been actively promoted by the Brezhnev regime in the form of "anti-Zionism." It surfaced in 1985, the year in which Gorbachev came to power, when Pamiat transformed into a motley collection of anti-Semitic, xenophobic, and fascist fighting groups. They were the first to state openly that Russia was deliberately being victimized. Soon, organizations such as the "interfronts" that had sprung up in non-Russian republics for the protection of the interests of local Russians (and whose activities were coordinated by the KGB) took on more and more Russian-nationalist and anti-Gorbachev overtones. The United Front of Toilers and the Soiuz faction in the Soviet parliament pleaded their cause in Russia. In the autumn of 1990 these forces joined hands with conservatives at the top levels of the CPSU, the army, and the KGB to bring a halt to what they saw as a dangerous policy by Gorbachev that threatened to lead to the breakup of the USSR. They tried to show their capabilities in Lithuania and Latvia in January 1991 and to prevent a new union treaty from being signed in August 1991. But before going into these events, we should perhaps take things from the start by analyzing the disestablishment of the USSR and the reincarnation of Russia in their consecutive phases.

THE FIRST FOUR STAGES OF TRANSITION

Analyzing the period in stages or phases is of course somewhat artificial. Still, such an analysis is acceptable since different key issues were at stake during consecutive phases, and events that have been of seminal importance separate them. The perspective in this phased historical description is that of Russia. That is to say that we will view events in the "environment" of Russia from the seat of the Russian government and parliament. This way of seeing things indicates the complexity of the situation, at least up to 1992, when Moscow was the government seat of both the Soviet Union and of Russia and when it was not always easy to "disentangle" Russian from Soviet developments. This was precisely the core issue at stake during the first period, from June 1990, when the RSFSR parliament issued its Declaration of State Sovereignty, to August 1991, when the coup against Gorbachev failed: with communist rule collapsing, how could the political entity that the communists had kept together for seven decades be saved? Could a true (con)federation come about that would do justice to Russia's central place—and if so, how? Was there a peaceful way for the transformation of an empire into a federation or confederation? How should such processes be coordinated with fundamental economic reform? Finally, could the transition be managed in collaboration with the Soviet leadership under Gorbachev? The answer to the last question came in August 1991.

The second period lasted only four months. A barrier had been removed by the failure of the August coup, and during the four months between August 1991 and January 1992 the central issue was not *whether* the Soviet Union would cease to exist, but how, in a constitutional-technical sense, this inescapable event would be realized. The CPSU had been banned. The search was for a formula allowing for maximum continuity and maximum protection of the domestic and foreign interests of Russia. Boris Yeltsin and his entourage thought to have found that formula by late November, and put it into practice during the next month. By New Year's Eve, the Soviet Union was no more.

The third and fourth periods will be dealt with in the next chapter. The third period started with Gorbachev's resignation as president of the USSR on 25 December 1991 and ended only in September 1993, when Russian president Yeltsin dissolved the Congress of People's Deputies and Supreme Soviet in violation of the Constitution. During this period, two complex issues were central to the concern of Russian politicians and opinion leaders. The first was whether it would be possible to safeguard constitutional and legal continuity (in deference to Russia's stated resolve to become a law-governed state) while implementing fundamental political and economic changes. In 1991, the Soviet leaders had been saved from this dilemma when, in the autumn of that year, the USSR Congress of People's Deputies effectively cooperated in the discontinuation of their state. During 1992, however, the Russian Congress of People's Deputies and Supreme Soviet were much less cooperative. Only after a failed attempt at a "constitutional coup" in March 1993, did Yeltsin, in the autumn, finally break with the supreme law of the land.

The second central issue during the period, intertwined with the first, was that of the consequences of the departure of the "Soviet environment." After President Yeltsin had, on 27 December 1991, moved into Gorbachev's Kremlin office, he and other Russian leaders became aware of a great number of questions following from the demise of the USSR. During the preceding period they had been preoccupied with the daily managing of the decline of the Soviet state, failing to anticipate many of the implications of its absence for Russian statehood. Now, as they tried to deal with one implication after the other, new dilemmas and unexpected developments would knock on their doors and bring them face-to-face with an uncomfortably complex reality. Power and policy became entangled in a paralyzing struggle over the new profile of the Russian state.

The fourth period started on 21 September 1993, and accelerated after 4 October, when parliamentary resistance had been smothered in blood and its leaders had been arrested. Once Yeltsin had finally made the decision to circumvent the Constitution, his aim was to combine a maximum of surrogate legality with full use of the fact that he had succeeded in paralyzing both the legislative and the judiciary powers—parliament and the Constitutional Court. An avalanche of often improvised decrees was the result. The period, and the year 1993, ended in a situation that gave rise to mixed feelings. On the one hand, the Russian political elite had by adaptation found a new common ground in a more assertive foreign policy, and there were indications that several CIS states were moving back into the orbit of Moscow. On the other hand, during the days following the general elections of 12 December 1993, it dawned on Yeltsin, Gaidar, and their colleagues that they had made crucial mistakes in assessing the mood of the population. Yeltsin's new Constitution was accepted, but the "presidential" electoral bloc "Russia's Choice" suffered a shattering defeat.

RUSSIA SOVEREIGN

From the very start, Boris Yeltsin played a leading role in the reincarnation of Russia. After a humiliating defeat inflicted upon him by Mikhail Gorbachev and the Communist Party's Central Committee, in October–November 1987, this former regional party secretary from Sverdlovsk had made a startling comeback in March 1989 when, in the first contested elections, Muscovites voted him their deputy in the USSR Congress of People's Deputies. He beat the party's candidate, factory director Brakov, with 89 percent of the vote. The victory was won over the intrigues of a Communist Party leadership that tried to manipulate voters to reject Yeltsin. In one big sweep it gave Yeltsin legitimacy, and testified to the trust in him by many Russians. To the dismay of Gorbachev (who never in his life, before or after 1989, won a competitive election), Yeltsin took the lead in charting the course for Russia's resurrection. By the spring of 1990, still a member of the party, he was one of the leaders of the parliamentary protofaction named "Inter-Regional Group of Deputies," and the main antagonist of Gorbachev. In June of that year, he led the newly elected Russian parliament in its attack on Soviet institutions. In July, at the CPSU's twenty-eighth congress, he gave up his party membership, stating that "as head of the republic's highest legislative power I must obey the will of the people and its plenipotentiaries" instead of "only the decisions of the CPSU."[8]

It was only too obvious that the Soviet president and the Communist Party were going downhill. Since 1986 the Communist Party's self-assurance had quickly drained away as a result of the open dialogue that Gorbachev had started and the impact it had had on society. The party's unified command structure was destroyed by the Baltic party organizations going their own way. In the elections of March 1989 and of early 1990 (to republican parliaments and local councils), members of the communist establishment had tasted a so-far unheard-of experience: defeat at the ballot box. In the minds of the state's subjects, the myth of the invincibility of communist power had begun to crumble. People discovered that the ballot box gave them power after all. Popular fronts had gained strength from the confusion in the party. The parliaments of Estonia (November 1988), Lithuania, Latvia, and Azerbaijan had adopted declarations of sovereignty, and on 11 March 1990, the newly elected Lithuanian parliament had boldly declared independence. Gorbachev's reaction—a boycott and a Law on Secession from the Union, making lawful secession virtually impossible—only served to strengthen the resolve of the anti-Soviet forces. Developments were going extremely fast. Only three days after the Lithuanian declaration, the USSR Congress of People's Deputies deleted the power monopoly of the Communist Party from the USSR constitution, and agreed to appoint Gorbachev as president of the USSR (a new institution), hoping he could make the most of a hopeless situation.

In the RSFSR, elections for its new Congress of People's Deputies (an institutional renovation that only the RSFSR had copied from the Union) had been held earlier that month; the Congress convened in the Kremlin on 16 May. On 29 May, with a margin of only four votes, it elected Boris Yeltsin chairman of the Supreme Soviet, the working parliament that was to be elected from among the Congress deputies. On 5 June, prompted by Yeltsin, the Congress voted Ruslan Khasbulatov first deputy chairman of the Supreme Soviet.

The agenda of the Congress was overloaded, the discussions were heated and lengthy, the issues before it of crucial importance. Topping the agenda was the need to take a stand on the question of the disintegrating Soviet state, and to bolster the interests of Russia in a new federal or confederal configuration that was to come about. One clear signal was the election of Yeltsin in spite of the objections that many conservative communist deputies expressed toward him. The other agenda item was the Declaration on State Sovereignty, voted with 907 ayes ("including the votes of all party functionaries and generals")[9] against only thirteen nays and nine abstentions. The verbatim report mentions that the vote triggered "stormy, prolonged applause and cries of 'Hurray, Hurray' from the hall"—reminiscent of Communist Party congresses of the past.

This time, the cries were not misplaced. Although the Declaration was of limited legal-constitutional significance, it sounded a strong clarion call. Its political significance, in the process of replacing the Soviet Union by something as yet undefined, was unmistakable. In the Declaration, the Congress stated its historical responsibility for the fate of Russia and its respect for the sovereign rights of all peoples (vsekh narodov) of the USSR, and it claimed to express the intention (volia) of the peoples of the RSFSR, when it "solemnly proclaims the state sovereignty of the RSFSR . . . and announces its resolve to create a democratic law-governed state as part of a renewed USSR."[10]

In fifteen points the Congress specified what it meant by state sovereignty within the USSR. Sovereignty, it said, was guaranteed by giving the RSFSR full powers in all state and social affairs, except those which would voluntarily be transferred to the USSR; by the supremacy of the RSFSR Constitution and of legislation on its territory; by arresting USSR legislation that conflicted with the sovereign rights of the RSFSR; and by giving the exclusive right to Russia's national wealth to the people of the RSFSR. With these provisions, the Declaration turned the existing relationship between USSR and RSFSR institutions on its head. Further, the Declaration said that the sovereign rights of the USSR's other fourteen union republics must be honored and promised that the RSFSR would unite with other republics of the union on the basis of a treaty. However, the right to separate from the USSR was stated explicitly.

The Declaration did not deal exclusively with the RSFSR's place in a rapidly changing environment; it also touched upon the structure of the Russian state itself. In point 9, a compromise text that had been proposed by Yeltsin said that the Congress "confirms the necessity of a material broadening of the rights" of the autonomous republics and the lower national and administrative units. All citizens, political parties, and movements were guaranteed equal rights in participating in public affairs. The Declaration concluded that it was the basis for drafting a new RSFSR Constitution, for the conclusion of a union treaty, and for the improvement of the republic's legislation.

By referring to the position of the RSFSR's autonomous republics and nonethnic regions, the Congress touched upon an issue that was to remain central to the struggle between Russia and the USSR and, after the demise of the USSR, to Russia's statehood as such. Two months before the Russian sovereignty declaration, the USSR parliament had adopted the law "On the deliniation of powers between the USSR and the subjects of the federation," granting the USSR's twenty autonomous republics (sixteen of which were located inside the borders of the RSFSR) the status of subjects of the federation.[11] This provision came to be used by Gorbachev as an answer to the "War of Laws," in which the republics effectively negated the power of federal institutions to have their decisions implemented. Treating autonomous and Union republics indiscriminately was also a way of lowering the "weight" of the major actors involved in bringing about a new union treaty. It was a tactic that greatly irritated Yeltsin and the Russian leadership. They accused the center of promoting a policy that could lead to the disintegration of the Russian Federation; Gorbachev in his turn accused the Russians of deliberately encouraging the disintegration of the USSR.

The signal of the first Russian Congress of People's Deputies was loud and clear. Within a few months, all other republics and even lower administrative units had adopted declarations of state sovereignty.[12] Amid slogans such as "The farther from Russia, the closer to Europe," the Ukrainian parliament adopted its declaration on 16 July. Following Lithuania (11 March), Latvia, Estonia, Georgia, and Armenia even proclaimed independence, albeit after a certain transition period. Common among these declarations was the claim of ownership of the natural resources of the region in question, the upgrading of their status, and the claim that the laws of higher state bodies would no longer automatically apply. In the meantime, the reactionary wing of the Communist Party, led by Yegor Ligachev and Ivan Polozkov, showed a growing resolve not to allow the Soviet Union to disintegrate further. The "loss" of the "socialist states" at the Western rim of the empire had been more than enough. Calls for Gorbachev to step down from leadership were heard from both wings.

In the "War of Laws," lower units denied higher units, up to the federal government in Moscow, the right to "order them around." Republican and regional leaders quickly put up trade barriers, choosing to first satisfy the demands of their own population before sending products to other regions. The republics made a start with the denial of central control over the exploitation and sale of their natural wealth. The centrally planned economy dissolved into an economic archipelago with little and erratic shipping between the islands. The military faced similar problems with conscription. In late July, the Ukrainian parliament ordered all Ukrainian conscripts stationed outside the republic to return home. Young people in some of the more radical republics were voting against Soviet power with their feet. Draft refusal spread like a contagious disease; in the autumn of 1990, only ten to thirty percent of the planned recruits reported for service in the Baltic and Transcaucasian republics.[13] Republics unilaterally appropriated the powers of the federal government, and the effectiveness of rule from Moscow evaporated. The Soviet Union became ungovernable.

On the day when the Russian Congress of People's Deputies proclaimed its Declaration of State Sovereignty, elsewhere in Moscow the USSR Council of the Federation met to discuss plans for a new union treaty. The leaders of thirteen of the fifteen republics decided to set up a working group to draft the document. During the fourteen months that followed, the redefinition of the relationship between the constituent republics of the USSR and central institutions was the center of attention, and this structured political events—until in August 1991 the coup ended all but the most obstinate expectations of forging a renewed bond under centralized control.

Constitutional and economic reform

On 22 June 1990, ten days after adopting its Declaration of State Sovereignty, the RSFSR Congress of People's Deputies, chaired by Boris Yeltsin, instructed the Supreme Soviet's Constitutional Commission (CC) to write the basic principles for a new RSFSR Constitution, and to submit them to a referendum. Taking the results of the referendum into account, the CC was to prepare a draft Constitution for the Congress's January 1991 session. The Congress wanted to have a new RSFSR Constitution in place before a new USSR union treaty (to the need of which Gorbachev had finally surrendered) and a new USSR Constitution were to be adopted. Talks between the USSR and the RSFSR on a new USSR union treaty began on 3 August, with Yeltsin demanding a confederation of sovereign states leaving only defense, internal security, and monetary affairs for the federal government. During summer and autumn, Gorbachev was negotiating with the Union republics for a new treaty, all of them demanding control over their resources.

The economy was in great trouble, and both USSR and Russian institutions were trying to reach political agreement on economic reform. Much was at stake, and many conflicting interests were involved. There was Boris Yeltsin, speaking for the interests of the RSFSR and some of the other republics, and set to outmaneuver Gorbachev. There was USSR prime minister Nikolai Ryzhkov, representing the interests of the federal economic bureaucracy and of Central Asian republics that had benefitted from the planned economy. And there was, of course, Mikhail Gorbachev, desperately trying to keep the USSR together (and himself in command), and experiencing great difficulty in making consistent policy decisions. They fought each other through plans for an economic reform in which the main issues were private property, price liberalization, the economic rights of the USSR's republics vis-à-vis the federal bureaucracy, and tax policy. Prime Minister Ryzhkov relied on the brain trust of Leonid Abalkin, his deputy for economic reform. In May of 1990, Ryzhkov presented Abalkin's moderate plan for the introduction of a "regulated" market economy to the USSR Supreme Soviet. Afraid of the social consequences of price liberalization, the parliament rejected it and demanded an improved plan by September.

Yeltsin and the Russian parliament wanted more radical and more rapid reforms. At the end of July, Gorbachev and Yeltsin agreed on the installation of a "working group" that had to come up with a plan for fundamental economic reform, to incorporate the ideas of both the Russian radicals and the Union moderates. During the month of August, the working group led by academician Stanislav Shatalin, a member of Gorbachev's Presidential Council, and the young economist Grigorii Yavlinskii prepared a plan for radical and swift reform that came to be known as the "Five-hundred-days plan."[14] It was this plan that had been intended by Yeltsin and Gorbachev to be presented to the parliaments of the USSR and the republics, instead of a revised Ryzhkov/Abalkin plan. But soon after it had started its work, Leonid Abalkin left the working group, and, against Gorbachev's orders, the economic bureaucracy of the USSR actively obstructed the work of the Shatalin-Yavlinskii group. The State Planning Commission and Finance Minister Valentin Pavlov refused to provide the group with essential statistical data. Consequently, by early September the Supreme Soviets were faced not with one, but with two conceptions of economic transition that, in the words of Shatalin, were "of two different blood types." President Yeltsin used another metaphor, saying that "one cannot combine a hedgehog with a snake."[15]

Although there had been considerable crossbreeding, fundamental differences remained, not only in their timing, but also in some of their basic conceptions. One essential difference was that Shatalin and his group had accepted the disintegration of the USSR as a fact of life. Taking the sovereign rights of the republics as a point of departure, his plan tried to save as much as possible of a common market. Ryzhkov and Abalkin, on the other hand, were not able to go beyond decentralization within the quasi-federal state, and the retaining of central control by the USSR's bureaucracy. In September, the RSFSR Supreme Soviet accepted the radical Shatalin-Yavlinskii plan "in principle." The USSR Supreme Soviet received no less than three plans: the Shatalin Plan; a revised edition of the Ryzhkov plan it had rejected in May; and an attempt at compromise between the two that had been prepared by Abel Aganbegian at the request of Gorbachev. With no plan accepted, the Supreme Soviet, on 24 September, granted Gorbachev special powers (up to 31 March 1992, a period of approximately five hundred days) for as yet unspecified reforms. While Yeltsin's Russia remained firm in announcing its intention to implement the Shatalin plan, the USSR Supreme Soviet, on 19 October, accepted yet another plan: Gorbachev's own "Presidential Plan," a watered-down version of Aganbegian's adaptation of the Shatalin Plan. It was "not so much a plan as . . . a statement of intent so general as to be unobjectionable to the various factions in the debate."[16] The Soviet parliament had disqualified itself by not being able to act boldly on the country's most pressing problem, reform of the economy. On 1 November the plan was to go into operation. On 31 October the Russian parliament adopted a law by which it appropriated all natural wealth and state property located on its territory.[17]

While politicians in Moscow were battling over economic and constitutional reform, during the summer and fall the country experienced increasing turmoil. The population was angered by shortages of bread, other food products, and cigarettes. At many places there was labor unrest. Communist Party members turned in their membership cards—or sold them; on the black market they went for prices ranging from thirty dollars up. Statues of Lenin were being dismantled or demolished. Just one indication of the mood in some parts of the country was that at the beginning of October the presidium of the Ternopol City Soviet in Ukraine confiscated all Communist Party and Komsomol property on its territory.[18] The Soviet Union vibrated with warnings of an impending coup. In Russia, agreement on a new Constitution could not be reached. On 12 November the Russian parliament's Constitutional Commission approved a draft,[19] but opposition against some of its provisions caused delays. In late November the referendum was postponed until the spring of 1991.

A Russian union?

One of the sensations of autumn had been the publication of Alexander Solzhenitsyn's views on Russia's future. Instead of answering calls to return from his retreat in the United States, the exiled author for the first time directly addressed the problems that his country was facing, and presented its people and its leaders with a few provocative suggestions.[20] There was no future for the USSR, and thus the negotiations on a new union treaty were a waste of time—even harmful. Through the mechanism of the USSR's empire, the non-Slav republics were sucking the juices of Russia. The process which Russia had started three months earlier with its Declaration of State Sovereignty was to be taken to its logical conclusion. Solzhenitsyn wanted Russia to take the initiative at decolonizing, and if necessary to force non-Slav republics to independence.

Solzhenitsyn wrote that Russia should throw off its empire—but it should not let go of its Slav relatives. He infuriated both Kazakhs and Ukrainians by brazenly proposing a new union to include Russia, Ukraine, Belorussia, and the northern part of Kazakhstan (to the Kazakhs in the South, Solzhenitsyn gave the option of deciding by referendum whether or not they wanted to join). This new union was to be called not a *slavic* union but the *Russian* Union (*Rossiiskii Soiuz*). Solzhenitsyn's insensitivity and lack of understanding of Ukrainian and Kazakh national feelings closely matched the attitude of many Russians. Boris Yeltsin commented that he was "intrigued by the idea of a union of the three Slavic republics."[21] The Solzhenitsyn essay was to structure the debate on Russia and its empire for many months to come.

In the meantime, news came that Mikhail Gorbachev had been awarded the Nobel Peace Prize. The prize accentuated Western gratitude for what Gorbachev and his minister of foreign affairs, Edward Shevardnadze, had done for disarmament, for the liberation of the countries of Eastern Europe, and for the normalization of their country's relations with the rest of the world. It symbolized Western acceptance of Gorbachev's Soviet Union as a reliable partner in international relations. But the irony was that at the moment when the Soviet Union was accepted as a cultured state, it stopped addressing the world with one voice. Next to *Soviet* foreign policy, several republics started up their own foreign policies, asking foreign governments not to take the positions of Gorbachev and Shevardnadze for granted.

In October, Andrei Kozyrev was confirmed minister of foreign affairs of the RSFSR. His first official act on 16 October was to sign Russia's first declaration of friendship and cooperation with a foreign country—Poland—three days after a similar declaration had been signed by the Ukrainian minister of foreign affairs, Anatolii Zlenko. Russia started to formulate its own foreign policy, heavily oriented to gaining acceptance and credibility among the countries of the Western world, Japan, and South Korea. Its other priority was the weaving of a diplomatic safety net of bilateral ties for the republics to land on should USSR structures collapse. The signing in November of long-term political and economic cooperation agreements between Russia, Ukraine, and Kazakhstan was the beginning of crisscrossing bilateral agreements among many of the USSR's republics.

The precautions that the republics were taking were not out of proportion, for the mood of the majority of USSR officials and deputies took a turn for the worse. The military, the KGB, and the party leadership felt pushed into a corner by what they saw as the increasingly provocative behavior of nationalist governments in the republics, particularly in the Baltic states. They took offense at the confiscation of property; the resistance to the draft; the blocking of water, electricity, and other supplies to military garrisons; and the increasingly difficult position of the Russian-speaking population in those states. One could hear Russian generals angrily pounding their fists on Gorbachev's desk, saying that this had to be over and done with once and for all.[22] In the Soviet parliament their cause was urged by Soiuz, a group of anti-Gorbachev communists that had been organized in February and had responded to Lithuania's independence declaration by demanding that Gorbachev place Lithuania under direct presidential rule. By the end of the year Soiuz claimed to be the parliament's second largest faction after the pro-Gorbachev communists (730 deputies, 32 percent) with 561 members (almost 25 percent). The Inter-Regional Group of Deputies, of which Yeltsin had been one of the founding members, had less than half their voting power (229 members, 10 percent).[23]

In mid-November Gorbachev gave in to the pressure of the military and conservative communists. He asked parliament to expand his powers once more. Some of the things he wanted (and got): a cabinet to replace the Council of Ministers, the institution of a vice presidency, and the right to appoint his own representatives in the regions to supervise and control the implementation of Moscow's decisions. Defense Minister Yazov repeatedly threatened the Baltic governments that his army would no longer tolerate their insubordination. KGB chairman Kriuchkov said on television that foreign intelligence services were conducting a secret war against the USSR, and that his organization would fight for the preservation of the Soviet state. The Communist Party's Politburo asked Gorbachev to take "all necessary measures" against the Lithuanian government. The Soiuz deputies and a National Salvation Committee put pressure on Gorbachev to declare a state of emergency and direct presidential rule, at least in the Baltic region. Foreign Minister Shevardnadze came under heavy fire for the "loss" of Eastern Europe and for his pro-Western policy in the Iraq crisis. Reports that the USSR might possibly contribute troops to the anti-Saddam coalition sent shock waves of indignation through the Soviet parliament.

The dark winter of 1990–1991

Gorbachev made a complete about-face. On 1 December he replaced his liberal minister of internal affairs, Vadim Bakatin, with Boris Pugo, who as leader of the Latvian KGB (1980–1984) and Communist Party organization (1984–1988) had gained the reputation of being a hard-liner. Boris Gromov, the last commander of Soviet forces in Afghanistan, was appointed Pugo's first deputy. In a decree signed the same day, Gorbachev ordered the KGB and the Ministries of Defense and Internal Affairs "to secure the defense and security of the USSR and the operation of its armed forces, internal troops, and border guards."[24] It was a license for military intervention against civil authorities in the republics. During the tumultuous December session of the USSR Congress of People's Deputies, a group of over fifty VIPs, including Patriarch Aleksii II, demanded of Gorbachev that he declare a state of emergency and direct presidential rule "in major conflict areas . . . to counter separatism."[25] The next day, Edward Shevardnadze angrily resigned as minister of foreign affairs, disappointed in the failure of Gorbachev to support him. "Dictatorship is coming," he said, concluding half a year of premonitions.

The year 1991 brought Boris Yeltsin, standing for Russia, many more occasions to profile himself as the champion of decency and judiciousness against the increasingly despairing Communist Party leader and USSR president Mikhail Gorbachev. Part of the deal Gorbachev had made was that the army and security organs would get more latitude in dealing with obstinate republics. The central issue of Soviet politics had become who was boss in the USSR. On 7 January, the Ministry of Defense announced it would send airborne troops to enforce the draft in the obstinate republics. Why airborne troops? The answer came within a few days.

It had been decided that the Baltic states would have to serve as an example of what would happen if separatist republics would not give in. But the secret plan was not very original, not foolproof, and had a number of gaps. On 10 January, Gorbachev threatened Lithuania with presidential rule if its leadership ("attempting to reestablish a bourgeois regime") would not stop violating Soviet law.[26] He tacitly suggested that he would abide by the scenario demanded by the Soiuz group of deputies, the Central Coordinating Council of Intermovements, and the National Salvation Committee organized in Moscow in early December. The following day, a "Lithuanian National Salvation Committee" announced it was taking control in Lithuania, and Soviet troops occupied Lithuania's Ministry of Defense and printing house. Soviet defense minister Yazov later defensively claimed that the Salvation Committee had requested help—a thin excuse suggesting that the scenario used by the Soviet Union in past foreign interventions was now being applied within the USSR.

On 12 January, Yeltsin and the RSFSR Supreme Soviet issued strong statements against applying force in the Baltic states. That same day Gorbachev assured the USSR Federation Council that no force would be used. But the next day, with CNN fixing the eyes of the world on the crisis in Iraq, fourteen people were killed and many wounded when Soviet troops stormed the radio and television center in Vilnius. Was it to punish Gorbachev for his lack of resolve? The military action and the setting up of national salvation committees, coordinated from Moscow, had been intended to trigger presidential rule—but the president had hesitated. Colonel Alksnis expressed the feelings of those who were digging in their heels for the preservation of the Soviet Union: "The president betrayed us. . . . Just imagine, a surgeon begins an operation, makes an incision in the body of the patient . . . and abandons him."[27]

Yeltsin made full use of the occasion, bringing heavy rhetoric to bear on the Soviet positions. As soon as he sensed the "political earthquake," he "placed himself deliberately in its epicenter."[28] In the heat of the crisis he traveled to the Estonian capital Tallinn to sign a joint declaration with the leaders of the three Baltic states condemning the intervention. He provoked Gorbachev and the central institutions by appealing to soldiers from his own republic not to use their arms against civilians in the Baltic states, and by threatening that the RSFSR would create its own army should there be attempts to undermine its sovereignty. One week after the Vilnius incident, he suggested to the Russian parliament that the best answer to Gorbachev's behavior would be to speed up the conclusion of a treaty between the three Slav republics and Kazakhstan.[29] Gorbachev exited the Baltic crisis more harmed than he had already been. There was little room left for doubt: either he had taken part in its planning and had bungled the execution, or he had not been informed; in both cases he showed signs of a lame duck—an impression that was to become only stronger during the months ahead.

Little more than a week after his new Cabinet chief, Valentin Pavlov, had been confirmed by parliament, Gorbachev, on 22 January, decreed a monetary-financial reform with the invalidation of fifty and one hundred ruble banknotes as its centerpiece. The protests by pensioners, the chaos at the unprepared banks and post offices, the invented stories of Pavlov (who first defended the measure as being directed against the "ill-gotten gains" of "speculators," and later claimed that his measure had only just averted an "economic coup" by "the West")—all this so soon after Vilnius—did not help to create an impression that the USSR's president and cabinet were competent. Irritation and anger at the USSR's central institutions increased when, three days later, it was announced that by 1 February militiamen (police) would be augmented by army troops and forces of the Ministry of Internal Affairs in patrolling the streets of the large cities. The monetary reform and joint patrols were part of a package of extraordinary measures that on 24 December had been urged on Gorbachev by Kriuchkov, Yazov, Baklanov, Pugo, and others "to fight crime"—measures for which Gorbachev had refused to take responsibility.[30] Before the month was out, a group of RSFSR deputies demanded that Gorbachev and Pavlov resign, that the USSR presidential structures be abolished, and that power be handed over to a coordinating council of republican leaders. By the time the year was out, there was indeed nothing left of the USSR but a council of leaders of independent states.

On 6 February, President Gorbachev appeared on television to urge Soviet citizens to participate in the 17 March referendum, which the Congress of People's Deputies had granted him in December. He urged the public to approve his efforts to preserve the USSR. What he did not say was that he intended the referendum to provide him with the legitimacy he had failed to receive due to the fact that he had never been elected in a free and fair public vote. It was a belated attempt to create a secondhand legitimacy to prop up his weak position and make up for his lack of authority. Whether the attempt was successful depends on one's position.

It was a curious referendum indeed. For the first time in the history of the USSR (and in world history), the president and parliament asked the people whether or not they wanted the continued existence of their state. Gorbachev claimed victory. With a turnout of about 80 percent, three-quarters of the voters on 17 March rewarded his efforts to preserve the USSR "as a renewed federation of equal sovereign republics." Even in Ukraine and in Yeltsin's RSFSR, 70 percent had voted "for Gorbachev"!

But the results could be interpreted in a different way. In six of the USSR's fifteen republics, the referendum had not taken place: the leaderships of Estonia, Latvia, Lithuania, Moldova, Georgia, and Armenia had effectively boycotted the referendum.[31] Nevertheless, on 21 March the parliament of the USSR declared "the decision of the people" (*reshenie naroda*) "final" and "having binding force" for the state institutions of the USSR and the republics within its territory. It did so because the referendum law stated that referendum results must be taken into account by state bodies, thereby implying that the parliaments of all fifteen republics now had no alternative but to support the revised draft of the union treaty that had been published on 9 March. But the position of Gorbachev and the USSR parliament could hardly undo the impression that, as far as the implementation of decisions taken by its political bodies was concerned, the USSR had ceased to function.

The confrontation between the central institutions on the one hand and "Russia" on the other gained intensity. The practical meaning of "sovereignty" was shown in the ability to enforce political decisions. Compliance to Gorbachev's decrees was seldom and sporadic. The Moscow City Soviet and the Russian government denied the central authorities a say in the appointment of a new Moscow police chief, and Gorbachev and his team tried in vain to prevent a pro-Yeltsin demonstration organized for 28 March by his grassroots support movement, Democratic Russia (DR). The deployment of fifty thousand troops in the streets of Moscow, John Morrison wrote, "was not so much a show of strength as a show of weakness."[32] Yeltsin felt strong, and went full throttle. In a speech to the RSFSR Congress of People's Deputies, he called for a roundtable discussion for communist and opposition leaders in an effort to create a coalition government for the USSR. The Congress was divided, and calls that Yeltsin was planning to institute a dictatorship were heard.

The political intrigues and fights in Moscow took place against the backdrop of strikes during March and April in the major mining areas of the USSR. By the third week of March, the strikes had spread to more than one-third of the USSR's coal mines and was having a disastrous effect on industrial production. The miners demanded wage increases and better living conditions. Echoing calls by Yeltsin, they insisted on the resignation of Gorbachev and the USSR Cabinet of Ministers. Originally, Cabinet Chief Pavlov demanded that they return to work before there could be talks on their demands; after he had given in and agreed to open talks on 25 March, strike leaders said they would only return to work after Gorbachev had been replaced by Yeltsin—or if Yeltsin would ask them to do so. Again, Yeltsin used the occasion. At the Congress of People's Deputies, at the end of March, he supported the miners' demand that the jurisdiction over the mines be transferred from the Ministry of the Coal Industry of the USSR to that of the RSFSR. Three weeks later, the Vorkuta Strike Committee made the transfer a condition for their ending the strike. On the symbolic date of 1 May, Yeltsin signed an order instructing the Council of Ministers to support and coordinate the process of transferring mines to RSFSR jurisdiction by their workers collectives.[33]

The final showdown: toward the August coup

With his position strengthened, Yeltsin went back to the negotiating table. On 23 April, at a meeting in Novo-Ogarevo called by Gorbachev, he signed a Joint Statement with the leaders of eight (Slav and Muslim) republics and the Soviet president.[34] The statement called for speeding up the conclusion of the treaty for a "Union of Sovereign States" (USS) and the adoption of a new constitution by the USSR Congress of People's Deputies within six months after the treaty. This was to be followed by elections. Gorbachev and the leaders of the nine republics recognized the right of the remaining six republics to decide their own pace in joining a new union, should they want to join at all. But in one and the same breath they added that only signatories to the treaty would enjoy most-favored-nation status. One of the concessions Russia had been able to wrest from Gorbachev was that control over the mines was to be transferred to the Russian government; another was that the autonomous republics would not be allowed to sign the union treaty on a par with the Union republics, but merely as members of the delegations of the republics in which they were located. This meant that Russia would not speak with "one plus sixteen" (or more) different voices, but with only one, controlled by Yeltsin. Yet many differences remained, one of them being that Russia and Ukraine held on to confederal conceptions of a new union that were radically different from those of Gorbachev. Five days prior to the Novo-Ogarevo meeting, representatives of the three Slav republics had met with counterparts from Kazakhstan and Uzbekistan to discuss a common position vis-à-vis Gorbachev and his draft union treaty. They had agreed to continue their consultations as long as the new treaty had not come about.[35]

The main struggle during this period was between Moscow and Moscow—the institutions and leaders of the USSR, located in the Kremlin, and those of the RSFSR in the "House of Soviets" (popularly known as the White House)—both on the Moscow River embankment. But this is far from saying that "Russia" and "the USSR" were united by the waters of the Moskva. To the USSR Congress of People's Deputies and Supreme Soviet, "Novo-Ogarevo" meant a suspended death sentence, for they would cease to exist (and the deputies would have to face elections) with the adoption of a new constitution. This made the parliament increasingly nervous. In Russia, opposition to Yeltsin, particularly from the nationalists, was gaining strength. One indication of such opposition had been an open letter to Yeltsin, published in January by twelve concerned citizens, including the leading nationalist authors Belov and Rasputin, village prose writers of days past, and the fascist journalist Prokhanov. They accused him of "contempt for Russia's history," "indifference to the fate of the Fatherland," "an inclination to engage in political games," and "incitement to civil war." They wondered why Yeltsin did not understand that by his efforts to break apart the USSR, he was contributing to the disintegration and "destruction of Russia."[36] The nationalists brought Yeltsin and the progressive forces face to face with questions that lay at the basis of the Gorbachev-Yeltsin rivalry: Would disintegration stop at the borders of the Russian Federation? Could "Russia" be treated (and could it treat itself) as an entity separate from the central institutions of the USSR? Was Russia's position indeed equal to those of the other republics? Was Russia not different because it had created the USSR, and should it not receive a special place in the confederal construction that would replace the USSR? "We cannot separate the Russian republic from the center," philosopher Yurii Burtin wrote, "we look back in history, and the center is somehow ourselves."[37]

Many political bosses and deputies in federal institutions saw their interests threatened by the turn that union treaty negotiations at Novo-Ogarevo were taking, by the increasing marginalization of central institutions, and by the alliance between Gorbachev and Yeltsin that had been in the making since late April. Panic-stricken, they resorted to desperate acts. On June 17, five days after Yeltsin had been elected president of the RSFSR, USSR Cabinet chief Pavlov asked the Supreme Soviet for expanded powers at the expense of president Gorbachev. Gorbachev was taken by surprise. Pavlov's sinister designs probably had been discussed with KGB chairman Kriuchkov, Defense Minister Yazov, and Interior Minister Pugo. Supreme Soviet chairman Lukianov may have been informed as well; during the discussion on Pavlov's request, he implored the people's deputies: "If we do not resort to extraordinary measures, the country will perish. Will perish—do you understand this? . . . There is no governing center in the country today. The cabinet is making this plea: 'Untie our hands, let us do something for the country. . . .'"[38]

President Gorbachev addressed the Supreme Soviet four days later. Meekly, parliament decided with an overwhelming majority to pass the Cabinet chief's request to the president "for further study."[39] In August, the Cabinet ministers and parliament chairman were to make another desperate attempt at seizing power.

Many republics, provinces, and even cities had used the occasion of the 17 March referendum to organize their own referenda or polls, either in place of or side-by-side with Gorbachev's plebiscite. In Russia, voters had approved of the institution of a Russian presidency, the president to be elected in a popular vote; the inhabitants of Moscow had voted for a directly elected mayor. On 12 June, Russia's new "independence day," Boris Yeltsin was elected president of the RSFSR. On 10 July, his hand on the constitution and the Declaration of State Sovereignty of the RSFSR, he was sworn in as the republic's first president.

Supported by an aggressive campaign organized by Democratic Russia, with his "running mate" Colonel Alexander Rutskoi, he had beaten five competitors: a former USSR prime minister (Ryzhkov, 16.9 percent), a former USSR minister of internal affairs (Bakatin, 3 percent), an army general and commander of the Volga-Ural Military District (Makashov, 4 percent), the chairman of a provincial soviet (Tuleev, 6 percent), and the leader of the Liberal Democratic Party of Russia, Vladimir Wolfovich Zhirinovskii (almost 8 percent). For Yeltsin and his reformers, the election had been a true democratic triumph. They tended to underplay signs of impending trouble. It was not so much the second place of Nikolai Ryzhkov, the candidate of those in the Communist Party and USSR establishment who wanted to stop Yeltsin and disintegration. It was that, taken together, the results of the Stalinist reactionary Makashov and the fascist Zhirinovskii showed that reactionary groups in the established institutions had the support of twelve percent of the population. A month before the elections, Zhirinovskii, then forty-five years old, had proudly proclaimed to be "the representative of the new generation . . . the ordinary middle sections of the population: two hundred rubles pay, a two-room apartment. Not the elite, and not the bottom, those from the prisons, the drunks, the hobos."[40]

Still, he saw himself as from the highly educated strata. Addressing the Congress in May, he had boasted to be "free from dogmas," to have come from a lawyer's family, and (in contrast to other Russian leaders) to be able to engage in a conversation with Mitterand, Kohl, or Bush without the help of interpreters. He had even addressed the Turkish-speaking Congress deputies in one of the Turkish languages to prove his command of languages.[41] Zhirinovskii had amply shown his skill at adapting his language to the sensitivities of his listeners.

There were reports that ever since his party had been the first to be officially registered, Zhirinovskii had been supported by the KGB. On the first of April 1990, the founding of the LDP had been prominently announced on the front pages of all major newspapers, and in late September Zhirinovskii had declared that the CPSU would be the best ally for his party.[42] In early December 1990 he had been one of the spokesmen for the newly created National Salvation Committee and had demanded that Gorbachev impose a state of emergency. The day after he lost the presidential elections, Zhirinovskii demanded the annulment of all votes for Yeltsin. Russian television saw similarities between his success and the rise of Hitler and Stalin.[43]

Leaders in the Communist Party, the army, and the KGB were growing restless due to the turn that the "Novo-Ogarevo" negotiations on the union treaty were taking. But not only they were restless. Opposition to the deals made by republican leaders and Gorbachev (and approved by one republican parliament after the other) was widespread. The reactionary Soiuz group in the Soviet parliament, reformers in the Russian parliament including committee (deputy) chairmen like Sergei Shakhrai and Yevgenii Ambartsumov, many of the parliaments of Russia's autonomous republics (insisting that they would sign the treaty as independent states)—all voiced their opposition. But Yeltsin could not be stopped. On 20 July he decreed the "departification" of all Russian state bodies, institutions, and state-controlled workplaces "to prevent the intervention of social organizations [read: the Communist Party] in the activities of state organs."[44] Ever since its foundation the Communist Party had operated through party "cells" by which the leadership controlled its members at their places of work. The communist cells (renamed "primary party organizations" long before) at ministries, administrative offices, universities, factories, stores, schools, and hospitals were to be disbanded by 4 August. The measure struck the Communist Party at its heart.

On 23 July, *Sovetskaia Rossia* published "A Word to the People," signed by twelve military, communist, nationalist, and cultural leaders, including First Deputy Minister of Internal Affairs General Boris Gromov, Chief of the Soviet Ground Forces General Valentin Varennikov, Vasilii Starodubtsev, Alexander Tiziakov (the latter three were coup plotters less than a month later), Soiuz chairman Yurii Blokhin, and the nationalist writers Yurii Bondarev and (again) Valentin Rasputin. In inflated language, they announced the creation of a patriotic mass movement: "Let us awaken, let us collect ourselves, let old and young rise for the country. Let us say 'No!' to the destroyers and aggressors."[45] It was an alarming sign. Since the previous autumn, warnings about an impending coup had not abated. The Cabinet had tried to pull off a "constitutional coup" by appealing to parliament to grant it Gorbachev's powers. Now some very high officials wrote that "the army and the navy, true to their sacred duty, will not permit a fratricidal war and the destruction of the Fatherland. . . ."

The Novo-Ogarevo negotiations, in which parliamentary chairman Anatolii Lukianov played a leading role, were still at an impasse. Several republics denied the new Union its own competence, ownership, and tax income. The signing of the treaty was postponed until September–October.[46] But one night at the end of July, Gorbachev met separately with Yeltsin and the Kazakh leader Nursultan Nazarbaev. They reached agreement on taxation, an issue of prime importance for the future of the Russian state and for the viability of a successor to the USSR. Gorbachev gave in to the demand that there be no federal taxes, and that all taxes would be collected by the republics. Only a fixed percentage of the collected taxes would subsequently be paid to the central treasury.

Lukianov felt betrayed by Gorbachev. Boris Yeltsin later wrote in his reminiscences that at this secretive midnight session, Gorbachev had also agreed to fire Kriuchkov, Pugo, and Pavlov after the treaty had been signed. Nazarbaev was to be the head of the government of the new Union. But from beginning to end, Yeltsin claims, their secret conversation had been monitored by Kriuchkov's KGB.[47] On 2 August, Gorbachev appeared on television, announcing that the RSFSR, Kazakhstan, and Uzbekistan had agreed to sign the treaty on 20 August. Other republics would hopefully be ready by 20 August or would follow at a later date.

It was now a matter of *kto-kogo*, to be or not to be. The bosses of the government and the army decided to fight their last battle. The signing ceremony was to be prevented. On 5 August, the day after Gorbachev had left Moscow for a vacation at Foros in the Crimea, they met in a KGB safe house named "ABC" and decided that emergency rule was to be introduced before 20 August.[48] Two days before the fourth draft of the treaty was published on 15 August, Prime Minister Pavlov warned of a "power vacuum" once the treaty had been signed, using these code words for saying that he and his colleagues would lose their jobs. Defense Minister Yazov felt that "for me personally and for many other comrades with whom I talked, it suddenly became clear that the collapse of the Union was bearing inexorably down on us."[49] The Presidium of the Cabinet met on Saturday, 17 August, issuing a statement saying that the draft treaty at hand would deprive the center of its power and would destroy the economic and political integrity of the USSR. What was not said was that preparations for blackmailing the USSR president into submission were in full swing.

The story of the self-destructive August Coup has been told many times, and the reasons for its failure have been analyzed by several authors.[50] It is still too early for its definitive history to be written. Here we should concentrate on the role Russia played, and on the coup's impact on Russian politics. For Russia and Yeltsin, the coup was a gift from heaven. When on 18 August a delegation of state and party officials confronted Gorbachev in his Crimean retreat, President Yeltsin was returning from Alma-Ata, where he and Nazarbaev had dotted the last i's for the treaty that was to be signed on 20 August. The next day, five hours after Radio Moscow had announced that Vice President Yanaev and a "State Committee for the State of Emergency in the USSR" (GKCHP, the Russian abbreviation) were taking over, Yeltsin gave a press conference in the White House, broadcast live by CNN, calling for Gorbachev's reinstatement.[51] Less than two hours later, television viewers all over the world witnessed the Russian president mounting a tank in front of the White House and calling for an immediate general strike. In the meantime he had signed his Decree No. 59, qualifying the State Committee's actions as a coup d'état and warning officials not to execute its orders. He appointed Konstantin Kobets to be Chairman of the RSFSR State Committee for Defense and assigned him the task of organizing the defense of the White House.[52] The next day Kobets was made RSFSR minister of defense.

Four days later the coup was over, its leaders arrested, the hated Dzerzhinskii statue facing KGB headquarters toppled, and Gorbachev back in Moscow—all this, to a great extent, thanks to Yeltsin's resolve—and (but this was not known at the time) to the help he had received from the U.S. National Security Agency that had provided him with sensitive information on which army units were supporting the plotters, and which were not.[53]

Russian reformers were in a state of euphoria, and their president tended to become overconfident. In a live broadcast on Russian television and CNN, he forced Gorbachev, in front of the Russian parliament, to read the minutes of the USSR Cabinet meeting of 19 August, where the ministers had been asked to show their colors, and where all but two of them had approved of the coup or had failed to oppose it. By then, Yeltsin could have known that cowardice was not limited to USSR ministers. Not only had most of the leaders of the USSR republics adopted a wait-and-see attitude during those four fateful days. When later, during the fall, Yeltsin's staff took stock of the behavior of lower administrations in the RSFSR, the result was shocking. In only 30 percent of the republics and other administrative units had the authorities openly declared their loyalty to the Russian president; in the remaining 70 percent of the territories the administrative elite had sided with the GKCHP or had adopted a wait-and-see attitude.[54]

As for the Russian fascists, they of course had not been sitting around doing nothing. On 23 August, some hours after the Moscow City Soviet had suspended the activities of Zhirinovskii's Liberal Democratic Party for its support of the coup, Central Television screened an interview with Vladimir Zhirinovskii that had been taped three days before. In it, the LDP leader supported the coup, stating that being a specialist in international law, he was confident that the GKCHP had legal authority, and that those who were of a different opinion were "rabble" and "state criminals."[55]

FALLING APART

The last four months of 1991 brought Russia to one of those rare periods in history when people and institutions, only dimly aware of what is happening, move almost compulsively in what seems to be a predestined direction. The failure of the coup had lifted the two mental barriers that had for so long blocked acceptance of the approaching end. The CPSU would have to go—the only question remaining was how to go about removing it. The USSR was doomed as well—but perhaps it could still be replaced by a new construction built from the bottom? Mikhail Gorbachev had great difficulty in accepting the drastically changed political situation—what to do about him? Russia was "steering its course toward a way out of Utopia"—but no one knew where it would land.[56] To many Russians, a complete disintegration of the Soviet state into fifteen independent states was inconceivable, and it certainly was not difficult to hang on to rational arguments against such development.

The republics and regions of the USSR had been closely intertwined in an economic network of which the nerve center had been the State Planning Committee (Gosplan) in Moscow. Agricultural produce, raw materials, semimanufactured products, and consumer goods had been hauled from one republic to the other; each and every one of the republics was thought to be dependent on most of the others for its economic survival. The importance of interrepublic trade to the economies of the republics (expressed as a share of their 1988 Gross National Product) ranged from 15 percent in Russia and 32 percent for Ukraine and Kazakhstan, to 76 percent for Turkmenistan.[57] During the previous twelve months they had acknowledged their interdependence by weaving an economic safety net under the Soviet Union. But that net was of diplomatic making and there were no strong guarantees that it would hold. Only Russia, with its enormous natural wealth, could be confident. Several other republics were said to lack a sound geographical or material base for an independent economy. Who in his right mind, so many thought, would want to forego the benefits of an economy stretching from the Polish border to the Bering Straits?

The logical error that was made at the time was that Armenia was not compared to Andorra. Tiny Andorra, until 1993 jointly ruled by the president of France and the bishop of Seo de Urgel in Spain, had a viable economy when, in 1993, it adopted its constitution and became member of the United Nations. This happened even though it lacked many of the resources of Armenia—or Argentina.[58] The point I want to make is that with the collapse of the USSR and the Soviet economy, most of its republics had but one long-term aim, to be reached in the shortest possible time: to restructure their economies in the direction of the capitalist market and specialize in sectors in which they would have a comparative advantage. In 1990, the "Five-hundred-days' plan" of Shatalin and Yavlinskii had stated economic "openness" (*otkrytost*) to be one of the eight principles of a market economy. The economies of the republics of the USSR were to be "consistently integrated with the system of worldwide economic relations."[59] In principle, each and every republic of the USSR could play its role in the worldwide division of labor. Reality might be an altogether different affair: the transition from a closed economy to a market economy would be long and painful, and would cost society dearly. The republics of the USSR could not have it both ways *and* become independent states, *and* continue enjoying the economies-of-scale (and subsidies) that the USSR had provided them with.[60]

Or could they? Humpty Dumpty was going to fall—this much was sure. But would there be horses and would there be men that could break the fall—or put Humpty together again? The CPSU could be excluded. Its central nervous system was crushed in the revolutionary turmoil. Yeltsin had the building of the party's Central Committee locked and sealed. On 22 August, with Gorbachev returning from Foros, he banned (on the territory of the RSFSR) the party's activities in the armed forces, the KGB, and the police. He had already banned primary party organizations at workplaces, and on 23 August he decreed the temporary suspension of Communist Party activities in the RSFSR altogether. The same day, Russia's pre-1917 tricolor was seen flying over the Kremlin, next to the hammer and sickle of the USSR.

Mikhail Gorbachev had returned to Moscow under a cloud, amid rumors that in some way he had been involved in the coup. The rumors indicated that he had lost all credibility among the population and among elites in the republics. Politicians in the West who dreaded the disintegration of the USSR were the only people left believing in Gorbachev. There was no way he could save the Communist Party. On 24 August he resigned as General Secretary. He advised the Central Committee to self-destruct. Five days later, the USSR Supreme Soviet ordered the Communist Party to cease its activities.

The developments of late August to early September showed once more the extent to which membership in the Communist Party had been a matter of opportunism. Nine out of every ten members of the USSR Congress of People's Deputies had been communists when they had been elected in 1989, yet on 5 September 1991 the Congress agreed to disband the USSR, the state that their party had created and had preserved for over seven decades.[61] It ruled "to support the pursuit by the republics of being recognized as subjects of international law and of becoming member states of the United Nations." The new Union of Sovereign States was to be "based on the principles of independence and territorial integrity of the states." But whereas preparations for signing a treaty on the USS were (once more) to be speeded up, the Congress also made provisions for republics that would decide against entering the union.[62] One republic after another was declaring its formal independence and asking the international community for recognition: Estonia, Latvia, Ukraine, Belarus, Moldova, Georgia, Azerbaijan, Kyrgyzstan, Uzbekistan, Tajikistan, and Armenia. Yeltsin's Russia refrained from doing so, preferring to use the possibility of a declaration of independence as a threat to put pressure on Gorbachev and the federal parliament. Ukraine's declaration was conditional, pending a referendum that was to be held on 1 December. Since Ukraine was essential to Russia, and since a separation was inconceivable, final arrangements on the post-USSR situation were held up until December.

In October the British weekly *Economist* announced the results of a readers' contest for a new name for the USSR. One reader had suggested RELICS, for Republics Left in Chaos by Socialism, another COMA (Confederation of Mutual Antagonism), and yet another (the undeserved winner) Gorbystan. The most original entry suggested a very simple solution: replacing the two S's in USSR by two F's—Union of Fewer and Fewer Republics. In its first ruling on 6 September, the new State Council of the USSR (with Gorbachev and the republican leaders as members) had recognized the independence of Lithuania, eighteen months after its proclamation had given a strong boost to the forces driving the republics of the USSR apart.[63]

There were attempts to break Humpty's fall. The last act of the USSR Congress of People's Deputies, on 5 September, had been to adopt a law on the state institutions and management of the USSR "in the transition period."[64] Such a period was declared by the Congress, hoping to put a halt to the further disintegration of power structures and to allow for "the coming about of a new system of state relations based on the will of the republics and the interests of the peoples."[65] In addition to the State Council, the last law of the Congress created an "Interstate Economic Committee" and a "Committee for the Operational Management of the USSR Economy" that were to keep the economy going.

The Congress had acted under pressure from the Russian leadership, which had threatened to declare independence if the law was not adopted. Later that month, RSFSR prime minister Ivan Silaev resigned in order to head the committees. One month later, on 18 October, agreement was reached between the leaders of eight republics, and a treaty on the creation of an economic community was signed in the Kremlin. It was meant to provide for a "common economic space" between Russia, Belarus, Armenia, Kazakhstan, Tajikistan, Turkmenistan, Kyrgyzstan, and Uzbekistan, and to lure Western governments into providing economic support. To participating republics it held out the bait of trade with Russia, the main supplier of energy and raw materials, at special prices below those on the world market. But important republics such as Ukraine, Azerbaijan, and Georgia (and Moldova) had their reservations and initially withheld their signatures. Although both Gorbachev and Yeltsin acclaimed the treaty as an important step in preserving a joint economy, it was mainly of symbolic significance. The treaty was to take effect after ratification by the eight parliaments. But it was little more than wishful thinking printed on parchment, and it was soon overtaken by events.

On 28 October, President Yeltsin presented the Russian Congress of People's Deputies his program for the radical reform of the *Russian* economy, pushing the Economic Community off the stage. A few days later, the Congress, by an overwhelming majority, accepted the basic principles of his plan and gave Yeltsin extraordinary powers for its implementation, including the right to remove local leaders and to appoint his own plenipotentiaries in the regions. They were to oversee the implementation of reform. The president chose Yegor Gaidar, a newcomer, as his deputy prime minister for economic policy. An experienced observer of the Russian economic scene wrote that "Russia apparently intends to go it alone and refuse to sell its marketable commodities to the other republics for funny money" (i.e., rubles).[66] Later, in November,

Yeltsin effectively blocked agreement on a new union treaty by refusing to grant Gorbachev his wish of creating a Union of Sovereign States that would be considered a state and would have its own elected president. The Russian president insisted that the USS be merely a confederation of independent states with a weak coordinating center. He was waiting for the 1 December referendum on Ukrainian independence and in the meantime pushing Gorbachev into a corner from which there would be no escape. The day preceding the communists' celebration of the 1917 October revolution was selected for the signing of a number of important presidential decrees.

In his 6 November decree "on the activities of the CPSU and the Communist Party of the RSFSR," Yeltsin claimed that the coup had shown "that the CPSU never was a party" but was only "a special mechanism for the formation and realization of political power."[67] It was sheer nonsense, but Yeltsin apparently felt that he had to find a way to set the *Communist* Party aside in order to finish it off. Its leadership had been responsible for the "historical cul-de-sac" in which the peoples of the USSR now found themselves, and their activities had been of an "anti-people, anticonstitutional" character. After the coup failed, they had not ceased their activities, and "as long as the structures of the CPSU exist," there would be no guarantee against renewed attempts at a coup. Attempts at reviving (*reanimirovat*) the party machinery were impermissible, Yeltsin wrote, and he therefore ordered the party's activities terminated, its organizational structures disbanded, and its property transferred to the state. With this medical metaphor Yeltsin obviously referred to Gorbachev, who, in August, had had the bad taste to ask for the Communist Party to be given "the kiss of life."

But the Communist Party proved to be a multiheaded Hydra. As Yeltsin was signing his decree, new communist formations popped out of a boiling mass of resentment. In Moscow they staged rallies and protest meetings that were looked upon with pity by the public. During 1992 and 1993 they gained strength. Neither was the Russian Communist Party willing to give up without a fight. Within a week it appealed to Russia's new Constitutional Court, protesting against Yeltsin's decree. In spite of the legal provision that "the RSFSR Constitutional Court does not consider political questions," this was to become one of the Court's political test cases.[68]

On 1 December, 90 percent of the voters in the Ukrainian referendum approved of the republic's declaration of independence. In presidential elections taking place at the same time, Leonid Kravchuk won just over 60 percent of the votes. In a telephone conversation with U.S.

president Bush the day before the referendum, Gorbachev had said that even if Ukraine voted for independence, this would not mean that it would secede from the USSR. The same day, Yeltsin had confessed that he could not imagine a Union without Ukraine.[69] During that fateful first week of December, both were busy at maneuvering. Threats and attempts at intimidation (border conflicts, civil war, catastrophe, interference!) went back and forth between the leaders in Moscow and Kiev. On 5 December, the Ukrainian parliament declared to annul the 1922 treaty by which the USSR had been created. The Ukrainians made it quite clear that they would not join a new union. Gorbachev and the USSR Supreme Soviet kept insisting on a treaty for their Union of Sovereign States. In a pathetic, defensively worded appeal on 3 December, the Supreme Soviet's Council of the Republics pleaded that it be given a role in the formation of the new union.[70] The next day, Gorbachev met with Yeltsin, and on the evening television news, Russians heard Gorbachev say that his role was now more important than ever before. The Interstate Economic Committee started dealing with the problem of how to apportion the USSR's foreign debt.

Speaking on television on 4 December, after his meeting with Gorbachev, President Yeltsin indicated that his thoughts went in the direction of a Slavic economic union that would exclude the Central Asian republics.[71] Solzhenitsyn's essay of September 1990 had born fruit: now that independence had come, none of the major republics felt like continuing to subsidize the relatively "poor" states of Central Asia. The scenario of Gorbachev and the Supreme Soviet was to reach agreement on a union involving all parties (republics, i.e., as yet not-recognized independent states) concerned. Russia and Ukraine feared that in such a construction they would have to make too many sacrifices. The leaders of the two biggest Slav republics decided to dictate the terms of a possible deal by creating their own union. It was the only way to force Gorbachev and the USSR Supreme Soviet to their knees.

During the weekend of 7–8 December, Presidents Yeltsin and Kravchuk met with Belarussian parliament chairman Stanislav Shushkevich in a hunting lodge near the Belarussian village of Belovezhskaia Pushcha. They agreed to a "Commonwealth of Independent States" (Sodruzhestvo Nezavisimykh Gosudarstv) (CIS) open to all former republics of the USSR—but on their terms. With the USSR they dealt once and for all: being the main signatories of the 1922 union treaty, they "established" (konstatirovat) that the USSR "as a subject of international law and a geopolitical reality" was in the process of ceasing to exist. From the moment the documents were signed, on their territories "the application of normative acts of third states, including the former USSR," was no longer allowed and the activities of its institutions were declared discontinued.[72] The Belarussian capital Minsk was to be the seat of the CIS's coordinating institutions.

Gorbachev had not been informed. He was furious. After meeting with Yeltsin and Kazakh president Nursultan Nazarbaev on 9 December, he insisted that the federal and all republican parliaments be heard on the agreements at hand. Gorbachev the lawyer demanded an extraordinary session of the USSR Congress of People's Deputies, insisting on the "constitutionality" of the transition and once again trying to manipulate people's confusion over (legal) legality and (political) legitimacy. On 11 December, the USSR Constitutional Supervision Committee backed him up, stating that the agreement on the USSR "ceasing to exist" had no legal force.[73] It took three more days for Gorbachev to surrender. On 10 December the parliaments of Ukraine and Belarus ratified the CIS agreement; two days later their Russian counterpart followed. That memorable 12 December, Gorbachev said that he would go if nine more republics would join the CIS. Most people, he said, would have given up long ago. But he could not control his anger over the fact that as soon as the CIS agreement had been reached, Yeltsin had telephoned U.S. president Bush, and only subsequently Shushkevich had informed him.[74]

The same day, the leaders of the five Central Asian republics met in Ashkhabad. They expressed their willingness to join the commonwealth, provided that they have equal rights with the three founding states. With the help of Kravchuk and Shushkevich, Yeltsin had forced his own conception of a confederation on the republics of the USSR and had sidetracked Gorbachev. Kazakh president Nazarbaev, one of Gorbachev's early political friends, volunteered that the president of the USSR was living in a fool's paradise.[75] The formal accession of the five Central Asian republics plus Armenia, Azerbaijan, and Moldova (turning CIS into an organization with eleven member states) was signed on 21 December in the Kazakh capital Almaty. The states explicitly recognized each other's territorial integrity, the inviolability of each others' borders, the "openness" of their borders, and the free movement of people and information. They agreed to a joint command for the strategic armed forces. Russia was awarded the prize of the Soviet Union's permanent seat (with right of veto) in the UN Security Council, and the three founding states took it upon themselves to seek admission to the UN for the other eight (Ukraine and Belorussia had been member states of the UN since its founding in 1945). The deal was done. But whether the commonwealth (*sodruzhestvo*) would really contribute to common wealth and friendship was still very much unclear.

Gorbachev and Yeltsin had met separately with the military leadership on 10 and 11 December to seek their support. Gorbachev was on the defensive and had no time for questions and answers. To the assembled military leaders his fifty-minute monologue raised more questions than it answered. When Yeltsin faced the marshals and generals at eight o'clock the next morning, he knew that the next day Kravchuk would take the armed forces stationed in Ukraine (excluding the nuclear deterrence forces) under his own command.[76] But he did not reveal this. Stressing that he came only for an "informal talk," Yeltsin told the military what they wanted to hear. The strategic armed forces would not be split up and would remain under unified command. Russia would not create its own army and ministry of defense unless it was compelled to do so. He promised a 90 percent raise of officers' pay by the first of January, wherever (outside or inside the RSFSR) they were stationed. To officers' families that had been forced to return from abroad, he promised better housing. After his one-hour speech, Yeltsin answered questions for thirty minutes. In contrast to Gorbachev's performance, Yeltsin's speech was occasionally interrupted by applause.[77] The next day, presenting the CIS agreement for ratification to his parliament, Yeltsin reported that the military leadership had "actively supported" him.[78]

Naturally, the military gave Yeltsin the benefit of the doubt. They had little use for Gorbachev's incantations about merging "his" USS with Yeltsin's CIS and having the parliaments of the USSR and the republics find a middle ground. But as political questions were resolved, new and urgent issues emerged. What would happen to the nuclear weapons stationed in Russia, Belarus, Ukraine, and Kazakhstan? On 16 December, Yeltsin had said that control over these weapons would be in the hands of the heads of the four new states and of a "supreme commander in chief." The other leaders gave strong signals that they would not move their nuclear weapons to Russia, but U.S. secretary of state Baker declared after his last visit to the Soviet Union that he had been assured privately that Belarus, Kazakhstan, and Ukraine would sign the Nonproliferation Treaty.[79] It dawned on many in and outside Russia that the birth of the CIS would be accompanied by grave problems.

On 17 December, Gorbachev and Yeltsin talked for two hours and agreed that the USSR would cease to exist on 1 January 1992. Two days later, with Gorbachev and the USSR Supreme Soviet still demurring, Yeltsin took control of all USSR structures and assets on Russian territory, with the exception of the Ministries of Defense and Nuclear

Energy. Small groups of discontents protested in Moscow against the end of the USSR. One of the frenzied speakers was Vladimir Zhirinovskii.

Signing decree UP-3162 on 25 December, Mikhail Gorbachev resigned as president of the USSR. The "right to use nuclear arms" he handed over to the president of the Russian Federation.[80] The next day the Supreme Soviet's Council of the Republics adopted a Declaration in which it meekly "established" (*konstatiruet*) that, with the creation of the CIS, "the USSR ceases to exist as a state and subject of international law."[81] Russia's neighboring republics had become foreign countries, soon to be termed "the near abroad." Seven decades before, the Bolsheviks had created an "unbreakable union of free republics" for the preservation of the Russian Empire.[82] Now it was up to Russia to pick up the pieces.

FOUR   *The Unremitting Crisis*

The worst is over. (Boris Yeltsin, October 1992, October 1993, April 1994) [1]

. . . the business about Russian fascism is also mystique, and that should be realized in the West. Because if it were not mystique they would have won the elections. They are not going to win anything anywhere. (Alexander Tsipko, 1990) [2]

Today, the whole world knows about me. (Vladimir Zhirinovskii, 1993) [3]

The shock was tremendous. In 1989–1990 Russia had "lost" the states of Central Europe, its outer empire. Now, on 1 January 1992, the republics of the inner empire had become "abroad." It had lost (or freed itself of) fourteen republics at its western and southern rim. Russia had lost its common borders with Czechoslovakia, Hungary, Romania, Turkey, Iran, and Afghanistan. A short stretch of common border with Poland remained in what was now the Kaliningrad exclave, an important Russian naval base on the Baltic Sea. The country's coastline on the Black Sea was reduced to roughly one-third of what it had been before; its naval base Sebastopol (Crimea) was now located in a foreign country. Sochi, the popular seaside resort, was still in Russia—but Sukhumi, 120 kilometers to the southeast was Georgian (or Abkhazian?) territory. Russia's Caspean Sea coastline was reduced to one-fourth, that of the Baltic Sea to less than one-fifth of its former length. The ancient city of Pskov was still Russian territory, but 120 kilometers to the northwest, Tartu, with its university dating from 1632, was now in independent Estonia. Belgorod was in Russia, while Kharkiv, seventy kilometers to the south, was in Ukraine. In all the foreign cities lived Russians, many of them in favor of independence but wondering what would happen to them under foreign rule. For Russians at home it would take a long time to get used to the idea that traveling from Belgorod to Kharkiv meant crossing an international border, however "transparent" that border might be. They were living in a shrinking state. Russian military ports and bases were suddenly located in foreign countries, some of them openly hostile. Its land borders were 3,000 kilometers longer than the borders of the USSR had been. The Moscow Military District had become a "front district."[4] It was small wonder that the marshals and generals were worried.

The social upheavals triggered by Gorbachev and fanned by Yeltsin had pushed Russia back from Europe at a time when Russia wanted nothing more badly than to be part of Europe and its civilization. With its hopes fixed on Western Europe, Russia was now isolated from the West by a buffer of not all too friendly former vassal states. This dramatic event could only have taken place with the Russian leaders and public under sedation to soften the shock. That sedative was the belief in the Commonwealth as a temporary substitute for the USSR. But the sedative worked only through the turn of the year. As Russian leaders sobered up, they were brought down to earth with a bump. The CIS agreements had been patched together under heavy time pressure; they were anything but the outcome of normal diplomatic negotiations, and the distance between their supposed importance and their diplomatic caliber was immeasurable. Moreover, the member states had differing expectations of the significance and future of the CIS. For the Russians, the CIS was a way of keeping the empire together, albeit in a different form and under a new name. But their closest relatives, the Ukrainians, had been determined in rejecting the new union (the USS) as patched together by Gorbachev, Yeltsin, and Nazarbaev after "Novo-Ogarevo." To the Russians, therefore, the CIS had been the only way to "preserve" Ukraine for Russia. The Ukrainians, with over 500,000 Soviet troops in their country, had signed and ratified the CIS agreement, expecting it to be a means to get rid not only of the Soviet Union but of Russia as well. To them, the CIS was no more than an instrument for dealing with the partition of joint property. In late December, the CIS member states had rejected Marshal Shaposhnikov's vague plan for a unified CIS army; they wanted no more than "joint" armed forces.[5] On 2 January, Ukraine announced that as of the next day all military stationed on its soil (excluding the strategic forces) would be subordinated to the Ukrainian leadership.

Foreign policy

A multitude of highly explosive issues jumped onto the Russo-Ukrainian political agenda. The Russian parliament claimed the Crimea for Russia, contesting Khrushchev's 1954 decision to cede the territory to Ukraine "as a gift" for its loyalty to the Russian state. The issue was closely intertwined with that of the ownership of the Black Sea Fleet (four hundred warships) stationed in the Crimean port of Sebastopol, which had been claimed by Ukraine. The vagueness of the term "strategic forces" came in handy. In December, it had been agreed that these forces would remain under joint command, and on 16 January 1992 the CIS states agreed that, as far as strategic forces personnel were concerned, they would administer oaths of allegiance to the CIS, with these personnel simultaneously swearing to serve their own states. The lack of a precisely circumscribed agreement on the concept (due mainly to the rushed negotiations of the preceding month) invited the Ukrainians to try their own definition by administering the oath of allegiance to Ukraine to officers and soldiers serving in the "grey area." They argued that the fleet was not part of the strategic forces. At the long-range strategic bomber squadron stationed in Uzin, they administered their oath to supporting tanker and transport regiments—not to the bomber crews themselves.[6] In both cases, the CIS command and the Russian military protested— and the coinciding of their positions strengthened Ukrainian fears that the Russians wanted to use the CIS as an instrument of their hegemonic ambitions.

In addition, there was the issue of tactical nuclear arms, on which it had been agreed that they would be moved from Ukraine, Belarus, and Kazakhstan to Russia. By mid-March, when half of the three thousand tactical warheads had been removed from Ukraine, President Kravchuk suspended the withdrawal, demanding international supervision of their destruction in Russia. After renewed negotiations, all tactical nuclear arms were removed by early May, but Western support for the position of Russia—and the West's lack of empathy for Ukrainian sensitivities— had been strengthened by Ukrainian policy. Negotiations on the removal of strategic nuclear arms proceeded slowly and with many setbacks, not least because during the process the Ukrainians discovered that they could ask a price: a price in terms of Western financial help and a security guarantee for a nuclear-free Ukraine. In order to make their demand more effective, the government stated on 12 November 1992 that all of the property of the Soviet armed forces on Ukrainian territory at the time of independence, "including the entire property of the Strategic Nuclear Forces, belongs to Ukraine."[7]

It took more than fourteen months of threats and negotiations before, on 14 January 1994, a trilateral agreement was signed by Presidents Clinton, Kravchuk, and Yeltsin. The deal was that the Ukrainian president would agree to the dismantling and scrapping of the 1,600 warheads of his country's 176 ICBMs in Russia in return for security guarantees, uranium fuel for nuclear power stations, and financial compensation. At the same occasion, the Russian and American presidents promised in writing that by 30 May 1994 their nuclear arms would no longer be targeted against any country. In resolving these last problems, said Yeltsin, "we put a full stop behind the Cold War."[8] Some of his critics were saying that a new Cold War had already begun.

Ukraine had been quite explicit, both in its resolve and in its distrust of Russian capabilities and intentions. On 23 May 1992, Foreign Minister Zlenko had joined his colleagues from the U.S., Russia, Belarus, and Kazakhstan in Lisbon to sign a protocol by which the four CIS states were recognized as parties to the START-1 and Nonproliferation treaties. The agreement was "so fragile . . . that during the signing ceremony Secretary of State [James Baker] asked all the parties to refrain from speaking in order to avoid reopening sensitive issues."[9]

These and similar issues (such as the status of Russians living in the "near abroad") demanded a Russian foreign policy that would go beyond simple formulas of friendship with the West, with Central Europe, and with the new neighbors, as tentatively formulated before the demise of the USSR. During its formative period, Russian foreign policy had been driven by the desire to get Russia accepted as a foreign policy actor, both at home and abroad, and had been subservient to the aim of doing away with the Soviet Union and its institutions.[10] Only during and after the failed coup had Western statesmen and institutions reluctantly granted Yeltsin and his foreign minister Kozyrev the recognition they sought. For a while, Russian foreign policy was wholly aimed at friendship with the United States and Western Europe, and Russia's "reintegration into the family of European civilization."[11] In April 1991, when (in the building of the European Parliament) Yeltsin made his first speech abroad in his capacity as chairman of the Russian parliament, his advisor Gennadii Burbulis had stated that "a revival of Russia is impossible outside the renewed Europe," whereas Europe could not fully realize its plans unless it would take Russia into consideration.[12] With a naïve trust in the deputies in Strasbourg, Yeltsin had announced Russia's desire to become a full member of the Council of Europe, the European Community, and the United Nations.[13] Russian politicians were still unaware of the possible impact that hurt Russian pride would have on their foreign policy.

Only a few months into 1992, the concept turned out to be one-sided, to say the least. As Russia stood on its own feet it came to realize the many implications of the demise of the USSR for its own identity and position in the world. The question indeed became whether the country was really standing on its own feet, or only "getting up from its knees" (Yeltsin's words), or was still prostrate before Western might. Russia was begging for money, its self-respect and sense of identity badly hurt by the loss of empire. Academicians and politicians engaged in a heated debate on the question of where between East and West the country's identity and interests were to be located. Now that it had cast off the illusions of communism, was its future in a tight alliance with Western democracies and capitalism? Some insisted that Russia was and would always remain unique. Others saw its place in bridging the gap between the East, particularly the Confucian systems of the Southeast Asian Pacific Rim, and the West. Still others presented Russia as a bulwark against the advancing menace of fundamentalist Islamic states. Or was the loss of the communist empire perhaps not to be taken too literally? Could it be reincarnated in a different, Russian nationalist form?

With the removal of Gorbachev and the USSR, both the nationalist opposition in the Russian parliament and the military came to have a stronger influence on foreign policy. Yeltsin and Kozyrev could not maintain their one-sided orientation toward the West. In deference to nationalist protests over the alleged maltreatment of the twenty-five to thirty million Russians in the "near" or "nearly" abroad, Kozyrev wrote in June 1992 that "we cannot allow the consolidation of nations within the CIS (or those that did not become members of the Commonwealth) to be accompanied by any infringements of minority rights."[14] The issue had great potential for those who resented the loss of empire and sought to make a political career out of the anxieties of some of the Russians in the Baltic states and Central Asia.

This had also, of course, been the case during the years preceding the end of the USSR. But in January 1991, Yeltsin had explicitly supported independence of the Baltic states—an independence that had been supported by major portions of their Russian-speaking population. Yeltsin and Kozyrev had tried to defuse the issue by stating their commitment but rejecting any nondiplomatic means for the improvement of the situation of the Russians outside their country. But soon after the turn of the year, the position of the president and the Foreign Ministry had started to move in the direction of that of their nationalist critics.

Parliamentary *spiker* Ruslan Khasbulatov and Vice President Rutskoi took strong positions against Foreign Minister Kozyrev, demanding a separate ministry for relations with the CIS countries. During the summer of 1992, rumors were spread that the Security Council had decided to remove Kozyrev from his post. The installation of the Security Council on 20 May 1992 in itself had undermined Kozyrev's ministry, for Kozyrev was a nonvoting member of the body. The Council, with Yeltsin, Rutskoi, Prime Minister Chernomyrdin, First Deputy Chairman of the Supreme Soviet Sergei Filatov, and Secretary Iurii Skokov as voting members, quickly took foreign-policy making into its hands.[15] The Supreme Soviet asserted its foreign policy role through parliamentary hearings and discussions on the ratification of treaties. In the course of 1992, the institutionalization of Russian foreign-policy making yielded no less than five main actors: the president with his Security Council; the Supreme Soviet; the Ministry of Defense, which had been established in May (the *Soviet* Defense Ministry had been turned into the CIS High Command in January); and the Foreign Ministry. The Ministry of Foreign Affairs came last; it did "not make fundamental decisions on foreign-policy matters," as its boss Kozyrev declared.[16] As had been the case in the Soviet Union, foreign and security-policy making were outside the realm of the government.

In June 1992, civil war broke out along the banks of the Dniester River in Moldova, claiming several hundred casualties. In September 1990, an extraordinary congress of people's deputies in Tiraspol had declared the independence of left-bank Moldova to counterpoise the then strong movement for Moldovian unification with Romania. The new Dniester Moldavian Republic (DMR), including the right-bank city of Bendery, was proclaimed to be a constituent part of the USSR. It had 740,000 inhabitants, 25 percent of them Russians, 28 percent Ukrainians. The area was of considerable economic significance, since a major part of Moldovan factories controlled by the ministries in Moscow was located on the left bank, and it produced 56 percent of all consumer goods and 33 percent of all the industrial goods of Moldova.[17] Four states (Moldova, Russia, Ukraine, and Romania), one army (the Fourteenth Soviet Army, stationed in the area, whose commander served as minister of defense of the DMR), the Cossacks, and three national groups (Russians, Ukrainians, and Moldovians) became entangled in the conflict.

In the course of 1990–1992, Moldovian legislation on language, citizenship, and education had served as explosive fuel for the conflict. The cause of the DMR became a rallying point for Russian nationalists of all sorts. Right-wing leaders such as Alksnis, Makashov, and Zhirinovskii visited this "last bastion of healthy communist order" and declared their support for the DMR. For less extremist politicians it served a purpose as well; they turned the conflict into a showcase for Russia's loyalty to Russians living outside its borders and used the conflict for pressurizing both Yeltsin and Kozyrev to adjust their foreign policy. Their champion became Vice President Rutskoi, who in April 1992 advocated official recognition of the DMR by the Russian Federation.[18] After the bloody skirmishes in June, a cease-fire became effective on 7 July. Two weeks later, President Yeltsin signed an accord with the Moldovian president Mircea Snegur, agreeing to the stationing of a peacekeeping force consisting of units from Russia, Moldova, and the Dniester Republic itself.[19]

The impact of the hurt Russian soul on foreign policy found expression in the positions of both the military and the parliament. The draft military doctrine published in spring suggested that maltreatment of Russians in the "near abroad" could be ground for Russian military intervention.[20] In an interview, Defense Minister Grachev said that "a powerful army raises the self-respect of the *narod*" and added that Russian soldiers were in the "near abroad" because "without us those people will start killing each other."[21] At the end of June, the parliament's Foreign Affairs Committee held a closed hearing with Minister Kozyrev on the sense of Russia's foreign policy. The report prepared by its chairman Yevgenii Ambartsumov stated that the basic doctrine of the Russian Federation should be to declare

> all of the geopolitical space of the former union its sphere of vital interests (in the way of the "Monroe Doctrine" of the U.S. in Latin America) and to get the world community to understand and recognize Russia's special interests in this space . . . and her role as political and military guarantor of stability in the whole of the space of the former USSR. We should get the G-7 countries to support these functions of Russia, right up to the subsidizing of rapid intervention forces (Russian "blue helmets").[22]

The idea was to be more or less forced on the other successor states of the USSR, for, Ambartsumov continued, future CIS and bilateral agreements would have to state Russia's right to defend the life and dignity of Russians in the near abroad.

In late 1992 the issue escalated and was linked, both by some Baltic governments and by the Russian government, with that of the withdrawal of troops from Estonia and Latvia. After all troops had left Lithuania, Yeltsin, on 29 October, deferred the withdrawal of troups from Estonia and Latvia, and explicitly linked further withdrawals with Baltic "respect" for the rights of the Russian-speaking population. In an official instruction to the Foreign Ministry on 30 November, he explicitly ordered it to make the development of economic ties with former USSR republics conditional upon their observing human rights for the Russian population.[23] Several international expert commissions that visited Estonia and Latvia came to the conclusion that the new legislation of these states was basically in agreement with international norms, although they criticized Estonia for excluding sizable portions of the Russian-speaking population (particularly former officers) from citizenship.[24] Nevertheless, in both states part of the Russian-speaking population had strong fears concerning their future, and real grievances over new legislation.

But in spite of the many demarches of Foreign Minister Kozyrev, Russian foreign policy toward the near abroad was not driven by concern for the standards of international law or for the position of their compatriots. The main driving forces were of an internal and foreign-policy nature: concern for the destabilizing effect of the return of millions of Russians to Russia, an inability (and unwillingness?) to receive them in an organized way, the need to counter the growing strength of ultra-nationalist and fascist forces, and the use to which the issue of the Russian "diaspora" could be put in claiming a Russian say over the countries of its former empire. Although Russian demographers and sociologists stated that large-scale immigration of Russian speakers from the near abroad was inevitable, the policy of the Russian government remained to keep them out and to simulate deep concern for their fate. An internal policy paper of the Ministry of Foreign Affairs stated in early 1993 that "our policy in this issue is aimed at the creation of optimum conditions for their integration in the political and economic life of the states of their permanent residence."[25] Just in case it might come to armed conflict, Russia, in early March, used discussions on revision of the UN Charter to try to get UN endorsement for a special CIS (read: Russian) role in peacekeeping in its own region. Speaking to the UN General Assembly in September, Foreign Minister Kozyrev said that "no international organization or group of states can replace our peacemaking efforts in this specific post-Soviet space."[26]

In Ukrainian-Russian relations, the issue of the Russian-speaking diaspora was particularly explosive since it was closely related to that of the contested Black Sea Fleet, stationed at the largely Russian port of Sebastopol in Ukrainian Crimea. In August 1992 Yeltsin and Kravchuk had tried to defuse the fleet issue by agreeing to a joint command for a three-year period, after which it was to be divided.[27] But in June the next year, the presidents agreed to speed up the process of splitting the fleet. Russian legislators immediately took revenge. On 9 July 1993, the RF Supreme Soviet decided to award Russian federal status to the city and environs of Sebastopol; this amounted to the Russian parliament unilaterally incorporating Ukrainian territory. The action was strongly condemned by President Yeltsin, who expressed his "shame," by the Foreign Ministry, and by Ukrainian authorities. The Ukrainian government appealed to the UN Security Council to intervene, saying that the dispute could threaten international peace and security. On 20 July, the Council adopted by consensus a statement by its president in which it expressed "deep concern" over the Russian parliament's decision, condemning it as "incompatible" with the 1990 Ukraine-Russian treaty. The conflicts between Russia and Ukraine over the Black Sea Fleet, Sebastopol, and the Crimea dragged on into 1994 and led to increasingly dangerous situations.

This jumble of issues was typical of how tight Yeltsin and Kozyrev were sandwiched between their perceived need to maintain friendship with the West, for the benefit of financial support for economic reform, and the demand by the military and the parliament that Russia define its interests and sphere of influence and formulate a more assertive foreign policy. Kozyrev had been on notice from the Congress of People's Deputies since that body had aquired the right, in December 1992, to approve the appointment of the foreign minister and three other key ministers. Parliamentary opposition to his policy had gained in strength. In November 1992, reactionary deputies published an article claiming to be based on American documents showing that top leaders such as Yeltsin, Poltoranin, Burbulis, and Lukin were secretly working as paid "agents of influence" for the CIA, implementing its strategy for the destruction of Russian statehood.[28] The Supreme Soviet urged the Foreign Ministry in December to use the Russian veto in the UN Security Council for blocking enforcement of the (anti-Serbian) no-fly zone in Bosnia-Herzegovina.[29] The military pressed their case by occasionally showing Yeltsin and Kozyrev their potential, when in the Moldova-Dniester skirmishes and in the Abkhaz-Georgian war they (most probably) acted on their own. The dumping of nine hundred tons of liquid radioactive waste into the Sea of Japan, four days after President Yeltsin had signed the "Tokyo Declaration" on 13 October 1993, raised suspicions as well that the military were acting on their own.

During 1992–1993, the policy position of Yeltsin and Kozyrev had gradually moved in the direction of the military and parliament; meanwhile they played on Western fears of a nationalist turn in Russian foreign policy and put such fears to use as a means to lead the wealthy West into recognizing a ruined Russia as an equal partner *and* into increasing its financial support. They skillfully used Western despair at the complexities of peacekeeping in the Balkans to claim a role of their own as the policeman of the "geostrategic space" of the former Soviet Union. They discovered how to take advantage of Western hesitation at the demand of Eastern and Central European states to be allowed shelter under NATO's security umbrella. In the autumn of 1992, Foreign Affairs had stated that one of its strategic tasks was to prevent a buffer zone between Russia and Western Europe from coming into being.[30] The new military doctrine accepted by the Russian Security Council on 2 November 1993 explicitly stated that Russia would consider repressions against Russians abroad, or "the widening of military blocs and alliances damaging its security interests," as potential sources of war, and the stationing of foreign troops in a neighboring country a "direct military threat."[31]

Russian politicians and the military finally reached a consensus on a platform that defined the Russian sphere of influence to be the states of the former USSR and those of Eastern and Central Europe. In the former, Russia claimed the right to adjudicate conflicts, if necessary by force and without the consent of the international community. In the latter, Russia explicitly rejected these countries being drawn into the Western collective security system or into the European Union. At the end of 1993, after two years of dissonance and political struggle, a senior observer concluded that "Russia's politicians, diplomats, and generals have worked out their differences" and had succeeded in formulating a coherent and disciplined foreign policy.[32] It should not go unnoticed that this consensus was achieved before the fascists and communists carried the day in the 12 December 1993 general election. During President Yeltsin's visit to Brussels, four days prior to the election, his spokesman Kostikov declared that "Russia considers itself to be a great power and the successor to the Soviet Union and all its might."[33] The Kremlin's foreign policy offensive had only just begun.[34]

Shock therapy?

With its land mass reduced to 17 million square kilometers and a population of almost 150 million (down from 22.4 and 290 million), Russia at the outset of its new era was still a formidable country—too vast, perhaps, to be ruled from one capital city. The question was indeed whether fundamental economic reform would not generate too much pressure on Russia's unified statehood. Such reform required the active cooperation of regional and local officials, whereas the overwhelming majority of regional and local administrative positions remained in the hands of the *nomenklatura*. Even if they were willing to execute the demands of Moscow's reform team, and if the legislation in which such demands was expressed was unambiguous, were local elites actually in a position to do this, considering the havoc that economic breakdown and reform created in local economies? Would they not be pressed to place the interests of their regions first? The legitimacy of the Soviet state for local rulers had partly been based on the subsidies that they and the factories that dominated their regions had received from the coffers of the treasury in Moscow. Should these subventions fall away, they would have to look elsewhere for generating income. This in turn would undermine the credibility of the Russian state.

Economic reform started with the liberalization of most prices. In January, consumer prices rose by nearly four times, and producer prices by nearly five times. After this "jump-start," the rate of inflation (not the prices) dropped for a while, but between October 1992 and March 1993 it was never below 20 percent per month.[35] During 1993, consumer and industrial wholesale prices rose by 940 and 1,000 percent, respectively.[36] If the price level of December 1991 was set at 100 percent, at the end of August 1993 it was 8,825 percent.[37]

This affected not only the population of Russia, but producers and consumers in many of the other former Soviet republics as well. The creation of the CIS had been followed "by less rather than more cooperation in the economic sphere."[38] For the new states, Russian price increases, particularly on fuels, became one of the main causes of reduction in industrial and agricultural output.[39] Through its exclusive control over ruble printing presses, Russia could influence monetary policy in the other CIS states.[40] However, ruble notes represented (in 1992) only 23 percent of all money in circulation (not counting dollars!). Some 77 percent was noncash money in bank accounts.[41] The national banks of the other CIS countries had been given the right to grant credit and thereby engage in noncash emissions themselves. Thus, at the time when there was an acute cash shortage, noncash money was brought into circulation in the CIS capitals, providing easy credit for national industries and payment for imports from Russia. Financial settlements between Russian and non-Russian enterprises often did not go through the Central Bank of Russia, but were made directly. These practices contributed to inflation in Russia and undermined its stabilization policy.[42] On 21 June 1992, President Yeltsin decreed the practice ended, and trade relations between the countries of the CIS were to be based on bilateral clearing. His decree did not solve the problem. One year later, on 30 June 1993, the Supreme Soviet suspended the providing of "technical credits" to cover the trade deficits of the other CIS states.[43]

The other centerpiece of reform was privatization. The phased program was to start with small-scale enterprises. As of 1 October 1992, 150 million privatization vouchers with a face value of 10,000 rubles each were distributed over the population. The vouchers could be used to invest in enterprises, to take part in investment funds, or to pay for goods, services, or cash. Some of the bewildered Russians used them to pay the dentist, to buy vodka, or as advance payment for their own funerals.[44] Nevertheless, the privatization scheme showed results, at least on paper. By late March 1993, one-fourth of Russia's 250,000 enterprises, mainly small enterprises, had been privatized. A private retail trade sector quickly made inroads into trading; its share of total retail trade rose to 23 percent in early 1993, sixteen times higher than it had been in 1991. But privatization of medium and large enterprises and of land proved more difficult, partly due to obstruction by parliament. Privatization was necessary, but in medium and large industries it did not (and could not) immediately lead to a drastic improvement in management and production. Many factories were faced with a lack of resources, energy, and markets. The threat of bankruptcy loomed large. In 1992, industrial production dropped 19 percent, oil extraction 15 percent, and agricultural production by an average of 8 percent. By the end of the year, overall net material product was down to 78 percent of what it had been in 1991; at the end of 1993 it stood at 68 percent—a drop of almost one-third in two years. During the first five months of 1994, overall industrial production dropped by another 26 percent compared to the same period in 1993.[45]

The way in which the Yeltsin-Gaidar reform package was implemented and repeatedly adapted during 1992–1993 made the shock therapy *à la Russe* into a parody of the market. Privatization benefited primarily those who had privileged information, experience in administration, and contacts. Members of the Soviet *nomenklatura* collected enormous fortunes in what came to be called *"prikhvatizatsiia,"* where *khvat(at)* stands for snatching. An argument could indeed be made that the policies were aimed at creating a class of nouveaux riches by the "initial phase of capitalist accumulation."[46] Those who had been at the "commanding heights" in the Soviet Union were best positioned to use their networks for getting rich quickly by trading, collecting shares, and posing as benefactors of Russia in the process; the Grand Sale of Russia's natural wealth made them into millionaires.

For the mass of the population, the consequences were catastrophic. Estimates of the percentage below minimum subsistence income varied with the assumptions used to compute them, but even the most conservative was impressive: one-third of the population (with 10 percent classified as "very poor") in 1993.[47] Particularly hard hit were pensioners and single-parent families. In December 1992, the real value of an average pension was only 86 percent of what it had been one year earlier. Such a pension was not enough to live on *and* not enough to die. An increasing number of people could no longer afford a funeral for themselves or their relatives. With this came the impact of a demographic decline that had started several years before Yeltsin and Gaidar had set out on their reform course. Population growth came to a halt in 1991, then declined. During the first six months of 1992, many regions of Russia reported over twice as many deaths as births.[48] In 1993 there were one million fewer births than during the previous year, and the population declined by 300,000.[49] Life expectancy took a dive. Russian families experienced a sharp deterioration in their diet; an increasing number of abortions, stillbirths and birth defects; and diseases and epidemics: tuberculosis, cholera, and diphtheria. During the first half of 1993, four thousand cases of diphteria were reported, nine hundred of them in Moscow alone.[50] Soup kitchens and night shelters were opened. Many workers and employees did not receive any pay for months; they kept working as long as the supply of materials and energy allowed. Others were in fact out of work, but were kept on, resulting in considerable hidden unemployment. By early 1994, unemployment (officially reported at 1.5 percent) was at least 10 percent of the workforce, and rising.[51]

Both the government and parliament had tried to prevent social unrest and to win the support of Russia's regions by granting generous subsidies to prevent layoffs and bankruptcies. Thereby they had undermined the fiscal-monetary stabilization policies of the minister of finance. A few months into 1993, the IMF had identified three interrelated trends that "created difficulties in achieving macroeconomic stabilization: the regional desire for greater political and economic autonomy; the evolving nature of fiscal federalism; and the vaguely specified division of political power between the Presidency and the legislative branch."[52] After his resignation in January 1994, Gaidar came to almost the same conclusion: "Russia never experienced shock therapy. Yes, there were deep reforms in the direction of privatization and price liberalization. But financial policy always remained soft and weak. . . . Pressured by the Supreme Soviet and the regions, the state coffer had to take more and more burdens that could not be supported. There simply was no shock."[53] It was perhaps too simply said. There had probably been *too many* shocks, but most of them had been of a noneconomic nature.

Disintegration

For all intents and purposes, Yeltsin, posing with the powerful of the earth at G-7 or European Union meetings, was in fact representing a country that had gone bankrupt.[54] Part of the blame went to a parliament that had obstructed the passing of essential economic reform bills and had authorized irresponsible public spending. Another part went to the regions. After the demise of the USSR, the question of their relationship with federal institutions had become one of great urgency, for the disintegration of the Russian Federation had started long before 1992. In 1990–1991 the autonomous republics had upgraded their status, taken an active part in the "War of Laws," and nationalized the natural resources and assets on their territory. In the past, the foreign trade of the Soviet republics and regions had "made *Moscow* prosperous but did not bring any wealth to the particular regions actually involved in the trade."[55] They now claimed the revenues of their wealth and work for themselves. The parliament and government of the vast, underpopulated, but very rich republic of Sakha-Yakutia, for example, had on 15 August 1991 transferred all enterprises to their ownership.[56] They smelled gold—and who could blame them?

Central authorities aimed at preserving Russian statehood through concessions to the republics. Mikhail Gorbachev had "provoked and steered" the then "autonomous" republics' wish to become subjects of the USSR; Yeltsin had initially reacted by promising them more autonomy inside the RSFSR than Gorbachev ever promised the USSR republics. As Sergej Saizew has noted, "Gorbachev was at best willing to *give* some of the center's power (to the USSR republics), Yeltsin incited the autonomies to *take* it on their own."[57] In this line, Yeltsin had, in August 1990, urged the Tatars to "take as much sovereignty as you like" and to "give the rest to Russia by treaty," suggesting a future confederation.

Of course, Yeltsin's initial support for the autonomy of Russia's regions did not ease his position after the USSR had ceased to exist. But in March 1992 he succeeded in having three federative agreements signed by almost all of the RF's eighty-nine constituent parts or, as they were called, "subjects." Tatarstan and Checheno-Ingushetia were the only two regions that refused to sign. The treaties "on the delimitation of areas of jurisdiction and powers" between the federal center and the regions were to be appended to the new constitution.[58] They were signed not only by the so-called autonomous formations (republics), but also by the territorial regions, a construction first suggested by Council of Nationalities chairman Ramazan Abdulatipov in October 1990. With this, however, new problems were created.

The first such problem was the difference in status of the federation's "subjects." Although the ethnic units as a whole represented only 13 percent of the population and 25 percent of the federation's economic potential, the republics and other "autonomous" units had the right to self-determination and were thereby first-class "subjects" of the federation. The provinces and territories had no such right and were only second class "subjects." The March treaties inaugurated a move away from an ethnically based federation in the direction of a territorially based federation. But the move was only partial. Due to the difference in status, the treaties had in fact created an "asymmetrical" federation. Land and other natural resources were said to belong to the people living in the twenty-one republics—but not to the populations of the sixty-eight other subjects. In contrast to the nonethnic entities, the republics had many characteristics of states, such as the right to adopt their own constitution. Besides, they were individually represented in the upper chamber of the Supreme Soviet, the federal parliament.

The second problem concerned serious legal defects in the Constitution itself: the rights of the autonomous subunits of the federation had not been precisely fixed. The autonomous units had the constitutional right to determine independently questions of administration, but there was no effective mechanism for the annulment of decisions that violated the Constitution of the RF. Dating from the time when the USSR existed, the formerly "autonomous" republics all had their own constitutions as well. When Tatarstan organized a referendum on its status within the Russian Federation, the Russian Constitutional Court ruled that the referendum violated the RF Constitution; but the court could not prevent the referendum, nor annul its results—for in organizing the referendum the state institutions of Tatarstan acted on the basis of their own Constitution, which said that Tatarstan was a state "associated with" Russia and that it had priority over the Russian Federation. By early 1993, in addition to the RF Constitution, Tatarstan and Chechnia had their new constitutions, and fifteen draft constitutions of republics were ready for adoption by their parliaments. The Constitution of

Chechnia declared the country an independent state; the draft constitutions of the republics of Tuva, Karelia, Sakha-Yakutia, Kalmykia, Buriatia and Bashkortostan proclaimed the primacy of their republics' laws over those of the federation, whereas the Bashkortostan Constitution reserved the right to secede from the Russian Federation.[59]

The leaders of several nonethnic regions were contemplating the upgrade of their status to that of republic. After the March crisis and the referendum of 25 April 1993, some of these plans were put into action. Soon, the struggle was defined in terms of the separatism of republics and even some nonethnic regions (i.e., provinces and territories). The term *separatism* served several of the parties to the conflict well, in particular Yeltsin's opponents in Moscow. The term had an inherent centralist bias, as it implied the splitting-off of areas from an entity that is best kept as a whole. "Separatism" by implication blames those who demand concessions from the center. In the difficult transition process from a quasi-federation to either a real (con)federation or a decentralized unitary state, the use of the term *separatism* by centralist elites served a clear political goal: to blacken the reputation of those demanding more autonomy and a redistribution of powers between the once almighty center and themselves.

The regional elites answered in kind to the accusation of separatism. After Chechnia and Tatarstan had shown that Moscow's power to resist disintegration was limited, many of them upgraded their status to *almost* that of an independent country. They seemed to be saying that if those politicians still motivated by an empire mentality insisted in defining the conflict in terms of separatism, then separatism is what they would have. In addition to Tatarstan and Chechnia, Bashkortostan and Sakha-Yakutia refused to transfer collected taxes to Moscow.[60] The soviet of Vologda province declared its sovereignty. On 14 May 1993, the Volgograd provincial soviet followed and declared that province was now a state. On 1 July, the provincial soviet of Sverdlovsk (Yekaterinburg) declared the province a republic, and one week later the soviet of Maritime Territory in the Far East followed.[61] On 9 July, the Cheliabinsk provincial soviet decided to start the process for becoming a "Republic of Southern Urals": local soviets were to express their views on the project. Not all of these declarations were to be taken at face value. The soviets acted mainly with the aim of increasing pressure on the Constitutional Conference meeting in Moscow to polish the draft Constitution, demanding that it level powers of provinces and regions with those of republics.

Separatism was set to work in order to force concessions from the institutions in Moscow. The real discussion concerned the extent of the concessions the center was willing to make. The acceleration of the process in 1993 seems to have been driven by the converging of two developments in the regions. First, in many of the regions, the state institutions—soviets and their executive committees—were still populated by former *apparatchiki*, elected in 1990. They had lost their Communist Party positions, but had held onto positions that had in the past been formal but now opened new possibilities. The main possibility—and the second development—was reaping the fruits of privatization and transforming oneself from party functionary into manager or businessman. Whether or not the regional elites worked primarily for their personal benefit or for the interests of their region, they had a stake in claiming as much power as possible. The authorities in Moscow, locked in incessant power struggles, had shown themselves impotent with regard to the performing of functions by which in the past they had tied the regions to the center: authoritative decision making on the redistribution of wealth and benefits among the regions, and providing both external and internal security.[62] The muddled power struggles between legislative and executive institutions, both at the center and in the regions, and the crisscrossing struggle *between* the center and the regions prevented compromise.

The Constitution guerrilla

During 1992–1993, the three policy areas discussed above served as the main reservoirs from which Russian politicians drew the arguments, demagoguery, chicaneries, dirty tricks, ill-conceived schemes, threats, and innuendos that they fired at each other. In the absence of established political rules, Moscow politics developed into guerrilla warfare. The sudden demise of the Soviet Union had left many constitutional issues unresolved and had burdened the new Russian state with a plethora of legacies that would be hard to overcome. We have seen in the previous chapter that constitutional renewal had in fact been started up in June 1990 immediately after Russia's Declaration of Sovereignty, but we have also witnessed how, until the end of 1991, this process had been dominated by the struggle against Soviet institutions. Only after Gorbachev and the Soviet Union had gone could Russia make a fresh start creating its own statehood and constitution.

One of the Soviet legacies was the peculiar state structure that had been written into the Russian Constitution (dating from 1978) and which had been adapted to developments since 1988. With the presidency, Gorbachev and Yeltsin had introduced a foreign element into the Soviet system. In that system, the Communist Party had ruled through the instrument of the Supreme Soviet, the institution unifying the highest legislative, executive, and judiciary powers of the state. The communists, in their understanding of the state, had rejected the separation of powers and had seen the Supreme Soviet as all-powerful, permitted to decide all state questions without exception. Lawmaking had been considered a purely instrumental activity for the benefit of the communist rulers. The members of the Council of Ministers had been only nominally responsible to the Supreme Soviet. New prime ministers had been selected by the party's Politburo, presented for approval to the Supreme Soviet, and had ritually been applauded by the people's deputies. The members of the Council of Ministers had subsequently been selected by the party's Secretariat and Politburo, presented to the Supreme Soviet by the prime minister, and, again, rubberstamped by that institution. Due to the use to which it had been put by the Communist Party, the Presidium of the Supreme Soviet had become a potentially very powerful institution. After the tinkering with the administrative structure in 1988–1991, the situation was somewhat different, but old reflexes and impulses showed their tenacity. With the introduction of the presidency, the professed desire to create a real separation of powers, and the upgrading of the role of the Council of Ministers, one of the main questions became how this body was to be viewed: as the executive arm of the president, or as an instrument of parliament? How was the newly evolving triangle between president, government, and parliament to take shape? Would the president be able to have his reform plans implemented through the heads of regional administrations and, later, the personal representatives he was appointing? Would parliament be able to use its ties with the soviets in the nonethnic regions to frustrate such implementation? And could power relationships crystallize at all in the absence of well-organized parliamentary parties?

The power struggle between parliament and president intensified in April 1992 and raged until the parliamentary leadership and vice president were arrested on 4 October 1993. A characteristic of this struggle was that conflicts over the profile of a new constitutional setup were fought not in the abstract, but through amendments to the constitution (and to laws) currently in force. Those in the parliament (led by chairman Khasbulatov) who desired a new Constitution with limited powers for the president, tried to further their cause by limiting the president's powers in the *current* Constitution. Parliament's power to adopt, amend, or block legislation and to change the current Constitution thus strengthened its position in the struggle for the new Constitution. It goes almost without saying that the Congress of People's Deputies soon regretted that it had limited *its own* powers for the period of one year. Its position was strengthened as well by the fact that there was no established procedure by which a new Constitution was to come into force; this procedure was to be decided during the course of the power struggle, with adoption by the Congress, by a referendum, or by an ad-hoc elected Constituent Assembly (or a combination of these) being the main alternatives.

The president's position was initially strong thanks to the legitimacy he had acquired as recent as June and August 1991. But soon, parliament started a campaign to regain the ground it had ceded to the president in November, when the president had been granted emergency powers, including the right to hold the position of prime minister and to appoint his own ministers without parliamentary consent. The jumble of issues at the beginning of 1992 (Ukraine, the Russians in the "near abroad," the Dniester Republic, inflation) gave communist and nationalist deputies plenty of ammunition for bombarding the president and his entourage and for joining in an informal "red-brown" coalition. More and more often, the vice president sided with them. Khasbulatov, who had once been Yeltsin's right-hand man in the campaign to weaken the Soviet government, made it his personal goal to pull the Russian government out from under the president and make it wholly responsible to parliament again. Soon after the August coup, Yeltsin's support started to crack, with Khasbulatov supporting Yeltsin (and blaming his close advisors Burbulis and Shakhrai for Yeltsin's mistakes) only so long as Khasbulatov had not been elected chairman of the Supreme Soviet. The Congress finally voted him into that position on 28 October 1991.[63] In late July, Khasbulatov, then acting chairman, signed a decision to create his own administrative office (*upravlenie delami*), including a "financial-economic department."[64] During the following years it stood him in good stead in broadening his power over the "deputies corpus."

Since 1990, Boris Yeltsin had benefited from considerable grassroots support provided by the Democratic Russia (DR) movement. Now that power relations had undergone fundamental change, a new definition of its relationship with the Yeltsin government was called for. The movement had been successful in the elections of 1990 and had nested itself not only in the Russian parliament (one-third of the seats), but in several major cities as well, including Moscow (282 out of 499 seats) and Leningrad (240 out of 400 seats).[65] But its organization was extremely loose, and torn by internal dissent. Many deputies soon stopped identifying with the movement. At the meeting of its Council of Representatives on

18–19 January 1992, the radical wing that wanted to turn the movement into a parliamentary opposition clashed with the progovernment wing. The movement developed into a "support team" for the president, but with President Yeltsin keeping DR at arm's length, refusing to provide leadership, and uncertain on how to deal with his opponents in the Russian parliament. The consequences were disastrous. On the basis of his study of DR history, Yitzhak Brudny expressed it in these words:

> DR's capacity and will were seriously undermined by Boris Yel'tsin's ambivalence about whether to compromise with, or confront his opponents [the nationalist-communist alliance in the Russian parliament]. . . . In the six months preceding the April 1993 referendum, Yel'tsin effectively prevented DR from becoming a major player in Russian politics, preferring to search for an intra-elite deal.[66]

A different player had come to the scene in the spring. It was the Civic Union alliance, and it initially held high hopes of being able to provide a middle ground from which to moderate the impact of the "red-brown coalition" of communists and nationalists—although some of its leaders shared that coalition's desire to recreate the USSR. The Civic Union alliance had been created in June by three political parties, a group of deputies in the Russian parliament (*Smena*) and a number of smaller organizations.[67] They were united by two aims: changing the direction of economic reform in order to prevent a total collapse of Russia's industry, and countering the forces of disintegration to save the Russian state. The parties joining in Civic Union were the Democratic Party of Russia, Russia's most solid party to date led by Nikolai Travkin, which had broken away from DR in November 1991; a former faction in the CPSU led by Alexander Rutskoi, the People's Party for Free Russia; and Arkadii Volskii's Russian Union of Industrialists and Entrepreneurs. The program of Civic Union demanded that the pace of privatization be slowed down, that state enterprises and labor be granted continued protection in the form of easy credits and indexed wages and prices, and that the Russian government disassociate itself from Western governments and international financial institutions.[68] In the autumn, Civic Union succeeded in convincing the Federation of Independent Trade Unions of Russia (FNPR, successor to the Soviet trade unions) that labor's interests lay in an alliance with the industrialists and administrators. Michael McFaul has characterized Civic Union as an organization that was temporarily successful in building "a social base comprised of old social groups that were now seeking to defend their newly-perceived interests."[69] As such, the Union had a profound impact on the events of the winter of 1992–

1993. The question was only whether this coalition of "old interests" would hold as reforms began to have an impact on society and disrupted old cleavage patterns.

The last months of 1992 witnessed an escalation of the power struggle between the president, his vice president, and parliament, with Yeltsin simultaneously manipulating the populist potential of his supporters in Democratic Russia and moving in the direction of the policies advocated by Civic Union. The struggle for power soon overshadowed other political events. All the major parties to the struggle—President Yeltsin, Vice President Rutskoi, *Spiker* Khasbulatov, and Constitutional Court chairman Zorkin—exhibited a lack of political restraint and "a blatant disregard of law and legal institutions," of procedural rules, and of the separation of powers.[70] Parliament and president acted just as they pleased, with no concern for legal niceties. Their struggle strengthened the impression among ordinary people and observers outside the Kremlin corridors that the top politicians of Russia were a group of irresponsible street fighters. In October 1992, President Yeltsin warned against the emergence of what he called "parallel power structures" in Moscow, and suggested that the next session of the Congress of People's Deputies be postponed from 1 December to the spring of the following year. Such a respite would of course have meant that he would keep his extraordinary powers for three or four more months: by October it was obvious that in December the Congress would not allow him to keep those powers. The Supreme Soviet, the local soviets, the "communist structures"—all were obstructing the reforms he and Gaidar were trying to implement. "I sometimes think," Yeltsin said in an interview, "that when this summer the Supreme Soviet was on vacation I could have signed a decree on land. But I did not want to show a lack of respect toward an elected institution."[71]

It was inadmissible, Yeltsin said, to convene the Congress of People's Deputies, for that assembly would have no "constructive questions, no new ideas" to discuss and would only want to dismiss his government. "Their main policy is to destabilize the situation." Yeltsin announced his decision that the time had come to put an end to his own efforts at trying to meet parliament halfway. "It is time to make use of power. And to act."[72]

Soon it became clear what Yeltsin had meant by "parallel power structures." Ruslan Khasbulatov was strengthening his hold on parliament through its Presidium. On 14 October, *Izvestia* reported that a man of Chechen nationality had been arrested in Moscow after he had threatened a taxi driver with a Makarov gun. The nationality of the man was of course no irrelevant information, for parliamentary speaker Khasbulatov was of Chechen extraction, and one of the major mafia gangs of Moscow had for a long time been the so-called Chechen mafia. Upon his arrest, the man claimed to be a nephew of Khasbulatov and he was found to possess both a weapons license and a permit to enter the Belyi Dom (White House). Less than two hours after his arrest, he was taken from the police station by a captain of the security service of parliament. Reporter Mostovshchikov of *Izvestia* continued his story with the claim that a security service consisting of up to five thousand armed men was operating in Moscow under the exclusive command of Khasbulatov; arms licenses were distributed by General Ivan Boiko, and the service was claimed to be a vehicle for arming Khasbulatov's Chechen family members. The Directorate for Guarding Sites of the Highest Organs of Power and Administration had been created in October 1991 by Khasbulatov without the consent of the Supreme Soviet. It controlled access to seventy-five government buildings. On 27 October 1992, Khasbulatov sent his guards to the *Izvestia* building. The same day Yeltsin ordered Interior Minister Yerin to disband the Directorate.[73]

Hostilities between Khasbulatov and *Izvestia* dated from March 1992, with Khasbulatov determined to subordinate the newspaper (independent since August 1991 and supported by Yeltsin) to his control.[74] The affair of his "private army" was the opening salvo in a new round of skirmishes. A shoot-out between the police and the parliamentary guard resulted in deaths; at a press conference four politicians loyal to Yeltsin, including Foreign Minister Kozyrev, issued a warning against what they called an impending "constitutional coup" by Khasbulatov's Congress; a few days later Vice President Rutskoi demanded that Yeltsin fire them. Ultranationalist and communist members of Congress founded a National Salvation Front aimed at the restoration of the USSR within its pre-1992 borders and at the resignation of Yeltsin, acting premier Gaidar, and their government. Yeltsin banned the Front, though he had no constitutional authority to do so, and ordered Khasbulatov's guard dissolved.

President Yeltsin and his political friends felt that they were in a no-win situation unless they polished off their main enemy. The Congress and the current constitution were seen to block fundamental political renewal. Their lack of patience and of diplomatic and strategic skills made them believe that a clear and dramatic break with the past would allow for a new start. If that break would mean unconstitutional actions, so be it. Yeltsin hinted that he was prepared to violate the Constitution in order to "save Russia." The Constitution, after all, protected the powers of a parliament that had been elected in the old times and that would not accept his draft Constitution. He alluded to the possibility of proclaiming a state of emergency and instituting presidential rule, even though he seemed aware of the fact that the Constitution did not give him the power to dissolve or suspend parliament. Just to be sure, he asked Western governments to condone possible unconstitutional acts on his part.

At the time, President Yeltsin was on better terms with Western governments and financial institutions than with most of the politicians of Russia—and this soon proved to be a liability. Soaring inflation and contracting production increased the social pressures on the population. For right-wing, nationalist, and communist forces it was easy to find juicy arguments against the policy of the government: it had thrown itself and Russia at the feet of Western capitalists, brought poverty and despair upon the toilers of Russia, was at least partly responsible for the demise of the USSR, and by its drastic policy was now threatening the integrity of the Russian Federation.

In November, President Yeltsin sought compromise with both Civic Union and with the heads of republican and regional administrations, hoping thereby to strengthen his position in the forthcoming session of the Congress that was to decide his special powers. But the intended deal with Civic Union (toning down economic reform by introducing new price controls and continued financial support for state enterprises) fell through, and the promises to the regional administrators (on local taxes, increased subsidies, and incorporation of the federation treaties in the constitution) were made on the president's incorrect assumption that the administrators would make the people's deputies from their region support Yeltsin in the Congress.[75]

The situation came to a head at tumultuous Congress sessions in December 1992 and March 1993, where Yeltsin was attacked by deputies of both Civic Union and the communist-nationalist Russian Unity group. Fistfights occurred at the December session. Yeltsin answered the refusal of the Congress to extend his emergency powers and to accept his prime minister Gaidar with threats to have the Congress dissolved with the help of a referendum. The December session ended in a compromise reached by Valerii Zorkin, chairman of the Constitutional Court. Yeltsin and Khasbulatov agreed to a referendum on 11 April in which the population at large was to decide whether Russia was to be a presidential or a parliamentary republic, that is, whether the president or parliament was to have the main say over the composition of the government. Yeltsin hoped that by the referendum the *narod* would help him get rid of the obnoxious parliament. In return for Khasbulatov's concession, he agreed to drop support for his acting premier Gaidar, one of the main targets of the Congress's displeasure. He accepted as the new prime minister Civic Union's Victor Chernomyrdin, a man who was expected to move with more caution than Gaidar. In addition, the Congress took the right to henceforth confirm the appointment of the ministers of foreign affairs, defense, security, and internal affairs.

This give-and-take was reached at the end of the session of Congress under great pressure of time, and the precise terms of the deal remained unclear. The April referendum was declared to be binding on all parties, and the deal assumed that the president, parliament, and the chairman of the Constitutional Court would be able in the intermediate months to agree on the precise wording of the question or questions to be presented to the public. The Congress formally called the referendum for 11 April, but needled the president by adopting a number of constitutional amendments that threatened his powers and were to take effect after the referendum.[76] The constitutional amendments served as a programmed guillotine, instantly severing the president's head the moment he would violate the Congress's terms of the deal.

Given the fundamental differences of interest and view between the president and the majority in Congress, it seemed unlikely that they would agree on the details of the referendum. And indeed, within a few weeks their war continued. Early in the new year, Victor Chernomyrdin sent smoke signals into the Moscow sky signaling that he wished to be considered the independent head of government, responsible only to parliament and not to President Yeltsin. Between late December 1992 and late January 1993, the naming and signing of government orders changed from "order of the government" signed by "V. Chernomyrdin" to "order of the Council of Ministers / government" signed by "Chairman of the Council of Ministers / government of the Russian Federation V. Chernomyrdin." The subtle implication was that not Yeltsin but Chernomyrdin was chief of the government. Soon, parliamentarians, the chairman of the Constitutional Court, and representatives of lower administrations expressed their doubt on the desirability of the referendum. Yeltsin tried to find a way to checkmate parliament. He and Khasbulatov bombarded each other with imputations—hardly the situation for quietly drawing up balanced questions for an important referendum. Both parties to the verbal war tried to ensure the support of the armed forces command.

The Congress reconvened on 10 March for an emergency session, and effectively curtailed the powers of the president. It rescinded its decision to organize a referendum on 11 April and decided that the constitutional amendments of December would take effect immediately. This meant that from now on Chernomyrdin and his Council of Ministers could circumvent the president in presenting draft laws to parliament. It also meant that decrees and orders issued by the president could be suspended by parliament pending a ruling on their constitutionality by the Constitutional Court. Finally, it meant that from now on the Constitution said that the president would automatically lose all of his powers in the event that he suspended or dissolved "any legally elected organ of state power." Yeltsin thought he was faced with the prospect of a ceremonial presidency. On 12 March he angrily left the session, saying that he would never return to this Congress. The next day, premier Chernomyrdin thanked the Congress for its confidence.

The president responded one week later with an ill-conceived constitutional trick. In a televised address he stated that he had signed a decree introducing a "special regime of government" (osobyi poriadok upravleniia) for the period until the crisis of power had been overcome. His staff had invented the term in an effort to sidetrack the Congress while circumventing constitutional provisions and legislation on emergency rule. The Congress and Supreme Soviet, Yeltsin said, would not be dissolved and their work would not be suspended. But any of their decisions suspending presidential decrees or directives were to be considered invalid. Yeltsin also announced a (constitutionally nonexistent) "vote of confidence" for 25 April, avoiding the term "referendum" because of legal provisions concerning referenda. The vote of confidence in the president, he said, would be accompanied by 'votes' on the draft Constitution and on the draft law on the election of a new federal parliament. The draft Constitution would be presented by the president and would contain a new type of parliament instead of the Congress and Supreme Soviet. Within hours, Vice President Rutskoi, Supreme Soviet deputy chairman Yurii Voronin, Procurator-General Stepankov, and Constitutional Court chairman Valerii Zorkin appeared on television, distancing themselves from Yeltsin's move. Zorkin, claiming to speak for the Constitutional Court, accused Yeltsin of attempting to stage a coup d'état. Addressing the president by way of the television audience, he was dramatic: "Boris Nikolaevich, believe me, I truly pity you. You have lost the chance of being Russia's saviour."[77]

The next day, the decree Yeltsin claimed to have signed was not published.[78] Soon it became known that Yeltsin's staff had asked Rutskoi and Security Council secretary Skokov to countersign the decree; they had refused and had urged the president not to appear on television. The affair created a great deal of indignation, confusion, and name-calling. The

Supreme Soviet convened; the Congress met on 26 March and learned that Yeltsin and Khasbulatov had reached an agreement. Furiously, it voted on the impeachment of Yeltsin *and* the dismissal of Khasbulatov. But the motions failed, and in the end Congress agreed to a referendum on 25 April. Nevertheless, confrontation had turned into mutual hatred. This worked out disastrously for the authority "Moscow" enjoyed in the regions. As one Congress deputy, a regional leader, commented: "In whatever way this will end, I am no longer interested in the federal powers."[79]

In the 25 April referendum, the population was asked to express its confidence either in President Yeltsin and his team or in parliament. A majority of 53 to 58 percent of the voters endorsed Yeltsin and his economic policy. But Yeltsin's jubilation at the overall results, reached in no small part thanks to the campaigning of DR, masked strong divisions within the country. In some regions he had been staunchly supported by over 70 percent of the voters: his home base of Sverdlovsk had topped the list with 84 percent, followed by Moscow, St. Petersburg, and some of the ethnic regions of the North, Siberia, and the Far East. But the referendum also exposed vast bands of discontent. In twenty-six (out of eighty-eight) provinces, territories, and ethnic regions, less than half the voters supported the president and his economic policy.[80] The first such band ran, not surprisingly, along the northern slopes of the Caucasus and almost sealed Russia off from Georgia and Azerbaijan. This band contained the republics of Dagestan, Chechnia (where the authorities prevented the referendum from taking place at all), Ingushetia, Karachaevo-Cherkessk, Kabardino-Balkar, and Adygei. It seemed no exaggeration to say that Russia had lost this area.

The second band ran from the central Urals right into the heart of European Russia and contained not only "rebellious" republics but traditional Russian areas as well: the republics of Chuvashia, Tatarstan, Bashkortostan, and Mordovia, and the provinces of Kursk, Tambov, Briansk, Penza, Orel, Ulianovsk, Smolensk, and Belgorod. To these could be added four thoroughly Russian provinces—Lipetsk, Pskov, Voronezh, and Riazan—where almost 50 percent of the voters had supported Yeltsin, and almost 50 percent had expressed a lack of confidence in him. This band of discontent came surprisingly close to the Moscow area, where Yeltsin was supported by three out of every four voters. The third band contained the vast Chita and Amur provinces, Altai territory, and the Mountain-Altai and Buriat republics, showing that support for Yeltsin was very weak all along the Mongolian/Chinese border up to—but not including—the provinces of the Far East.

Yet the overall results were interpreted as a victory for Yeltsin, in particular since two-thirds of the voters had expressed a demand that early elections for the Congress of People's Deputies be held. The leadership of the Congress was put on the defensive, but Yeltsin's draft Constitution of 30 April was nevertheless rejected. Amid continuing disputes about its profile and the procedure for its adoption, the president convened a Constitutional Conference. The Conference started its work on 5 June 1993 with about seven hundred members, representing the subjects of the federation and the most important forces of the country. Its tasks were to prepare and agree on a text for a new Constitution and to propose a procedure for its adoption. The Conference made some progress, but fundamental differences of interest remained. No agreement could be reached on the status of the federation's subjects. One extreme position wanted to upgrade all nonethnic units to the status of republics, which would turn the RF into a confederation with a decorative center; the other would downgrade the republics and create a unitary state with one single constitution and unified state power over the whole territory. Representatives of a majority of the Russian provinces and territories demanded, on 25 June, to receive equal status with the other subjects of the federation. During the days that followed, the leaders of Sakha-Yakutia, Tatarstan, and Komi expressed in the newspapers their insistence that their republics retain a special status compared with nonethnic entities.

Disagreement also remained on the kind of republic that the RF was to become. Many members refused to accept Yeltsin's wish to become the "single head of state" of the federation. Yet on 12 July the Conference accepted the text of a draft Constitution with 433 votes (74 percent). After the Constitutional Conference had adjourned, Yeltsin stated that, following discussions in the regions during summer, he wanted the Constitution to be adopted—one way or another—during the autumn. But the summer did not bring a miraculous coalescing of interests. Both parties continued lobbying. In August the president tried to assure himself of the support of the heads of the republics by agreeing to create a Council of the Federation as the upper house of a new parliament, in which each subject would have two appointed representatives. This done (and provoked by the Congress's repeated obstruction of privatization legislation), Yeltsin decided to have another try at breaking the deadlock.

At eight in the evening on 21 September he appeared on television, explaining to the Russians that he had signed a decree (Number 1400) suspending parliament, instituting a new but temporary state structure with a Federal Assembly as parliament, and calling for elections for a new lower house of parliament (the State Duma) on 11 and 12 December.[81] An outline of the state structure in force, until a new Constitution could be adopted by the Federal Assembly, and rules for the election of the Duma were published three days later. Of course, all decrees as of Number 1399 were in violation of the written Constitution, but that Constitution was to be overruled anyway. Amid calls for simultaneous elections for a new parliament *and* for a president, Yeltsin on 23 September decreed early presidential elections for 12 June 1994, the day on which he had been elected president three years earlier and on which, under current legislation, he could stay on for two more years. In public remarks later during the fall, his spokesman went back on this promise, although the presidential decree was left intact. Obviously, Yeltsin wanted to await the outcome of the elections.

Preparations for the presidential coup had begun in early September with visits to army units. The army command was not at all eager to intervene in the quarrelling of politicians. Yet Yeltsin succeeded in assuring himself of the support of the Ministry of Defense and the Dzerzhinskii, Taman, and Kantemir Divisions. On 18 September, he signed decrees replacing Oleg Lobov as first deputy prime minister, appointing Yegor Gaidar in his place, and interpreting Articles 121[7] and 121[8] of the Constitution in a way that could not be seen as other than an anticipation of the reaction of parliament to the decree that he was to sign three days later. In Decree 1398, the president had claimed that he could not be replaced by the vice president other than by decision of the president himself. Khasbulatov and Rutskoi warned the public that a "Yeltsin dictatorship" was at hand.

Parliament, led by Khasbulatov, reacted immediately, stating that with his Decree Number 1400, Yeltsin had, on the basis of the constitution, automatically made an end to his being president. The guillotine swished down. At twenty-five minutes after midnight on 22 September, Alexander Rutskoi took the oath of president before an emergency session of the Supreme Soviet. Yeltsin's ministers of defense and security were fired, and parliament appointed its own ministers, Achalov and Barannikov. Before 21 September, Russia had suffered *dvoevlastie* (double power) for quite a while, with the government and parliament acting as rival power centers. Perhaps the term *troevlastie* (triple power) could be coined, for the regions had developed into a third center of power. Now Russia actually had two presidents and two ministers of defense.

In the days that followed, the most stubborn parliamentarians barricaded themselves in the White House and received support from a motley group of extremist and nostalgic birds of different feathers. Water, the power supply, and telephone communications were cut, and the parliament was increasingly isolated while Yeltsin and the government went out of their way to present an image of business-as-usual to Russia and the world. Parliamentary appeals for support drew only limited groups of demonstrators in Moscow, not the millions of strikers that Rutskoi and Khasbulatov would have liked. Some of the regions were furious, not the least because Yeltsin's dissolution of parliament deprived them of the financial gain that they had received as a result of the rivalry between the two. On 29 September, Siberian leaders demanded that Yeltsin and parliament resolve their differences—if not, they would proclaim a Siberian Republic and close down the Trans-Siberian Railway.[82] During the first days of October, negotiations initiated by the patriarch of the Russian Orthodox Church seemed to bring results, but the events of Sunday, 3 October, effectively excluded compromise.

Ever since late September, when the standoff between the parliament and the president had been turned into a physical standoff between the Kremlin and the barricaded White House, it was obvious that the side that would lose would be the side that fired the first shot. Western governments, with a great deal of experience in dealing with sieges, lock-ins, and terrorist attacks, beseeched the president to have patience and not to attack parliament. The other side, having locked themselves into a fortress, was not exposed to critical advice, and this proved fatal. Disappointed at the lack of effective support from the country, or overconfident of the support of at least some of the military—or both—Alexander Rutskoi, on 3 October, roused a mob of demonstrators in front of the White House to storm and capture the office of Moscow's mayor and the television studios at Ostankino. Hostages were taken in the mayor's office and "Ostankino" was attacked at the cost of lives and great damage. With this, the occupants of the White House had provided President Yeltsin with a casus belli to deal with them once and for all. Late in the afternoon, Yeltsin returned to the city from his country residence, declared a state of emergency in Moscow, ordered censorship, and called in troops.

The siege of the White House ended in blood, shocking many Russians. Tank attacks on the parliamentary building started at seven A.M. on 4 October; later in the day, the burning building was taken and the leaders, including Khasbulatov, Rutskoi, Barannikov, Dunaev, Achalov, Makashov and some twenty-four others, were taken into custody and moved to Lefortovo prison. Now the question was: how to use the momentum for maximum benefit.

For a start, the loot was hauled in by heavy rhetoric. In a television speech two days later, Yeltsin presented himself as the person who (with the help of the military) had once again saved Russia, now from a carefully prepared "armed mutiny" aimed at the installation of a "bloody communist-fascist dictatorship." The White House, he said, had become a "citadel of terrorism" and a "symbol of treachery and betrayal." This "seat of civil war in Russia had been put out."[83] News media loyal to the president resounded with indignant cries about the "fascist gangs." Presidential advisors and ideologues evidently were well aware of the demagogic potential of the fascist label. Two months later the elections showed that they had fooled mainly themselves.

A NEW CONSTITUTION, A NEW PARLIAMENT

During the days following his signing of Decree Number 1400, Yeltsin had been very busy at improvising and signing an avalanche of decrees meant to make optimal use of the constitutional vacuum that he and his supporters had said they wanted to avoid but had, in fact, created. An important reason for the flood of decrees was the utter lack of preparation or strategic planning during the period preceding Decree 1400. Some of the decrees were infested with errors, contradictions, and inconsistencies. Others were overruled by new decrees within days. Yeltsin wanted to bring the standoff between him and parliament to an end. But he had no clear idea of what exactly he wanted, no well-prepared plan, no strategy that he and his staff had thought through. In his published reminiscences he later testified that he had discussed the move and its unconstitutionality with his friend Helmut Kohl, the German chancellor, but that the planning had been rather amateurish. Yeltsin thought that the campaign for the December elections would lure his opponents to vacate the White House, and he had made no preparations whatsoever for the possibility of an armed confrontation.[84]

And thus once again, as in March, his policy was erratic even at the moment when he was determined to make a clean sweep. Although on 21 September he decreed rules for the operation of the state "during the transition period until the adoption of a new Constitution," the political actors during this period became players in a game where the rules were changing constantly.

Ten days after Decree 1400, the president replaced his rules for the election of the Duma with new ones. Three days after the crackdown at the White House, he "established," in a decree, that the Constitutional Court was unable to function, and he in fact suspended the court's activities. At the same time, he decreed a "temporary legislative order." Four days later, again, on 11 October, the president decreed that the upper house of the Federal Assembly, the Federation Council, was not to consist of the chairmen of the soviets of the republics and regions (which he had in the meantime called upon to disband, following with their suspension on 22 October) and the heads of their executive administrations. The Council's members were to be elected on 12 December as well (the date had been changed on 1 October). On 15 October he decreed that a plebiscite on the draft Constitution was also to take place on 12 December and that the Constitution was to enter into force at the moment of its publication after a positive vote. When finally its draft was published, on 10 November, it showed that the president had expanded his own powers vis-à-vis the future parliament and in relation to the regions. The regions had lost their leverage, and after some demurring they gave up their resistance. As new decrees were written and signed, the president faced new problems and the need to change rules laid down in earlier decrees with so much resolve. The lack of preparation showed.

With the publication of Yeltsin's take-it-or-leave-it draft Constitution on 10 November, the new constitutional structure of Russia was more or less settled. More or less: because the second part of the Constitution (intended for the period 1994–1995) made some important exceptions to its first part. The State Duma was to consist of 450 deputies, half of them elected by proportional representation, the other half from 225 single-seat constituencies. The deputies to be elected on 12 December were to sit for two years, although their constitutional term was fixed at four years. The 178 deputies in the first Federation Council were to be elected (for a two-year term as well) in double-seat constituencies. All rules (for the election of the Duma and the Federation Council, and for the plebiscite) were decreed for the occasion, although the election rules were based on an electoral bill that had been drafted by a group of deputies and experts from the Supreme Soviet's Constitutional Commission under the leadership of Boris Strashun (an electoral specialist of the Institute of State and Law) and Victor Sheinis.[85] They had designed a variation of German electoral legislation in an effort to stimulate the development of parliamentary parties and coalitions. So-called electoral associations were introduced as the central actors in the electoral campaign, allowing not only political parties, but also movements and other groups that had been registered with the Ministry of Justice to join forces in an effort to collect enough votes for passing the 5 percent threshold. The associations were allowed to nominate their lists for the 225 seats to be distributed by the system of proportional representation, but they could nominate candidates for the single-constituency vote—and for the election of the Federation Council—as well.

Ultimately, thirteen electoral associations (and many "nonparty" candidates) competed. They were provided with free radio and television time. But for radical and moderate progressives the outlook was bleak, due to their inability to keep together. Members of Yeltsin's government ran for different associations, such as Russia's Choice (led by Yegor Gaidar and tacitly supported by Yeltsin) and the Party of Russian Unity and Harmony (PRES, the "party of the regions," led by Sergei Shakhrai). The differences between the platforms of the progressive parties were impossible to fathom for the average voter, who was fed up with politicians anyway; and in the single- and double-seat constituencies, voters often had no idea to which of the blocs individual candidates belonged.[86]

During the electoral campaign, President Yeltsin kept aloof from party politics and stressed over and again that adoption of his Constitution was of the utmost importance in preventing chaos. He went so far as to threaten opponents not to campaign against the Constitution, by which he violated one of the plebiscite rules he had laid down himself: the rule that "citizens of the Russian Federation and social organizations have the right to unhindered campaigning for or against the draft Constitution."[87]

Yeltsin got the Constitution he wanted—but not a roaring electoral success. On 20 December the Central Electoral Commission (CEC) stated that with a turnout of 54.8 percent, 58.4 percent of the voters who turned out had approved of the Constitution, and 41.6 percent had voted against it.[88] On 15 October, Yeltsin had ruled that the Constitution would be adopted if 25 percent of the eligible voters would approve of it: a minimum of 50 percent "yes" votes from a minimum turnout of 50 percent. If we want to gauge the degree of support of the electorate, a different presentation of the results than that of the CEC is called for. The electorate (in the sense of the 106 million citizens registered as voters) can be divided into three groups: 45 percent abstained by not reporting to the polls, a poor 31 percent voted "yes," and 22 percent rejected the constitution.[89] Compared to the referendum that had taken place on 25 April, the new results showed the erosion of support for the Russian president to continue slowly, but without stopping. In April, when asked whether they trusted Yeltsin and approved of his social-economic policy, 37.6 percent of the electorate had answered positively to the first question, 33.9 to the second (58.7 and 53.0 percent of the total voter turnout of 64 percent).

During the days following the 12 December elections, many Russians were shocked by the victory of the fascists and the communists. Revanchist and nationalist parties succeeded in gaining a majority of Duma seats. Against this bad news, the good news might have been that for the first time Russia had had free and fair parliamentary elections. Western monitoring missions reported to have seen little or no fraud.[90] But later it was reported that there had been fraud on a massive scale, benefitting the fascists, communists, and the Agrarian Party. Alexander Sobianin, a nonvoting member of the Commission, even claimed that the turnout in the Constitution plebiscite had in reality been only 46.1 percent, not enough for the Constitution to have been adopted.[91] President Yeltsin kept silent; CEC chairman Nikolai Riabov shrugged off all complaints.

Boris Yeltsin had forced a Constitution with very wide powers for the president, with the risk of continuing deadlock once that president was faced with an obstinate majority in the State Duma.[92] Soon he had to swallow the amnesty the Duma granted to his enemies of August 1991 and October 1993. He had obviously counted on an electoral victory of the parties supporting him. What he got in the end was a Duma in which the ultranationalist and fascist Liberal-Democratic Party of Vladimir Zhirinovskii claimed the highest number of proportional-representation seats, and both the Communist Party and the conservative Agrarian Party made a strong showing. In his television speech of 6 October, Yeltsin had claimed triumphantly that he had saved Russia from civil war and a dictatorship threatened by "a union of the swastika with the hammer and sickle."[93] With his help the fascists and communists now had won a strong position in the democratically—or not so democratically—elected parliament.

FIVE *Transition à la Russe:*

An Interpretation

A state without an all-powerful monarch is an automaton. At most it can reach the level of the United States. And what is the United States? A corpse. (Nikolai Gogol, 1850)[1]

Russia's struggle with Soviet communism produced many scenes right out of the theater of the absurd. In the beginning, Russian political circles had been optimistic about a new Constitution and government for the RSFSR. On 6 August 1990 Boris Yeltsin had announced a contest (with a first prize of five thousand rubles!) for the best draft federal treaty. Entries were to be submitted by 15 October to a jury chaired by Ruslan Khasbulatov. At about the same time, Russian prime minister Silaev appeared on television appealing for candidates for the Council of Ministers and giving a telephone number for applicants to call.[2] Another original idea had been expressed a few years earlier in an effort to short-circuit the confusing process of adopting a new Soviet Constitution. After a long discussion on constitutional reform at Moscow State University, one of the university's law professors had cried out in despair: "Let us put an end to this once and for all by adopting the Constitution of the United States in full." The audience did not burst out in laughter or jeers. The audience nodded in approval.[3]

In 1991, one of the early hopefuls for the Russian presidential elections was Roman Kalinin, leader of the Libertarian Party. His nomination was rejected by the electoral commission. Kalinin had wanted the elections to be complemented by a lottery in such a way that one in every ten thousand voters who voted for him would have won ten thousand rubles.[4] The idea was not so far-fetched. In Soviet quasi-elections, voters had always received a handout when reporting to the polls. Two and a half years later, voters elected Anatolii Kashpirovskii, a popular television faith healer and "president" of the "Research Foundation on the A. M. Kashpirovskii Phenomenon," to the State Duma.[5] He was listed as one of the twenty-three "nonparty" candidates of Zhirinovskii's "Liberal Democratic" Party—a party with an ideology that was the antithesis of liberal democracy. Soon after the first election results came in, Economic Freedom Party leader and one of the election's losers Konstantin Borovoi gave a news conference flanked by no less than five psychologists. Borovoi accused Zhirinovskii of having won the elections by engaging in sinister tampering with Russian minds through a mass campaign of "television hypnosis." It was, Borovoi said, "the first time in the history of mankind that this has happened," and it was dangerous. The psychologists gave his story a solid scientific basis by stating that Zhirinovskii's technique was that of creating an "aura" by skillfully combining the pitch of his voice, the expression of his face, and his use of language.[6] Again, it was not so terribly far-fetched. Like Adolf Hitler, Vladimir Zhirinovskii was gifted with great oratory talent, and like Hitler he knew how to appeal to the subconscious fears and desires of people who had been thrown off their balance; both were masters in manipulating the subliminal self.

Amusing (and disgraceful) was the sight of the developing triangular relationship between the Russian president, Vice President Rutskoi, and the minister of foreign affairs. In the conflict over the Dniester Moldavian Republic, Rutskoi made himself the highest official spokesman for the conservative-nationalist opposition in parliament against Yeltsin's and Kozyrev's cautious policy. Open conflicts between members of the administration occur in democratic countries; they often lead to one of the members tendering his resignation, but in postcommunist Russia they were fought to the bitter end. "In a situation almost unprecedented in democratic states," three students of the conflict wrote, "the vice president of the Russian Federation expresses the attitudes of the parliamentary opposition just as much as the attitudes of his government." In April 1992, Rutskoi and Foreign Minister Kozyrev both visited the capitals of Moldova and the Dniester Republic. "Rutskoi proclaimed that the Dniester republic 'has existed, exists, and will continue to exist,' while Kozyrev seemed to be running after him with a fire extinguisher."[7]

Where president and vice president would take opposing political stands and fight each other with corruption charges, in parliament one and the same deputy would voice opposing policy statements and con-

sider himself a member of different parliamentary groups. "What parliamentarianism is this," Vladimir Umov wrote in 1993 (using the qualifi-
cation "political phantasmagoria"), "where one and the same deputy will
not only manage to be a member of several 'fractions' (groups), but will
also act by the, for democratic representation unbelievable, principle of
'one person, many voices'?"[8]

This short anthology of *absurdnaia politika* has not been compiled
with the aim of ridiculing Russia or the Russians. It has been presented
to underline the very peculiar character of the transition that Russia is
going through. In chapter 2 I discussed the circumstances that set Russia
apart from other countries in transition. These are the very long duration
of communist rule and the enormous size of the country; the destructive legacies of Marxist-Leninist ideology and the Soviet economy; the
concurrence of transition with decolonization; and the identity crisis it
has brought about. Still, this unique combination of features is not sufficient reason to reject an analysis of the Russian transition against the
background of experiences elsewhere in the world. In the same chapter we have seen that democratic experiences and values have not been
altogether absent from Russian political history. Through comparative
analysis, this chapter aims to contribute to an understanding of the Russian condition. Some believe that Russia is a special case for which the
general experiences and comparative literature on transitions are use-
less. Indeed, Russia *is* special. But its peculiarities should not be taken
to mean (as many nationalists in Russia do) that Russia is so special a
country that our concepts do not apply; a culture that can only be understood in terms of itself. This disastrous neo-Slavofile view is one of the
obstacles to be overcome in turning Russia into a civilized society ruling
itself through a responsible state.

TRANSITION—TO DEMOCRACY?

Transition is the interval between one political regime and another, a
period of extreme uncertainty because the "rules of the game" are not
defined, but are indeed the subject matter of the game itself. The first
three and a half years of the Russian transition have displayed a "multilayered chess game" with players resorting to all sorts of tricks in order
to bend the emerging rules in the direction of their personal or group
interests. It is too early to state that this transition has come to an end,
the criterion for its end being the general acceptance of a new set of
rules and a general perception that "abnormality" is over. Normality is
when those active in politics come to expect each other to play accord-

ing to the new rules of a democratic regime.[9] Perhaps they will. Since December 1993, the Yeltsin Constitution has defined the rules of a new game, and in 1994 the players have abided by these rules, strengthening them in the process. But the underlying economic, social, and political problems of Russia are still far too unsettling to allow us to speak of the Russian transition in the past tense. Such can be the case only after the state has proven to itself and to the country that it is in command.

This raises the problem of whether the new game really is "democracy," and if so whether it has come about by design or by default. Some have argued that the political changes in Central and Eastern Europe were a revolution against communism, but not necessarily *for* any single thing.[10] As far as Russia is concerned, it is obvious that part of its transition was an elite-driven revolt against the USSR, so that the question should be answered in the context of Russia's place in the Soviet state. From early in the transition of Russia it seemed that both political leaders and the public entertained quite specific goals. They all wanted the liberation of Russia from Soviet-communist rule. A considerable part of the population wanted a quick entry into the world community of civilized states, and a quick restructuring of the economy resulting in prosperity. Some wanted human decency and respect; others merely wanted to retain their power and wealth in changing circumstances.

One of the main causes of the disenchantment with democracy has been the misconception by many that democracy breeds prosperity. In Russia as elsewhere in Central and Eastern Europe, many considered democracy an instrument for reaching the ultimate goal of prosperity. We have seen in chapter 2 that the new professionals of the Soviet Union showed highly democratic attitudes. At the time, before the advent of the Gorbachev era, such attitudes were noncommittal. In early 1993, Russian citizens still saw political opposition and press freedom as essential elements of democracy. But when asked which single characteristic they considered "the most important feature of democracy," *economic* prosperity was mentioned more often than any one of the political characteristics.[11]

The frustration and agonies of the population as a whole are expressed in seemingly contradictory data. In the April referendum, a small majority of the voters endorsed Yeltsin's economic policy, yet eight months later many of them expressed their disappointment by voting for political parties that promised to slow down or put a stop to economic transition. What this shows is that more detailed analysis is called for. What it also does is to illustrate Huntington's argument for the positive effects of disappointment in the process of democratization, referred to in chapter 2. The Russians' expectations of democracy are being lowered. It is a process that takes time. Possibly, the moral authority and anticonsumerist message of Alexander Solzhenitsyn, who returned to Russia in May 1994, can help in bringing about more realistic expectations of a Russian-type democracy. What the contradictory data on political behavior say about the significance of the eudaemonic mode of legitimation to the present-day Russian regime is a point that will be taken up in the next section.

We should not dismiss the positive effect that unrealistic expectations may have had in the recent past. If Gorbachev had had realistic expectations, he would never have started his *perestroika*. Had Russian reformers been fully aware of the risks and complexities of transition, or had they held the same pessimistic view of the Russian condition as some historians, they would never have engaged in the struggle for renewal. In Russia, as elsewhere in Eastern Europe, democracy remained for many "an ill-defined objective with diverse associations"—but an objective nevertheless.[12] For the populations in Central Europe and at the Western rim of the Soviet Union, democracy often implied a "return to Europe," but Russia was schizophrenic—Russia was both "West" (Europe) and "East" (Asia)—thus, uniquely in Russia, a crisis of identity was intertwined with the question of the institution of democracy. Did Russia really want a Western type of liberal democracy? *Is* Russia, in the mid-1990s, a democracy? If, as pointed out in chapter 2, minimal democracy is understood to be a system of rule in which "rulers are held accountable for their actions in the public realm by citizens, acting indirectly through the competition and cooperation of their elected representatives," Russia under the Yeltsin Constitution is such democracy, even though the cooperative aspect of contemporary Russian politics leaves much to be desired. On many of the indicators discussed earlier, it remains a weak and vulnerable democracy.

The arguments against this evaluation often heard in Russia are that the old *nomenklatura* elite now lodge in the new structures of power and that the democratic process is constricted by corruption, by the inroads organized crime has made into politics, and by the all-powerful bureaucracy. The argument goes that as far as interests are concerned, nothing has changed. To this argument the reply should be that Russia is not unique: many more democracies operate or have operated in an environment of corruption, organized crime, and powerful bureaucracies. And as far as the role of the *nomenklatura* is concerned, the economy and politics need their administrative experience. A new pristine elite cannot be raised from one day to the next. The absence of a civil service with its professional code is troubling but cannot be helped in the short run. While ruling in changing circumstances, some of the *nomenklatura* may by default adapt to the rules of democracy while others fall prey to organized crime. I will return to this topic at the end of this chapter.

LEGITIMATION AND CITIZENSHIP

Zhirinovskii's electoral victory in December 1993 has illustrated that life-and-blood people do not necessarily act in accordance with rational models of political theorists. They may vote antidemocrats into power. The (rational) explanation is quite simple, and was expressed lucidly by philosopher Grigorii Pomerants when, in 1992, he commented on Zhirinovskii's strong showing in the 1991 presidential elections:

> I do not think the millions of people who voted for Zhirinovskii really failed to understand what sort of nonsense he represents, or that they do not understand today that the country cannot be fed by selling water from Lake Baikal for a dollar a glass. The *narod* is not that stupid. But sometimes people are seized by a retrograde (in the words of Dostoevskii's underground man) desire to give common sense a kick. . . . And the buildup of absurdity may end with an explosion.[13]

The kick dealt to "common sense" has a lot to do with the profound legitimation deficit of the new Russian regime. Generally postcommunist societies have to deal with a legitimacy vacuum since they simply lack an established system to legitimate.[14] Social-eudaemonic and goal-rational legitimation are excluded due to the serious problems of economic transition and to *any* "telos," other than minimal well-being and security, having become discredited. Leslie Holmes has suggested that this may be one of the reasons why the predominant modes of early legitimation in postcommunist societies have been the official nationalist and charismatic ones. When finalizing his book in late 1991, Holmes further stated that "in all of the existing postcommunist states," where there is no "established system" to legitimate, "even the regime is as yet insufficiently consolidated and stable for there to be meaningful talk of legitimating it."[15] If we turn to Russia, what can be said about the legitimation of Russia's political system and its rulers by late 1993, after the new constitution had been adopted in the December referendum?

Concerning the eudaemonic mode of legitimation, the results of the April 1993 referendum are illuminating. The referendum took place almost sixteen months into the economic transition, at a time when people were suffering from inflation and when the outlook for the future was bleak. To the question whether the voter approved of the socioeconomic policy of the president and the government during 1992, a nationwide average of 53 percent of the voters answered yes, and 45 percent no. Obviously, the population was deeply divided, with a considerable number of regions rejecting the president and his policy, including central provinces such as Belgorod, Smolensk, Kursk, and Tambov, where around 60 percent of the voters indicated disapproval. Some people may have been willing to take economic pain for the sake of a more prosperous future in a market economy for their children, but many were not. Yet, eight months later, in the Duma elections, the attractively simple message of Zhirinovskii was rejected by most Russians. The majority of the electorate did not vote for his (and their) hurt feelings, but for parties instead that stood for certain (socioeconomic) *interests*, however conservative they might be. This can be interpreted as supportive of democratization. Only to the extent that the Chernomyrdin government and the Duma succeed in balancing these interests and providing for stabilization will they possibly in the far future contribute to eudaemonic legitimation.

What about Yeltsin's personal legitimacy as president of Russia? Was it primarily of the charismatic kind? It seems not. During 1992–1993 his popularity, as measured in opinion polls and referenda, gradually declined, but popularity should not be confused with legitimacy. It was generally acknowledged that Boris Yeltsin was the first ruler of Russia to be elected in a democratic way, thus ascribing to him (and his office) full legal-rational legitimacy. Yes, he was a former regional party boss inclined to the periodic consumption of excessive amounts of alcohol; he was lacking in essential political skills; he was given to periodic over- (and under-) reactions; but he was still the legal and politically legitimate president as long as the population at large was not aware that he violated the law. But Yeltsin lacked legitimacy in one important respect. In the course of 1992–1993 his legitimacy became more and more shaky among the "staffs", that is, his vice president, the leadership of parliament, and his plenipotentiaries and other rulers in the republics and provinces. Over time, his manipulative attitude toward his most active supporters in Democratic Russia (DR) harmed his legitimacy as well. Many of his own appointees "deserted" him and thereby contributed to the struggle over interests and power that so irritated the Russian population.

In 1990, Sergei Shpilko of the Center for the Study of Public Opinion used the term "social infantilism" to characterize the Russian population's lack of those values necessary for a democratic political culture. People are not used to shouldering responsibility, he said; they delight in blaming others and in seeking scapegoats.[16] That remark underlines the difficulty of getting rid of attitudes deeply ingrained in Russian political culture and fostered by the communist regime. Yet the remark is also too general. In chapter 2 we saw that the professional elite and the younger "suppies" in particular support many of the basic values of democracy. At the basis of the Gorbachev revolution lay an undercurrent of profound social change. The economic development programs and social engineering of the communists begat a society in which the professional elite became a driving force for democratization. Can it be that the democratic values and attitudes to which they testified were no more than gratuitous remarks? Or were such attitudes real and have since evaporated in the heat of transition? Is it possible that the findings of research projects on political culture have lost their meaning with the election results of December 1993? In other words, is there a future to responsible citizenship in Russia?

No doubt the events of 1992–1993 have put democratic political culture under severe strain. The Russian citizen (and the Western observer) who believes in honesty and fair play in politics is considered a simpleton. As before, Russian politics is said to be about intrigues, cheating, self-enrichment, corruption, money-grabbing, privileges, and connections—and the stakes have been raised. During the process of intermittent democratization, the norms and values of democratic behavior have been overshadowed by personal and patriotic interests. In such circumstances it is indeed difficult to resist the temptation of cynicism.

Democracy, as we have seen, requires people to be capable of playing the roles of both citizen and subject, and to do so in a responsible way. It places rights and obligations on both citizens and the officers of the state. For "freedom, once it reaches maturity, exercises self-restraint through responsibility." In Russia, however, "the sense of responsibility suffered systematic demolition" from the Soviet system, "which drove people to pass responsibility off to the state, to intermediary institutions and enterprises, to someone else."[17] This may be an exaggeration—but the gap between individual democratic values and actual political behavior remains wide. It can be narrowed only as transition progresses without major disturbances.

The consolidation of responsible citizenship is particularly difficult due to the painful process of psychological emancipation from historical hang-ups. Many Russians suffer from a victimization complex in which they attribute all their ills to the harm inflicted upon their innocent selves by outsiders. It is a mechanism, a reflex, for shifting responsibility for individual behavior to "outsiders," be they Jews, gays, the neighbors, *kulaki* (successful farmers), the communists, Western intelligence services, non-Russian nationalists in the Baltic states and Transcaucasus, Presidents Gorbachev and Yeltsin, the IMF and the World Bank, or the Congress of People's Deputies led by Ruslan Khasbulatov. It is also a reflex that easily gives rise to all sorts of conspiracy theories. Both the political events of 1990–1991 and (in a somewhat different way) those of 1992–1993 document that the Russians' historical proclivity to justify imperial policies in terms of their being victims of the evil outside world has not spent its force. For some reason, "the Russians do not allow themselves to forget their past suffering," an inclination that has led Simon Dixon (in 1990) to sigh that "it is hard to overstate the degree to which Russians are capable of exaggerating their own vulnerability."[18] This basic insecurity has contributed to a reaffirmation of Russia's imperial ambitions in the "near abroad" as documented in the new military doctrine. For the time being, these ambitions are dampened by the country's economic decline. On the other hand, they are strengthened by the desire of the Western powers to have a benign hegemonic Russia—if such were at all possible—that is in command of the situation in Eastern Europe and beyond. By supporting the demand for a special Russian peacekeeping role in the "near abroad," the Western powers sabotage the democratization of Russia and the growth of responsible citizenship.

Democracy requires of its citizens a certain minimum of trust and responsibility: trust in each other and in their politicians, and responsibility for their own life. It is an almost impossible task to start a process of democratization in a country like Russia, where such attitudes are weakly developed. Political forces such as the Russian nationalists, who see their whole world outlook and their interests threatened, have no difficulty in taking advantage of these impulses and reflexes and thereby slowing democratization down, or bringing the process to a halt. Dealing with Russia, it is difficult to share Giuseppe Di Palma's optimism, documented in chapter 1 (pp. 20–22), precisely because his observations help us to zoom in on the essence of Russia's troubled condition. The counterarguments abound. Copying the "art" of transition has often had negative consequences and sometimes made things worse. Russia's problems, to use an understatement, are somewhat more complicated than those of Spain and Uruguay. Even after August 1991 and October 1993, types of rule other than democracy are still available—for example nationalist dictatorship. And in spite of Di Palma's expectation, in the Russian mind there is a close relationship between democratic legitimacy and economic performance. In view of the events of the period covered in this book it would be preposterous to claim that "the point of no return on the path to democratization is at hand." Even though contemporary Russia is a "minimal democracy" in the terms defined above, it is impossible to pin down a "point of no return." At best, the democratization of Russia will continue by fits and starts.

POLITICAL DEMOCRACY, CIVIL SOCIETY, AND THE CAPITALIST MARKET

Transitions from communist rule involve not only the redefinition of the individual's relationship to the state (civil rights). At least as important is the regeneration of independent relationships between individuals in society: the transformation of a society dominated and manipulated by the party-state into a *civil society*. Civil society is considered to be "the independent self-organization of society, the constituent parts of which voluntarily engage in public activity to pursue individual, group, or national interests within the context of a legally defined state-society relationship."[19] In other words: the soccer club, the choral society, the churches, the schools, the trade union and employers' federation, the media, the national chapter of Greenpeace or Amnesty International— all acting independently and free from state interference. A basic premise for postcommunist transitions is that for civil society to develop (and ultimately to support a democratic state structure), the state has to make major concessions by withdrawing from society. This involves recognition by the state that it has no exclusive access to public affairs, and that independently organized citizens have a right to activities in public life.

The dilemma involved in a successful emancipation of civil society is a complicated one. To start with, the all-powerful party-state has to limit its own powers over society. But a passive "go-ahead" attitude is not enough. Simultaneously the party-state must actively help civil society to free itself by providing for legislation that allows social organizations to throw off party-state tutelage. Emancipating social organizations (including, for example, the press) should have recourse to new laws and access to an independent judiciary to fight government departments and local administrations that try to sabotage the new course. To make matters even more complicated, once the regeneration of civil society has reached a certain stage, the state should withdraw even more by limiting its legislation on civil society to the bare minimum, that is, to guaranteeing basic human rights.

To what extent has the emancipation of civil society in Russia been successful, and to what extent has it gained cohesiveness? In answering these questions, we should compare the Russian situation to that of other postcommunist states. In the countries of Central Europe, social movements such as Charta '77 (Czechoslovakia, founded 1977) and Solidarity (Poland, 1980) were able to play an independent role in the collapse of communist rule because of the relatively widespread support they enjoyed. The dissidents of the Soviet Union, however, were more isolated—although some of them, such as Andrei Sakharov, Alexander Solzhenitsyn, and the group that since 1968 distributed the *Chronicle of Current Events* were respected by many people. Dissidents could do little more than publicly hold the state accountable to its own legal standards. In 1970 Andrei Amalrik advised behaving "as if party and state leaders were bound by the law even though it was commonly understood that this was not the case."[20] But only a handful of people had the courage to do so. During the 1970s and the first half of the 1980s, many Soviet citizens—young professionals in particular—opted for less confrontational opposition, in particular the compliant political activism, social activism, and "contacting" identified by Bahry and Silver (see p. 63). Combined, dissidents and young professionals formed "a pool of social actors ready to respond to Gorbachev's challenge."[21] After party leader had called for their help in resisting the conservative party apparatus, tens of thousands of small-scale social organizations (*neformaly*), protoparties, and popular fronts for the defense of *perestroika* testified to an emerging civil society. In the Soviet parliament of 1989–1990, their cause was argued by the Inter-Regional Group of Deputies, organized by Sakharov and Yeltsin. But almost all of them were small, underorganized, and lacking in financial means.

Since 1989, new legislation on social organizations and on the press has helped civil society to disengage from the state.[22] However, complete emancipation has been hampered by the ingrained tendency of most Russian lawmakers, including the president and his entourage, to consider the regulation of relations in civil society one of the tasks of the state. In the course of the struggle over a new Constitution during 1990–1993, several drafts contained chapters on civil society, suggesting that the development of civil society was to be the result of the realization of constitutional provisions. The Constitution adopted in December 1993 had no such chapter, but still contained many provisions enabling institutions of the state to interfere with the independent self-organization of society.

In spite of these drawbacks, it is an indisputable fact that if compared to the situation in the mid-1980s, Russian civil society has made a remarkable comeback. The promotion of free enterprise and privatization and the emerging private retail trade and services sector have stimulated the coming about of economic organizations and pressure groups. A great variety of independent newspapers and weeklies are available to the public. Churches and cultural and environmental organizations have regrouped and gained in influence. In December 1993, thirteen parties and coalitions contested the proportional-representation seats in the State Duma. And organized labor, one of the main actors in civil society, has ultimately found a new place. Its recent history provides a typical illustration of the peculiar way in which Russian civil society has emancipated from communist rule.

Trade unions

The trade unions were the only mass organization that remained intact after the collapse of the Soviet system. More than 80 percent of the membership of the Soviet trade unions continued their membership after the coup attempt of August 1991 and into the period of postcommunism.[23] Names were of course changed—the Federation of Independent Trade Unions of Russia (FNPR) was the Russian successor to the Soviet-era All-Union Central Council of Trade Unions—but the old trade unions proved to be much more resilient and attractive than new (anticommunist) trade unions that had come into being after the miners' strikes of 1989. In fact, as two observers of the trade union movement have written, by 1992 "the 'old' and the 'new' unions had effectively swapped roles," with the traditional Soviet trade unions developing into an independent opposition and the alternative and anticommunist unions collaborating with the government of Yeltsin and Gaidar.[24]

Two basic facts underlie the (reformed) Soviet trade unions' success right up to the end of 1993. The first is the simple truth that even during a transition, people have to make a living. Too often, the social consequences of monetary and industrial reform were played down or brushed aside. Not once did the Yeltsin-Gaidar government negotiate agreements with the trade unions without the intention of keeping its part of the deal. The 1991 law on wage indexation was not observed; the Ministry of Finance "made a deliberate practice of refusing to provide state-owned enterprises, and even government departments, with the funds they needed to pay wages on time," and wages went unpaid for many months. By the summer of 1993, trade unions and the government "were effectively at war with one another."[25] After the October events, the government dealt the unions a heavy blow.

The second circumstance is that during 1992–1993, the union's antagonist was not industry and management, but the government—a government desperately trying to bring order to the postcommunist chaos, a government that also felt compelled to act on the advice of Western monetarists. The once-collaborationist Soviet trade unions, now fighting an anticommunist government, transformed into the one and only organizational instrument of labor. This could happen as a result of the traditional functions they had had for workers during the Soviet period, and because of the behavior of the alternative trade unions after the collapse of the USSR.

Labeling the Soviet trade unions "collaborationist" is deliberately using a negative term that obscures their true position in Soviet society. The trade unions had, of course, been "part of the system," for in the Soviet Union there had been no escape from the communist system short of dissidence and imprisonment. Their leadership had been manipulated by the Communist Party. Labor union policy was little more than the implementation of the socioeconomic policy decided upon by the CPSU's Politburo. But the content of that policy proved to be of great importance for the role that trade unions could play during early post-communism.

All workers and employees in the Soviet Union knew that their unions were not independent, and that they would never organize industrial action against state industries for the satisfaction of workers' demands. But all the same, the unions were of great use to them, and they knew that they would put themselves at a great disadvantage by foregoing trade union membership. Wages and fringe benefits were decided by the Moscow bureaucracy, but the local trade union branches could do a lot to make life for the individual worker and his family more pleasant, or at least less disagreeable. The local union representatives were crucial in the distribution of social and economic benefits: sickness and maternity allowances, the allocation of housing, providing workers with scarce consumer products through their own channels, the admittance of children to day care centers, the organization of leisure activities and holiday trips. To the individual worker, it was important to maintain a good relationship with union leaders. The local trade unions controlled property and vast financial resources (including the "social insurance fund"), allowing them to perform these distributive functions for the population; the money came from the state budget.[26] In addition, union chapters played a central role in negotiating with management on labor safety and on individual labor disputes; quite often, union officials succeeded in undoing wrongful dismissal by the management.[27] The fact that these distributive powers often invited misuse and corruption by union officials could not undo the usefulness of union membership to the individual worker.[28]

Nothing of the sort was available to the anticommunist unions that had come into being after 1989, placing them at a great disadvantage vis-à-vis the "old" unions that maintained their nationwide structures and (until October 1993) their control over the social insurance fund. The old unions had remained untouched by Gorbachev's *perestroika*. There had been some labor unrest—a partly political coal miners' strike in the summer of 1989—but the unions had refrained from "making trouble." The old unions easily withstood the challenge of new unions such as the Independent Union of Miners (NPG) and the Association of Socialist (later *Social*, until the adjective was dropped entirely) Trade Unions (SOTSPROF). These new unions had originated in the strike committees of 1989, and in the struggle against the communist system. Once that system had gone, their leaders supported president Yeltsin and his government. It was no surprise that these structures—new, inexperienced, with little organizational strength, and shutting their eyes to the fact that many of the government's decisions were hostile to workers' short-term interests—"failed to win the majority of workers on their side."[29] As the old unions sprang back onto the scene and started to fight the Russian government, the new unions began to receive government support and were hedged in. This and the recurring splits and financial scandals led to their early demise. Many of their leaders went into business, administration, or politics.

The reconstituted Soviet labor unions, however, had difficulty in formulating a vision and a strategy for the future. During the first two years of postcommunism, their message contained little more than the "left conservatism" worded by Andrei Isaev, one of the many anticommunist activists who had reached a leading position in the "new-old" unions. His message said that the important changes that had been brought about, thanks to their opposition in 1986–1991, now had to be defended from the neoliberal reaction. In the mixed economy they stood for, private enterprise should coexist with a strong state sector. The welfare achievements and successful industries of the Soviet period demanded the former leftists to challenge the Russian authorities and their "shock therapy," and obliged them to summon people to struggle. Of the government the unions demanded the indexation of wages and a minimum wage at subsistence level. To the troubled working population they became "the sole all-Russian structure through which something at least might be achieved."[30]

In the summer of 1993, Russia saw the first nationwide collective industrial actions organized by trade unions since the beginning of the century. There was massive labor unrest in many parts of the country over the government's violation of a wage agreement that had been negotiated with the FNPR, with at one point as many as one and a half million workers and employees taking part. But after the October events in which the unions had proven helpless in organizing a *political* strike, the government finally dealt them a heavy blow by stripping them of exclusive control over the social insurance fund, and threatening the FNPR with dissolution.[31] Exclusive control by the unions was replaced by a construct in which the government was to manage the fund "with the participation" of the nationwide trade unions. The government position was that the trade unions had only managed, not owned, the social insurance fund. In October it ordered "government property" in use by the unions, such as administration buildings, holiday homes, boardinghouses, and sanatoriums to be transferred to the fund. It was the last stage in the unions' emancipation from the Soviet system. The once-Soviet FNPR had developed into an independent trade union, fighting for the interests of those who suffered the direct consequences of economic transition, and an important structure in postcommunist civil society.

The new middle class and centrist politics

The trade unions, uniting workers and educated professionals, were one of the forces making for the emancipation of civil society from the state. Another such force could be a middle class based on the new professionals who had been bred by the Soviet system. During the first four years of the 1990s the new professionals, whose profile has been sketched in chapter 2, have been caught up in a relentless struggle over power and interests. Some of them have gone into politics and administration, others into business. But by far the biggest portion of this social category has been faced with increasing insecurity, unemployment, and a frustrating struggle for survival. Most of them have withdrawn from political life, finding an easy excuse for doing so in the repugnant behavior of "their" postcommunist politicians.

Is this indeed the new middle class that is to provide the stabilizing and integrating core of civil society? And if so, why has this middle class by 1994 not been able to produce a forceful political movement or party to represent their interests, to keep extremists in check, and to bring order to Russian politics? Half the Russian population considers itself part of the middle class, and seven out of every ten politicians claim to represent centrist movements or parties.[32] Yet most of this is wishful thinking or deception. As Vladimir Umov has argued, postcommunist Russian society has many "crystal nuclei" for a slowly developing middle class—skilled workers, small-scale entrepreneurs, technicians, teachers (in public as well as private education), lawyers, doctors, government employees, shopkeepers, craftsmen, and starters of new service industries. But they are isolated. They have not yet succeeded in creating a community of interests held together by a shared sense of identity.[33] The new Russian middle class is developing, but its genesis will take a long time and is threatened by the fact that in the meantime no other institution or person can take upon itself the performance of its functions.

The process is threatened as well by the center losing ground as Russian society is being driven apart into the superrich, a mass of pauperized professionals, and a destitute "underclass." In spite of privatization and the limited contraction of the state sector, it remains exceedingly difficult for aspiring members of the middle class to achieve the independence from the state that they need. In the words of Umov, "the authorities [*nachalstvo*, the bosses] of all kinds are not in the least interested in their [the middle class's] independence." The values, behavioral patterns, and professional ethics of the middle class "cannot possibly be imitated or imported"; they can only grow on the basis of Russian traditions in an environment devoid of social upheavals or cultural fractures.[34] Considering the atomization and insecurity of Russian society, Umov in the summer of 1993 saw the real possibility of a "flight from freedom" into fascism—a development that would disrupt the emancipation of a free middle class.

But surely, one could object, there are positive signs such as the founding of the centrist Civic Union in June 1992, its alliance with the Federation of Independent Russian Trade Unions in autumn, and, a few months later, the appointment of Victor Chernomyrdin to the position of prime minister? Civic Union's days of glory lasted only a few months.[35] By the summer of 1993, the coalition had disintegrated; in the December elections one of its remnants—the Civic Union for Stability, Justice, and Progress, with Arkadii Volskii as top candidate—could not even pass the 5 percent threshold for the State Duma. The reason for its short-lived success was that the union "was created to represent individuals and social groups advantaged by the *old* Soviet socioeconomic system who then sought to secure a *new* political and economic role in Russia's postcommunist society."[36] Umov, after analyzing the union's 1992 program, bitterly remarked that "if this is an economic reform program of the end of the twentieth century, then history has really ended, although not in the way of Francis Fukuyama."[37] The go-slow program, demanding preservation of subsidies to state enterprises, price controls, and a deceleration of privatization, in no way promoted the development of a Russian middle class. The union itself fell apart as privatization created new lines of cleavage between the old *nomenklatura*-managers and new industrialists, and as workers came to understand that their interests were not necessarily in line with those of company directors and managers. But Victor Chernomyrdin remained, and his power increased considerably after the December elections.

Returning to the questions posed in the first two chapters of this book, we see that the educated professionals who had been the social base for Gorbachev's *glasnost* and *perestroika* did not easily translate into a middle class that could stabilize postcommunist society. They had been no more than one of the nuclei for an independent middle class that could only reach maturity after the emancipation from communist rule. But the guidance of reform from the top, the many dislocations, and the almost permanent crisis drove Russian society away from the center. In these polarized circumstances, the middle class had a hard time getting to its feet. The demoralized population became increasingly susceptible to extremist and nostalgic forces such as the fascists and communists. Thereby, Russia proves Jon Elster right in his "impossibility theorem," summarizing the necessity and impossibility of simultaneous economic and political reform. Full-scale reform has indeed been impossible; in the meantime, civil society and the middle class jerk along.

LEADERSHIP AND PACTS

Several authors have observed that in contrast to the countries of Central Europe, the Russian transition has mainly been an intra- and interelite affair in which social organizations and the masses have played only a limited role—primarily as workers going on strike for economic benefits or political goals. Social groups were not included in the on-and-off negotiations during the first phase of transition. Among transitions the end of the Soviet Union was exceptional, Timothy Colton wrote, in that "it was crafted, not by representatives of the state in concert with a political opposition and private groups, but by public officials alone, working for the most part behind closed doors. The compact reached was one *among governments*, meaning by this time the cooperating republic governments."[38] During this early period of Russia's transition, pacts were made in Novo-Ogarevo and at the Belovezhskaia Pushcha hunting lodge. In both cases they provided the framework for further negotiations. But after the CIS pact with the leaderships of most of the other USSR republics had provided the Russians with a way to dispose of the USSR, pacts for democratizing Russia "on the installment plan" did not come about until after the December 1993 elections and the adoption of the Yeltsin Constitution.

Pacts are not necessary to democratization, but other transitions have shown that they can be highly beneficial. Russia had to forego them primarily for two reasons. First was the absence of established links between elites and their possible social base and the speed with which that social base was changing. Civic Union held the promise of playing a main role in pacting, but its strength soon vaporized. Democratic Russia might have become a pacting partner, had Yeltsin provided more consistent leadership. The second obstacle was the absence of contingent consent. Earlier it was stated that the essence of pacting is that the parties concerned either forego or underutilize their capacity to harm each other and guarantee not to threaten each other's autonomy or vital interests. In doing so, they grant each other a "shadow of the future" in the form of contingent consent. If they are capable of doing so, they thereby show to have internalized one of the essential principles of democratic rule. Although in the struggle over a new Constitution we have seen several attempts at reaching compromises, pacts never came about or, in the case of the pact between President Yeltsin and the federation's subjects, they soon broke down.

One of the fascinating questions of the Russian transition is indeed why, at least up to December 1993, the main actors were not willing to forego the possibility of harming each other. Toward an answer, one may cite the traumas left behind by communism and the fact that almost all persons concerned were ex-communists not particularly given to a "leap of faith." Many of them had suddenly been catapulted to high positions, whetting their taste for power. As long as a new Constitution was not adopted, they lacked a long-term perspective and expectations of working with their adversaries for a long period of time. From the very beginning of the period (June 1990), the promulgation of a new Constitution was on the agenda, implying for all actors that sooner or later there would be a break which could harm their personal interests. In a situation of dramatic economic decline and social insecurity, but also of unprecedented opportunities at self-enrichment, the political positions of deputies in parliament and in the regional and local soviets became closely intertwined with their personal interests. Political rationalizations for personal interests were easily found. Here as in other respects, the Russian transition has the character of a vicious circle. In December 1991, Moscow deputy B. Vyzhutovich said that "one can govern democratically only through democratic structures. Taking control through totalitarian structures (and we have no others) in a civilized way is a hopeless endeavour."[39]

Lacking an outside power that could force a new Constitution on Russia, the new Constitution had to come out of intense political struggle. Only after this Constitution came into force and the opposition in the new State Duma had united did President Yeltsin, in March 1994, issue a call for a "Civic Accord" between all parties and political groups to regulate their conduct for a two-year period.[40] The "Social Accord Agreement," as it came to be called, was signed on 28 April 1994 by the president, the government, parliament, almost all major political groups, regional and republican leaders, and, on 5 May, by more than one hundred leading businessmen and bankers. It is doubtful whether this agreement can be classified as a pact in terms of the transition literature discussed at the beginning of this book. True, its main aim was to bring stability to the Russian state, to prevent further bloodshed, and to grant all of the signatories a "shadow of the future." But the Social Accord had not been the result of negotiations between conflicting parties and did not provide the framework for further negotiations on new "rules of the game." Such rules, including a two-year transitory period, had been fixed in the new Constitution. The obligations that the signatories took upon themselves added nothing of any significance to what was already regulated in the Constitution and the criminal code and enforceable on the basis of these two documents. The real meaning of the Agreement seemed to lie elsewhere. For President Yeltsin it was a way of showing that he was still in command. Probably it was also intended as an instrument to test the loyalty of other politicians toward the Russian president, an instrument that the president could put to use should he have to deal with disloyalty again.

Transition through pacting requires strong leadership. It is difficult to find a Russian leader who showed the rare combination of qualities making for such leadership: vision, patience, immunity to stress, restraint, a willingness to overcome resentment, and commitment to democratic procedure. Particularly after the USSR had gone and the stakes had been raised, the leading actors, including Yeltsin, failed in these qualities. The battle over economic reform and the new Constitution turned into guerrilla warfare, the kind of zero-sum game where society stands to lose from the lack of responsibility of politicians and the low quality of their leadership. Lack of vision and strategic thinking were particularly strong in President Yeltsin, who further showed a lack of leadership by not being able to restrain himself from taking privileges from his "enemies," by his leaning on a staff of dubious quality, by underestimating the importance of strengthening his ties with society, and by his tendency to interpret all controversy as a clash between loyal followers and disloyal enemies.

Before the agreement of April 1994, neither President Yeltsin nor the other leading actors did much to foster the tolerance that is so necessary for sustained democratization. In their escalating war they set a bad example for society. The labeling of each other as "dictators," "fascists," or worse; the dirty tricks; the cheating on compromises reached; the allegations of corruption; the vindictive taking away of the perks of high leadership from adversaries—such phenomena will not have created the impression that in Russian political behavior much had changed.

It is perhaps unfair to criticize Boris Yeltsin for his inadequate leadership. Here was a communist party boss from Sverdlovsk who had been catapulted into the maelstrom of Moscow politics at the time of the Soviet Union's system crisis, who had shown a great deal of courage (and impulsive behavior), and who had in the end won the trust of many Russians. Considering his qualifications and life history up to 1990, his task was almost impossible. Yeltsin understood the workings of the "command-administrative" system of days past all too well, but the basics of capitalist economics and political democracy were beyond him. Referring to the March 1993 attempt of the Congress of People's Deputies to impeach him, he showed his confused thinking by writing that "as any schoolboy understands, Congress cannot impeach the president because it has not elected him."[41] Congress *did* have the power to impeach him. Perhaps he was mistaking the new impeachment procedure, based on the idea of the separation of powers, with the recall procedure for people's deputies that had existed in the Soviet Union? Yeltsin was the first Russian president to be elected by the people; in his thinking, the overconfidence that he took from this fact pushed constitutional niceties to the margins.

Moreover, he could have had no idea of the difficulties, or the time frame involved in the Russian transition, and no expert in or outside Russia could have provided him with advice. It was, as Yeltsin said himself, a journey through a taiga without paths, where no one had tread before. This showed in an insecurity about strategic goals and an inevitable lack of consistency in his policy. As late as October 1992, Yeltsin would see no contradiction in simultaneously (in an interview) raising pensioners' and unwed mothers' incomes without any mention of the cost to the state coffers; promoting "shock therapy" for transiting to a "normal, civilized market" economy; and stoutly denying that Russia was "returning to capitalism": "Russia is a unique country," he said; "she will not be socialist, and neither will she be capitalist."[42] During the preceding two years, he had many times promised that the worst would soon be over. Now again, he would say in one and the same breath that "the situation at the moment is difficult," "the worst is behind us," that no later than April 1993 prices would be stabilized, that it would be naïve to expect the Russians' psychology to change quickly, and that it would take many years of hard work by the government before the Russian population would be receptive to reforms.

INSTITUTIONAL CHOICES

The main four institutional choices that have been made in the course of the Russian transition have left a strong imprint on political developments. The first such choice was the decision to copy the Congress of People's Deputies from the USSR. On the level of the USSR, the 2,250-member Congress had been elected and installed in 1989. Of all fifteen republics, only the RSFSR had decided for a Congress from which the smaller working parliament was to be elected. The second choice was the introduction of the presidency in Russia, in a situation of heated controversy over the place of that presidency between parliament and government. The third choice concerned changes in the electoral system. When in October 1989 Russia opted for its own Congress of People's Deputies, it decided against the dubious innovation that Gorbachev had introduced in 1988: the appointment of one-third of the USSR Congress's deputies by social organizations most of which at the time were still controlled by the Communist Party. All of the 1,068 deputies to the RSFSR Congress were directly elected, 900 from nonethnic single-seat districts and 168 from ethnic single-seat districts.[43] Up to December 1993, the district system that had been in use in the Soviet Union was preserved. It was, however, of no little significance that real elections were a new phenomenon. The very first, but still limited, experiments which allowed some of the voters a choice, dated from 1987. In the March 1989 election of 1,500 deputies to the USSR Congress, it had not yet been mandatory that the ballot paper in a single-seat district contain more than one candidate. These elections had produced a limited number of dramatic victories and defeats. But it was only in early

1990, when republican parliaments and lower bodies were elected, that most of the electorate was presented with the opportunity to make real choices between different candidates. The fourth and final choice was Yeltsin's Constitution, adopted in December 1993. It replaced the parliament inherited from the Soviet era by a Federal Assembly; redefined the relationship between parliament, government, and president; abolished the position of vice president; and introduced the electoral technique of proportional representation for half the number of seats in the State Duma.

Of central importance was the introduction of the presidency. Referring to Douglas Verney's observations quoted in chapter 1, we see the singular way in which Russia democratized its "monarchical power." Verney had identified roughly two historical ways for this to happen: either the government was "pulled from under" the king and made responsible to the legislature while the king retained the largely symbolic function of head of state, or the king was substituted by a democratically elected president. For the sake of argument, it seems not too far-fetched to substitute the CPSU for "the king" in this historical example. After all, in the Soviet Union the CPSU had reigned supreme, being the twentieth-century manifestation of the Autocrat. In 1990, when it had become obvious that the CPSU was failing and Russia and other republics were asserting their sovereignty, the despairing party had agreed to the institution of the presidency, hoping that by this instrument General Secretary Gorbachev could at least keep the USSR intact. The quasi-democratic USSR had been ruled by a cabinet-type government, with the CPSU pulling the strings behind the scenes. The short-lived experiment of 1989–1990 (the USSR Congress of People's Deputies and Supreme Soviet with the Ryzhkov government) had shown the party that in an increasingly competitive environment where it suffered a severe legitimation deficit, it could not "hold things together." The CPSU did not want to lose its power. The party accepted the presidency as an extra instrument for its general secretary to reaffirm control over the country.

Thus, in March of 1990, the "king" had been replaced by the not-so-democratically elected president-king Gorbachev.[44] One year later Russia improved on this arrangement by opting for a presidency itself, to be elected directly by the people. Being in opposition to the Communist Party and its president-king Gorbachev, Yeltsin's presidency was the first true presidency in Russia. At a time when legitimacy was quickly being washed away from Gorbachev's presidency (both among his staff and among the people at large), the new Russian president received strong legitimation. This was particularly so when a group of plotters, including the chief and members of the USSR Cabinet of Ministers, tried to turn the clock of reform back in August 1991.

But the presidency came to Russia in a situation in which its powers vis-à-vis parliament and the government in Moscow had not yet crystallized, and in which the president had to give proof of his ability to establish effective control over the rest of the country. President Yeltsin tried to recreate the *vertikal* of power (and the regional clientele) that had been lost when the Communist Party structure had collapsed. He appointed chiefs of administration and governors in the regions, but soon had to face their limited power (due to obstruction by regional soviets) and limited loyalty. With the issues of a new Constitution and economic reform topping the political agenda, fights over power distribution between president, parliament, and the regions turned into a relentless tug-of-war.

The struggle lasted two full years and wasted lots of energy that might have been applied to more constructive purposes. Perhaps Russia would have fared better if in 1991 a presidential system had not been introduced? The question is not entirely hypothetical. One of the issues in designing a new state structure was the disproportionate power of parliament—and of the Supreme Soviet's Presidium in particular. It can well be argued that had the presidency not been introduced, it would have been even more difficult to bring about a balanced separation of powers. As chairman of the Supreme Soviet (the position he held until he was elected president in June 1991), Boris Yeltsin would perhaps not have felt the urge to limit the powers of his own institution, as, in fact, his successor Khasbulatov did not. Had Yeltsin remained in this position, parliament would probably not have ceded the unique position it claimed on the basis of outdated communist constitutional doctrine. The historical function of the presidency may have been precisely to do away with lingering Soviet conceptions of the role and place of parliament and the soviets, and to break their resistance. By 1994 it produced a situation where Russia had a more or less normal parliament—and a rather abnormal presidency.

Whether the presidential system is the best that contemporary Russia could wish is a different question. After the installation of the Federal Assembly, the arguments against the presidential system presented in chapter 1 weigh heavy. The procedure written into the Constitution for dealing with a deadlock between president and parliament over the appointment of the chairman of the government does not guarantee that such a deadlock can indeed be resolved. It can, in fact, produce a sequence of dissolutions of parliament by the president and votes of no confidence by parliament.[45] Under the presidential Constitution to which he has fully committed himself, President Yeltsin holds wide powers, including that of issuing decrees. But at the same time he can no longer deny the legitimacy of parliament. He can no longer argue, as he did so often during the crisis of 1992–1993, that he is the only government official freely elected by the people. He still considers himself the plenipotentiary and incarnation of the whole *narod,* the mythical personification of its will—an elected king. But the Duma has forced him to accept the resignation of two of the architects and foremen of market reforms, Ministers Gaidar and Fedorov (Finance). He could not prevent the freeing from prison of his hated adversaries of August 1991 and October 1993. Yeltsin has neglected to reflect on the impact of political realities upon the presidential system that he wrote into his Constitution. On the other hand, he enjoys wide legislative powers, which he uses to the fullest extent. His stream of decrees, which are not too fussy about the law and the rights of the individual, pose a grave danger to Russian society. The president's rule by decree can easily degenerate into the abuse of power.

Electoral reform has produced unexpected results as well. In 1993, proportional representation with a 5 percent threshold was introduced for the election of half the number of deputies to the State Duma in order to inspissate the party system while putting up a barrier against extremist political forces. The innovation contributed somewhat toward an improvement of the party system, but was only a small first step. The tenacity of old habits showed in that one-third of the deputies on the eight party tickets, among which 225 seats in the Duma were distributed, had been listed as having no party affiliation whatsoever (*bespartiinyi*).[46] Preservation of the district system was no alternative either, since that system can only work properly if supported by the type of strong parliamentary parties that were still lacking in the Russian political arena. After the new Constitution was adopted and the Federal Assembly had convened, the primitive party system remained one of the main weaknesses of responsible and representative government in Russia.

CLEAVAGES AND PARTY SYSTEM

Yeltsin's greatest failure has been his lack of resolve in building and leading a strong political movement or party. His weakness showed in an ambivalence between the role of leader of a political party or movement and the role of national leader above the parties, seeking compromise between different elites and factions. He failed to turn Democratic Russia, the one movement by which he was seen as leader, into a strong reform party that would be identified with the reform process. He therefore bore part of the responsibility for the fact that DR never became a parliamentary party, and for its declining role in the course of 1990–1993.[47] In the 1990 elections, individual candidates had been supported by DR. Its vigorous organization, its anti-*nomenklatura* ticket, and its attention to real grievances of the voters had resulted in victories in several cities and in a strong showing in the Russian parliament. But the deputies had not been elected as party members. Once elected, they remained individuals not subject to party discipline, and there *was* no discipline in the DR groups in the soviets.

The traumatic legacy of Leninism made it difficult for strong parties to emerge. There was an aversion to party discipline and leadership. In the few parties that were organized along disciplined lines, such as Nikolai Travkin's Democratic Party of Russia (DPR), founded in May 1990, the leadership was vulnerable to charges of dictatorial tendencies, so that here, too, splits occurred. Still, with about 18,000 members in August 1991, DPR was, after the CPSU, one of the best organized political parties in Russia.[48] Loose movements uniting both organizations and individuals, and led by collective boards including the different factions within the movement, were considered to be more democratic than strictly organized political parties. The members of these boards had shown a tendency to quibble, leading to many splits.

The missing link between President Yeltsin and a mass party was part of this legacy. It was fixed in Article 1 of the law on the (Russian) president that had come into being when, in the spring of 1991, Gorbachev was still both president of the USSR and leader of the Communist Party. Rejecting the mixing of executive and party-political functions that had characterized communist rule, the legislators had written into the law that during his presidency the person in question would have to suspend his membership in political parties and social organizations and was barred from holding any other positions in state or social organizations.[49] The provision implied that the Russian president would stand above all parties and would be the symbol of national unity and the driving power of politics. In his reminiscences discussing the situation of the spring of 1993, Yeltsin expressed his attitude on his own role and on that of other state institutions and political forces. There was in 1993 an abundance of power structures, civil servants, and institutions, he wrote. Russia had a highly developed, "civilized" population. And yet there was "anarchy." Instinctively borrowing Stalinist imagery, Yeltsin wrote that the anarchy could be explained in one way only: "The drive system doesn't work. And so the machine doesn't operate. In the end everything must submit to one single, sharply defined principle, law, institution. Roughly speaking, someone in the country must be in command. That's all. . . ."[50] He almost said it: "L'état—c'est moi."

In November 1991, when he had dealt the *coup de grâce* to the CPSU, Yeltsin had argued that it had never been a political party. The curious attitude that he developed toward political parties in the course of 1990–1993 was influenced by his own changing role (from Communist Party member, elected in 1989 to the USSR Congress of People's Deputies on an antiparty ticket and over strong obstruction by CPSU authorities, to president of the Russian Federation) and by the decline of the CPSU. Shortly after he had been elected chairman of the Russian parliament, he had resigned from the CPSU, with a line of reasoning that implied that should the chairman of parliament be a member of a party, he would have to execute that party's orders and instructions. Shortly after the August coup of 1991 he had signed a decree on the Council of Ministers in which he prohibited "interference of parties and other social associations" in the activities of the government.[51] Seen in retrospect, it was a strange thing to say—for one would think that in a democracy, indirect (through parliament) and direct "interference" of political parties and lobbies in government decision making is their main purpose. These instances testify to a continuing ambivalence in Russian conceptions of political parties that is particularly strong in the country's president.

The settling down of political parties into a more or less consolidated party system was hindered not only by the stiff resistance of outlived conceptions. It was also frustrated by the fact that during these tumultuous four years the cleavage pattern of Russian society was constantly on the move. New center-periphery cleavages were piled on top of rapidly changing socioeconomic cleavages, making for an opaque image of society and its crisscrossing pattern of interests. The high hopes that some Russians had of the centrist Civic Union soon faded to nothing.

GOVERNABILITY

Many of the issues discussed above converge in the issue of governability. As was said in chapter 1 (p. 44), governability depends on the combination of weak and strong society and government. On society's side of the equation, we now see that Russian society has strengthened since the onset of Gorbachev's reign. Russia's population was already highly educated when intellectuals gained considerably in independence. Both the intellectuals and the general public now have much more access to information about society and politics than before. Since the demise of the Communist Party, they can organize freely in autonomous organizations. Although radio and television are still dominated by the government, the public has more access to these institutions than before. Finally, in spite of a general weariness with politics, a considerable portion of the public is "mobilized" in the sense of being aware of the issues on the political agenda. By 1994, Russian society may not be strong, but it is certainly much stronger than before.

Government, however, is much weaker than before. Its infrastructure, financial and coercive resources, and instruments of propaganda and socialization have been in constant overhaul and disarray for over five years. As a result, the accuracy of its information about society is to be doubted; and its capacity to reach consensus about policy and to assure its execution and implementation is restricted. The governing elite (in the sense of government and parliament in Moscow, and administrative and representative structures in the regions) is divided; conflicts on legitimacy continue. And finally, on the question of the presence of either popular legitimacy of the system and the regime or the ability of the government to terrorize society into submission, the situation is alarming. In 1993 President Yeltsin expressed his regret over the weakening of government in his subdued admiration for Tsar Alexander III (1881–1894), and communist leader Leonid Brezhnev (1964–1982). Their reigns, of course, were inhumane. But during the rule of Alexander, Yeltsin wrote, Russian society and industry made great progress, and "the Russian state was finally accepted in the family of civilized peoples." He added that Brezhnev's "heavy-handed but . . . very consistent administrative hardness had a number of wholesome effects."[52]

Boris Yeltsin was not alone in his nostalgia for strong leadership. By the mid-1990s, the central issue of Russian politics had become whether the state would be able to withstand the onslaught of organized crime. The criminal element in Russian society, one observer wrote, was in the process of "hijacking the state."[53] Speaking about Russia, one cannot fail to notice the destructiveness of this factor. A discussion of the governability of Russia would be ludicrously irrelevant without mention of the extent to which both society and the state are being weakened by crime. Only a few years into the Russian transition, the explosion of crime had become the single most important factor making for a possible change of its course in the direction of autocratic dictatorship. Prompted by the pervasive impact of crime, the "iron fist" theme will be at the center of the country's Duma and presidential elections of 1995–1996. Since 1993, Russia has the dangerous construct of a weakened president in a strengthened presidency. This president has in 1994 taken all law enforcement agencies under his direct control and has decreed a relentless fight against crime. His appointment of law enforcement executives does not require parliamentary approval. His decrees prompt them to greater efforts, in words suggesting that legal protection of the individual does not matter all that much. An excuse for a clampdown and a return to authoritarianism is easily found: crime is threatening the survival of the state.

Crime is penetrating everything. Corruption is everywhere. And they have not come out of the blue. During the reign of Leonid Brezhnev, the "Soviet mafia" had settled in the communist *nomenklatura* network; corruption and criminal protection had become the lubricant of a politics of patronage and clientelism.[54] In 1976, a former party official had published (abroad) an essay titled *Party or Mafia: The Plundered Republic*.[55] The Communist Party apparatus encapsulated organized crime, thereby holding it more or less in check. Then the party collapsed and the new Russian state was caught up in internecine warfare. During 1992–1993, President Yeltsin and his opponents bombarded each other with corruption charges. The Interdepartmental Commission for Fighting Crime and Corruption, created by Yeltsin in October 1992 and placed under the leadership of Vice President Rutskoi, was no more than a framework for such charges. During the same period, privatization offered a radiant future to the mafia and former *nomenklatura* officials. Inflation, deprivation, and insecurity made everybody susceptible to the lure of money. Border controls slackened; security officials were on the take. Soldiers guarding ammunitions depots could easily be bought.

"Russia is pregnant with crime," *Argumenty i Fakty* reported in April 1994, adding that "it is widely known that it is impossible to be just a little bit pregnant." Data released by the Russian Federation's public prosecutor's office showed that in 1993 murder and manslaughter (including attempts) stood at the frightening level of 29,213, up 27 percent from the previous year.[56] For every 100,000 inhabitants there were about sixteen cases of murder or manslaughter, compared to nine in the United States and one in the Netherlands.[57] In 1987, on the territory of the RSFSR, the total number had still been below 10,000; then it rose to 15,566 in 1990 and 23,006 in 1992. Compared to the previous year, robbery in 1993 went up by 32 percent to 40,180 cases; assault and battery resulting in serious injury went up by 24 percent, arms theft by 23 percent to 1,396 cases, "open stealing" by 12 percent, and rape by almost 6 percent. Theft was the only category where a slight drop occurred, at a level of almost 1.6 million cases. The total number of registered crimes in the Russian Federation more than doubled from 1.2 million in 1987 to 1.8 in 1990 and 2.8 in 1993. In 1993, 12,431 of the registered crimes were committed by organized gangs, 3.5 times as many as in 1990. For participating in organized crime, 1,394 police and state officers were prosecuted.

By 1994, the territory of the Russian Federation was divided among several thousand criminal gangs. Almost all policemen and public officials were corrupt. Ties with former *nomenklatura* officials and criminal manipulation of the privatization process had resulted in large sections of private industry, retail trade, banking, hotels, and service industries ending up in the hands of organized crime. The shopkeeper, director, bank, or hotel manager who was not being forced to pay protection money had become a rare exception. Organized crime was thought to account for 30 to 40 percent of the Russian GNP. Between 1988 and 1990, the average number of policemen killed annually had been 149; in 1993 it stood at 185. Even public prosecutors were no longer safe: in 1993, 120 of them fell victim to crime, and two were killed. The hiring of hit men had become rather inexpensive and quite frequent; in 1993 the prosecutor's office registered almost twenty assassinations per month. With an eye on the elections of 1995–1996, criminals even created their own political parties.

Organized crime did not stop at Russia's borders. Links had been established with gangs in the other CIS countries and in Central and Western Europe. These conglomerates were dealing in everything, including prostitution, refugees, drugs, and fissionable materials. Some American and European experts were deeply concerned about the expanding "nuclear black market" and the nuclear "smuggling infrastructure" that was being set up.[58] Reports on the interception of illegal shipments of uranium and plutonium suggested more about the possible use of such materials to terrorist organizations than was warranted by the technical feasibilities of the production of nuclear arms. Nevertheless, the possible illegal sale of *complete* arms did present a danger to international security.

The impact of crime on society and politics was shattering. Compared to the mid-1980s, society had been strengthened, but at the same time it was permeated with crime and would probably not be able to "defend itself" if a renewed tyranny presented itself as the ultimate solution to the criminalization of Russia.

This brings us to the final theme of this chapter: revenge. Why has there been no revenge, no putting the past behind? Why have the criminals of the communist era not been hunted down and called to account? During the early phase of transition, calls had been heard to *Davai nam nash Nurenberg*, "give us our own Nuremberg trial." Nothing came of it. During 1990–1991, there were limited instances of revenge in the form of attacks on local party headquarters. Shortly after the coup attempt in 1991, philosopher Grigorii Pomerants wrote that "in Russia [as opposed to other republics of the USSR], the nationalistic awakening did not become influential, despite the efforts of the chauvinists. The masses of the people hated the Party mafia much more."[59] If so, why have the masses not taken the party mafia to court?

Settling past accounts with former oppressors can be a divisive issue during transitions, and has been so in many Latin American countries. It has also been an issue in Germany after unification, and in other Central European countries. Why not in Russia? The answer is that first, in Russia the communist elite managed the transition and adapted to the new situation, and second, in communist Russia the line between "good" and "evil" had been blurred even more than elsewhere. There were very few people who had not compromised themselves during communist rule. Although the masses had hated the "party mafia," they had adapted to their rule by exploiting that rule to the best of their abilities. President Yeltsin and his advisors, almost all of them former Communist Party members, have stated that after the coup of August 1991, they knowingly made the decision "not to repeat the gruesome example of the Bolsheviks," and to exclude a purge of the security organs and the Soviet bureaucracy. They would not allow a "day of reckoning."[60] This was laid down in print in Yeltsin's November 1991 decree, by which he banned the Communist Party; in point two, it ordered all government and administrative institutions to prevent persecution (*iskliuchit presledovanie*) of citizens for the mere fact that they were Communist Party members.[61] But was such persecution likely? Is Yeltsin to be credited for preventing it?

John Morrison was quite correct when he asked the rhetorical question whether nobody in Russia was guilty for having propped up the old system. He referred to a "middle-aged Russian philosopher" who said that "the real loss is not fear but guilt. Everyone in Russia is suffering from a complex of innocence. Nobody wants to take responsibility for what has happened."[62] This innocence complex is in line with the historical tendency of Russians to see themselves as victims of wrongs inflicted upon their nation by foreigners, and to justify their conquests of foreign lands as a vindication of such wrongs.[63] Excuses were easily found. The expertise of the Soviet bureaucrats and administrators was vital. And in the end, of course, those who live in glass houses should not throw stones.

CONCLUSION

I simply believe that we shall not perish amid the debris of Utopia and empire (Grigorii Pomerants, philosopher and former dissident, 1992)[1]

We wanted to have everything, and immediately. We got . . . the exact opposite. (Sergei Baburin and three other deputies, November 1992)[2]

On 14 December 1992, addressing foreign ministers assembled in Stockholm for a meeting of the Conference on Security and Cooperation in Europe, Andrei Kozyrev created a shock wave that reached the farthest corners of the world and came to be known as his "wake-up slap." The basic conception of Russian foreign policy had been changed, Kozyrev said. Russia demanded that NATO stop trying to strengthen its military presence in the Baltic states and CIS countries, and its interference in the internal affairs of Bosnia and Yugoslavia. "If not," he added, "we reserve the right to take the necessary unilateral steps to defend our interests. . . . In its struggle, the current government of Serbia can count on the support of great Russia."[3]

Further, Kozyrev said, the norms of CSCE agreements did not fully apply on the territory of the former Soviet Union. In its "postimperial expanse," Russia was "to assert its interests using all available means, including military and economic. We will insist that the former republics of the USSR enter into a new federation or confederation without delay. . . ." And all those who thought that Russia would follow the fate of the Soviet Union, he warned, should not forget that Russia was a state capable of standing up for itself and its friends. A deathly silence descended upon the ministers of foreign affairs. American secretary of state Larry Eagleburger turned pale and left the hall.

After half an hour of alarm and confusion, Kozyrev explained that his speech had been a hoax. The text he had read had been a compilation of the demands of "not even the most extreme opposition in Russia" and had been meant as a trick to alert the international community to the danger of their taking over foreign policy.

One year later, Kozyrev's nightmare had materialized, and he was in fact the executor of precisely the policy that he had cautioned against in the past. At the end of 1993 Russia regained its foreign policy confidence in claiming to be a great power. It declared the "geopolitical space" of the USSR its sphere of influence, to be policed by Russia alone. It rejoiced at, and stimulated, the reintegration tendencies that were clearly visible in some of the other states of the CIS—they had discovered that they could not live without Russia after all. It vetoed the accession of Central European states to NATO. In February 1994 it claimed its first major diplomatic success, stating that Russia had effectively prevented NATO air attacks on Bosnian-Serbian artillery in the hills around Sarajevo by prevailing upon their Serbian blood brothers to retreat. Euphoria gripped Russian policy makers, who felt that they had rediscovered their self-confidence. With the United States, Russia started defining its sphere of influence in the Balkans and splitting up Bosnia in the process. Yeltsin's new security advisor Yurii Baturin gave a cynical summary:

> The U.S. considers Russia to be a developing country. In an economic sense that may be true. But in the past we were no trendsetter on the world market either, and yet we were seen as a great power. Why? Because all feared this country packed with nuclear weapons and an enormous army. Now the West fears that in the chaos of collapse there will be an explosion that will affect Europe or other parts of the world. Based on this criterion, therefore, we remain a great power.[4]

Russia is to be addressed in terms of "Thou," said Yeltsin, not on a first-name basis. If Russian self-assurance can only be based on a sense of being feared by the rest of the world, there is indeed good reason for renewed self-confidence. The threat of uncontrolled trade in arms, nuclear accidents and environmental disasters spilling over Russia's borders, mass migrations of biblical proportions, the criminalization of states, nuclear or other blackmail by robber barons and robber states, Russian interference in neighbor states and the instability this might cause—

these cumulative dangers pose frightening prospects for the countries of Central Europe, NATO, and Asia. Russian ambitions in the "growth industry" of peacekeeping operations in the CIS countries capitalize on Western fears by a casual attitude as to the conditions of peacekeeping, an attitude that favors Russian expansionist interests.[5]

In August 1992, Konstantin Eggert, commenting on parliamentary recommendations for Russian foreign policy, had said that the Supreme Soviet's expectation that the international community would voluntarily grant "Moscow" the exclusive task of "Eurasian gendarme" was "ludicrous" because such a role would result in wars that would mean the end of the democratic development of Russia itself.[6] He failed to see at the time that this Russian pacification doctrine was in for a favourable reception among both the embattled Russians and Western diplomats frustrated by their failed attempts to bring order to the Yugoslav chaos and impressed by the new instability in the remnants of the USSR. Over the years, Vladimir Zhirinovskii and other nationalists had expressed the same idea in less diplomatic terms, more appealing to the wounded Russians. Zhirinovskii had promised that if elected president, he would "start by squeezing the Baltics and other small nations" by contaminating their populations with radioactive waste, and stop only "when they either die out or get down on their knees."[7] The attractiveness of the "Russian gendarme" concept was boosted by the Western countries' unwillingness to counter Serbian policy in Bosnia-Hercegowina in such a way that Serbian (and Russian) leaders would get the message that there were limits to the West's tolerance of aggression and genocide. The failure of Western policy in the Yugoslav crisis told Russian nationalists that the West was not prepared to get involved in the problems of the East, and that Western governments might indeed feel relieved if and when Russia would take on the role of gendarme in its "own geopolitical space."

The return of hegemonic ambitions to the center of the Russian political stage was also stimulated by the often uncritical attitude of Western leaders toward the Russian president. Their reaction to his dissolution of parliament in September 1993 was ill considered, to say the least. In their fear of the possible alternative for Yeltsin's rule they put all their bets on Yeltsin. They tended to forget that Yeltsin would not last forever and that in fact his days might soon be over. Then what? That question was too difficult and too threatening for politicians in Western countries. In their support for the Russian president they tended to borrow his biased analysis of the political situation in Russia, and thereby to throw dust in their very own eyes. Shortly after the Moscow White House had been smoked out on 4 October 1993, British prime minister Major went as far as to say that "Yeltsin deserves our *uncritical* support."[8] It was small wonder that he was shocked when the results of the December elections came in.

After the loss of empire, the deeply felt need of many Russian rulers to be feared is an intervening complication in redefining their nationhood. The unsavory blend of emotions raises the question of the wisdom of Western help as long as the Russians have not resolved their contradictory attitudes and continue blaming their predicament on outsiders while at the same time feeling wronged because of insufficient help by the same outsiders. The events of 1990–1993 have resulted in a situation where a simpleminded split between "Western-oriented democrats" content with the Russian Federation in its present borders and "neo-Slavofile/Panslavist expansionists" is harmful to our understanding of the link between domestic and foreign policy. The Western-oriented tendency among Russian policy makers has had to incorporate some of the ideas and demands of the neo-Slavofiles. The urge to recreate some sort of empire in the "geopolitical space" of what once was the Soviet Union is manifest in almost all shades of the Russian political spectrum. The question now is whether the Western powers are well advised to support these forces.

Since early 1992, Western states and international financial organizations have pledged substantial amounts of economic assistance and support. Western assistance was asked by the Russian government as part of a tacit deal in which Russia agreed to promote the transformation to a capitalist market economy (promising Western producers a new market) and to behave loyally to Western concerns in the international arena, particularly in the UN Security Council. In more diplomatic terms, it was stated by Western and Russian leaders that "the democratic and economic reforms under way in the Russian Federation are of tremendous significance not only for the people of Russia but also for the entire world," for the Russian Federation's successful transition to a market economy and its "smooth integration into the democratic international community are indispensable factors for increasing stability in the world and making the process of forming a new international order irreversible."[9]

Some in the West, however, doubted the wisdom of providing aid to Russia on a massive scale. It was argued that the Russian economy, being in an extremely sorry state, could not possibly absorb the amounts of aid that were intended; most of the money provided by taxpayers in the West would go down the drain the way it had in the past in many Third

World countries. Why provide Russia with 1.5 billion dollars in support, as the G-7 pledged in 1994, if that amount equaled the amount of capital flight from Russia *per month?* Why the absurdity of Western countries providing Russia with one-twelfth of the amount of money that Russian carpetbaggers were withholding from their own economy?

In evaluating this argument, we could treat Russia as if it were the loser of a major war like World War II. Of course, Russia in 1992 differed in many respects from Germany, Italy, or Japan in 1945—I will return to the differences later. But there were similarities as well. Russia *had* lost a war—the Cold War—and it had lost much of its empire in the process. Its leadership and part of its population suffered a crushing psychological defeat, comparable to that of a war lost. Russia's economic and social infrastructure was not destroyed by wartime hostilities, but with the exception of military industry the economic infrastructure was in an extremely poor state due to long neglect. Could the assistance provided by the West make a difference in the reconstruction of the country? It is helpful to consult empirical evidence.

In a quantitative study of the costs of major wars and the power redistribution resulting from such wars, A.F.K. Organski and Jacek Kugler found in 1977 that countries that took an active part in, and subsequently lost World War II, recovered in a surprisingly short span of time, that is, within twenty years. They named this the "Phoenix Factor." Of more significance to our subject is their finding that this kind of recovery was not related to the help provided by the war's winners; in their words: "losers do not rise from the ashes because winners pick them up and help them to their feet."[10] Comparing the amounts of aid (in totals and per capita) given by the United States annually between 1948 and 1961 with the relative growth rates of the recipient economies, they found that growth and foreign aid were

> almost wholly independent of each other. Such relationship as may exist is negative: the countries that received most of the aid for the longest period performed worst. The United Kingdom received much more aid on a total and per capita basis than France; France received much more than Italy; Italy much more than Germany; and Germany much more than Japan. Yet it was Japan that enjoyed the more rapid rate of recovery, followed by Germany, Italy, and France, with the United Kingdom bringing up the rear.[11]

Organski and Kugler concluded that for recovery from war, foreign aid is not very effective and that the forces that are really important for recovery "lie within the devastated nations themselves."

If Japan and Germany were the quickest to recover (with the least assistance in quantitative terms), this may have something to do with their history and culture, or with the fact that both the introduction of democracy and the reconstruction of the economy were guided by the occupying powers ("démocratie octroyé"), or with both. In both countries, the "traumatic period" lasted only about ten years, from the mid-1930s to 1945, and after that period the population could in no way "sit back and relax" from the strains of the wartime period. In Russia, however, the traumatic period lasted much longer, and its most important quality was the holding back of the "translation" of deep social changes to political and public life. When by the early 1990s Russia's new professionals could finally throw off their communist straightjacket, they had to begin building what had existed in Germany and Japan long before World War II.

Should we conclude from this that Western economic assistance is of no use, and that our politicians are wasting our tax money by spending so much of it on Russia and other East European states? In order to answer this question, due consideration should be given to the special circumstances of Russia and to the many different forms of economic aid. Not all of them need be equally wasteful. Moreover, the question should not be considered on economic-financial terms exclusively. It may be so that even economic assistance that does not contribute to economic recovery in statistical terms still has great psychological value. Such assistance— and the political leverage it provides to proponents of democracy in and outside Russia—may help prevent relapses into authoritarian rule. To the populations suffering an inevitable drop in well-being, assistance is a signal of solidarity from the affluent West and may thus boost their energies.

Both Whitehead and Hadenius have found that in Third World countries, the importance of American manipulation of trade and aid relationships should not be underestimated; they have been a stimulus for democratization in the Third World, even though the United States has occasionally promoted undemocratic regimes out of anticommunist motives. Statistical analysis of an abundance of data showed Hadenius that by means of its trade relations, the United States has "exerted an important influence on political institutions overseas."[12] Obviously, the G-7 countries are hoping for this effect in their selective use of aid and trade for the promotion of democracy in Central and Eastern Europe.

Some policy advisers in the United States and Western Europe argue for a strong policy aimed at promoting the spread of democracy by way of the adoption of an international guarantee clause for the maintenance of constitutional democracy that would authorize international intervention in countries where democracy is in danger.[13] They seem to be swimming against a strong tide, for behind the 1990 crest of Huntington's "third wave of democratization" lies a yawning trough. The problem of this "reverse wave" is not so much the political "revenge" of the ex-communists in several Central European states and in Lithuania, Russia, Belarus, and Ukraine, where in 1992–1993 they scored resounding electoral victories. In spite of their return to power, most of the political elites in these countries may very well remain committed to the rules of democracy. But the question is whether they will be able to live up to that commitment in the face of the onslaught of increasing instability and the struggle over scarce resources caused by poverty, crime, and environmental degradation. Increasingly, and too soon after the euphoria of 1989–1990, the forces of reason and moderation are being cornered by destitute and angry mobs, led by populist demagogues. There seems to be no escape from "normal politics" getting infected by their aggressive bugs. The "new ways of life" that Ken Jowitt saw as possibly resulting from the "Genesis situation" of 1990 may yet come about.

Nevertheless, the Zhirinovskii scare of late 1993 and early 1994 should not cause us to close our eyes to the institutionalization of democratic procedure in present-day Russia. The criminalization of the state in Russia is sometimes compared to the "democracy" of Chicago politics in the 1920s and 1930s, "with Al Capone having access to nuclear weapons."[14] The instability caused by social stress invites comparisons with Weimar Germany; the corruptness of Russian rulers and their ties with organized crime are not unlike those of the Italian Christian-Democrat (and Socialist) *nomenklatura* in recent decades. But in taking stock of the interim results of Russia's continuing transition, we should avoid easy comparisons and look at the facts.

A brittle and battered democracy is crawling out from under the rubble of the Soviet system. There is a new constitution, more democratic and consistent than the previous one in spite of the wide powers that it grants the president. The power of the soviets has been broken, and there is a new parliament coming to grips with the rules of democratic procedure. A new relationship between the Federal Assembly and the government is being built. New local and regional councils have been elected. Free and fair elections, which had been suppressed for no less than seventy years, are making a comeback—accompanied by reports of electoral fraud. In the economy as well as in society and politics, private initiative is stimulated. The significance of these processes for the establishment of democracy is not to be disparaged. At the same time, results by way of democratization having reached a "point of no return" are not to be expected before the next century. During the late 1980s and the early 1990s, Mikhail Gorbachev repeatedly claimed that *perestroika* had *now* finally become irreversible; but he never intended his policy to end the way it did. Later, Boris Yeltsin claimed over and over that the worst was finally over—just a few times too many. There is more to come. In their expectations of the pace of democratization in Russia, both they and some Russian and Western observers have exhibited an unrealistic lack of patience. If for Japan and Germany twenty years was a short span of time for recovery, how could one expect such recovery in Russia in an even shorter time period?

There is a lot that democracy *cannot* do for Russia. It cannot in itself bring prosperity. It does not guarantee that each individual or group interest will be satisfied by public policy, or even that the give-and-take between conflicting interests will be fair and equitable to all. It cannot be considered incompatible with the concentration of economic power in the hands of a small elite, many of whom have gathered their riches in dishonest ways. It cannot provide a guarantee against extremism and instability; it cannot turn chauvinists into tolerant cosmopolitans. The new politics of Russia is heavily mortgaged by conceptions from the Soviet past that tend to make Russian democracy into a very specific type. Both in the new Constitution and in the minds of the president and the new elites, the attitude toward civil society and the role of political parties is harmful to the development of a strong society and a strong government. The slow and painful process by which Russia's citizens learn these lessons is inescapable on penalty of renewed tyranny. All of this may seem self-evident, but in the context of the fluctuating Russian expectations of democracy, it is worth repeating: democracy is not the cure-all for social ills; it is merely a way of governing with the maximum realistically possible participation of those who are affected by public policy.

The democratization of Russia may experience relapses and decelerations. But it is a transition all the same, and in spite of Tsipko's conviction expressed at the head of chapter 1, knowledge of transitions in other parts of the world does help us understand Russia's specific pain. Transitory processes are different in all countries, and theorizing (and generalizing) about them does not imply that there are "general regularities" (Tsipko) or one single "transition model" which individual countries should "fit."

It is not at all easy to find an explanation for the tragicomedy of Russia's "exit from Utopia." In Russia, the problems of transition are more complex than elsewhere in the world. Part of the reason is that the transition concurs with decolonization, the "double rejective revolution" to which both Holmes and Motyl have referred. But there is more to it than the mere synchronism of two independent developments; the two processes have been interrelated. The forces of nationalism, unleashed by Gorbachev's early attempts at limited democratization, turned into an independent force driving transition along while at the same time putting obstacles on the road to democracy. This seems to be an essential part of the explanation. But where is the rest? It is too easy to project Russian history onto the present and future by stating that Russia was, is, and can only be ruled in an authoritarian way. Democratizing tendencies were clearly visible both at the start and at the end of the twentieth century. It is also too easy to put the exclusive blame on communism, for the traumas of communism are not insurmountable. Moreover, in spite of communist rule, democratic attitudes and ideas found a wide reception among educated professionals. Perhaps it is simply the social infantilism and victimization complex of the Russians that make their endeavors hopeless? But if so, what have they been caused by, and to what extent can these ills be changed? And is it justified to put all Russians in one box?

Perhaps we should ask who is interested in the consolidation of democracy. Some authors feel that such an interest is not a necessary condition for a transition to democracy, and that democracy can come about more or less "by default." But conceivably it would help to have a strong society and social groups with a stake in democratic rule and due process of law. If posed thus, we see Russia's shaky position. There are only the first beginnings of a new middle class. Society and the state are in danger of being swallowed by organized crime. Economic stabilization will take a long time, not to speak of recovery. In these circumstances, assessing the situation of Russia and its near future depends primarily on whether the person making that assessment is an optimist or a pessimist by nature. Pessimists will have no lack of arguments for doomsday scenarios. But the evidence against a smooth continuation of the Russian transition is so strong that the survival instinct impels one to resist the temptation of turning into a prophet of doom. It is therefore appropriate to finish with the last words spoken on 20 December 1990 by Edward Shevardnadze in his capacity of foreign minister of the USSR, just after he had angrily announced his resignation to the Congress of People's Deputies and had warned against an impending coup: "And still I believe, I believe that dictatorship won't make it, that the future is for democracy and for freedom."

CHRONOLOGY *1990–1994*

1990

20–21 JANUARY. Electoral candidates from over twenty cities agree to found Democratic Russia electoral alliance for RSFSR and local elections in March.

7 FEBRUARY. Central Committee of the CPSU accepts change of Articles 6 and 7 of the USSR Constitution that fixed its power monopoly.

4 MARCH. Election of deputies to the first RCPD and to lower soviets in the RSFSR.

11 MARCH. Newly elected Lithuanian parliament declares independence.

14 MARCH. UCPD amends Articles 6 and 7 of the Constitution, dropping constitutional power monopoly of the Communist Party and instituting a USSR presidency.

15 MARCH. Mikhail Gorbachev elected president of the USSR by the UCPD.

26 APRIL. USSR law on the delimitation of powers between the USSR and the subjects of the federation.

16 MAY. Opening of the first RCPD.

26–27 MAY. Founding congress of the Democratic Party of Russia elects Nikolai Travkin party chairman.

29 MAY. RCPD elects Boris Yeltsin chairman of the RSS with 535 votes for, 502 against (necessary for election: 531 votes).

4–5 JUNE. Yeltsin proposes RCPD to elect Ruslan Khasbulatov as first deputy chairman of RSS; Khasbulatov is elected (5 June) with 604 votes. In the days following, RCPD elects members of Supreme Soviet.

12 JUNE. RCPD adopts Declaration on State Sovereignty; USSR Federation Council discusses plans for new union treaty and sets up working group; Yeltsin and Gorbachev meet and agree to work together.

13 JUNE. First session of new RSFSR Supreme Soviet.

20–23 JUNE. Founding congress of the RSFSR Communist Party; the RCPD ends 22 June.

16 JULY. Ukrainian Supreme Soviet declares Ukraine a sovereign state; Leonid Kravchuk elected (23 July) chairman of Ukrainian Supreme Soviet.

2–31 AUGUST. Economic working group installed by Gorbachev and Yeltsin prepares "Five-hundred-days plan."

30 AUGUST. Tatar Supreme Soviet declares Tatarstan the sixteenth union republic of the USSR, and no longer part of the RSFSR.

2 SEPTEMBER. Dniester Moldavian Soviet Socialist (later: Dniester Moldavian) Republic proclaimed in Tiraspol, Moldova.

11 SEPTEMBER. Shatalin's "Five-hundred-days plan" approved in principle by RSS.

18–19 SEPTEMBER. Publication of Solzhenitsyn's article "How We Should Reconstruct Russia" in two newspapers.

24 SEPTEMBER. USS grants Gorbachev special powers until 31 March 1992, to implement economic reform by decree.

1–9 OCTOBER. RSFSR government postpones implementation of "Five-hundred-days" program until 1 November; RSS votes to begin transition on that day.

11 OCTOBER. RSS confirms appointment of Andrei Kozyrev as RSFSR Minister of Foreign Affairs; Kozyrev proceeds to formulate new Russian foreign policy.

19 OCTOBER. USS approves Gorbachev's "Presidential Plan" for economic reform; RSS's Council of Nationalities discusses (eighth) draft federal treaty for the RSFSR.

20–21 OCTOBER. Founding congress of Democratic Russia.

12 NOVEMBER. RSFSR Constitutional Commission approves draft of a new RSFSR Constitution.

19 NOVEMBER. Yeltsin and Kravchuk sign RSFSR-Ukrainian agreement, stressing it is between two sovereign and equal states.

24 NOVEMBER. Publication of first draft for a new USSR union treaty.

3 DECEMBER. RCPD allows limited private ownership of farm land. USS approves of draft USSR Union Treaty.

12–15 DECEMBER. RCPD amends the Constitution; instructs RSS to draft a law on the election of the RSFSR president; decides to set up republican security committee.

17 DECEMBER. Fourth session of UCPD opens in the absence of Lithuanian deputies, who consider the USSR a foreign state; Gorbachev calls for a referendum on the future of the USSR.

20 DECEMBER. Edward Shevardnadze resigns as USSR minister of foreign affairs, out of frustration over lack of support from Gorbachev; warns of impending coup.

26 DECEMBER. Nikolai Ryzhkov retires as USSR prime minister.

1991

10–20 JANUARY. Baltic crisis. Gorbachev threatens Lithuanian parliament with presidential rule; attempt at Soviet coup in Lithuania and Latvia. Valentin Pavlov appointed (14 January) chairman of the USSR Cabinet of Ministers.

17 MARCH. Referendum on the future of the USSR and (in the RSFSR) on the creation of the presidency and (in Moscow) a directly elected mayor.

23 APRIL. In Novo-Ogarevo, Soviet president Gorbachev and the heads of state of nine Soviet republics sign a joint statement on speeding up a new union agreement.

24 APRIL. Laws on the president of the RSFSR and on presidential elections in the RSFSR enacted by parliament.

12 JUNE. Boris Yeltsin elected president of the RSFSR in Russia's first democratic presidential elections ever. He receives 57.3 percent of the vote with a turnout of over 74 percent; the other contenders: Ryzhkov (16.9 percent), Zhirinovskii (8 percent), Tuleev (6 percent), Makashov (4 percent), and Bakatin (3 percent). Gavriil Popov (with running mate Yurii Luzhkov) elected mayor of Moscow with 65.3 percent of the vote.

17–21 JUNE. USSR Cabinet ministers, led by Valentin Pavlov, try to wrestle power from President Gorbachev.

18–20 JUNE. President-elect Yeltsin visits U.S. and has talks with President George Bush.

10 JULY. Boris Yeltsin sworn in as president of the RSFSR.

18–21 AUGUST. Coup attempt by the "State Committee for the State of Emergency"; Gorbachev is "saved" by Boris Yeltsin.

20 AUGUST–22 SEPTEMBER. Estonia, Latvia, Ukraine, Belarus, Moldova, Georgia, Azerbaijan, Kyrgyzstan, Uzbekistan, Tajikistan, and Armenia declare independence; only the Baltic states (Lithuania had declared independence on 11 March 1990) acquire international recognition.

23 AUGUST–5 SEPTEMBER. President Yeltsin orders the Communist Party of the Soviet Union to suspend its activities on the territory of the RSFSR. The Central Committee building at Staraia Ploshchad is sealed up (22 August). The Russian national flag flies on the Kremlin, next to the Soviet flag. Gorbachev resigns (24 August) as general secretary of the CPSU and advises its Central Committee to dissolve itself. The USS orders the CPSU to cease its activities (29 August) and the fifth (extraordinary) meeting of the UCPD agrees to the dissolution of the USSR (5 September).

18 OCTOBER. Treaty on an economic community signed by President Gorbachev and representatives of eight republics; Azerbaijan, Georgia, Moldova, and Ukraine withhold signatures.

28 OCTOBER. RCPD elects Ruslan Khasbulatov chairman of the RSS.

6 NOVEMBER. President Yeltsin bans the activities of the CPSU and the Russian Communist Party on the territory of the RSFSR.

9–10 NOVEMBER. Second congress of Democratic Russia.

1 DECEMBER. In a referendum, the Ukrainian population confirms Ukrainian independence.

8 DECEMBER. In Minsk, the presidents and prime ministers of the Russian Federation, Ukraine, and Belarus declare the USSR dissolved and found a Commonwealth of Independent States.

17 DECEMBER. Yeltsin and Gorbachev agree that by 1 January 1992 the USSR will no longer exist.

25 DECEMBER. USSR president Gorbachev resigns.

27 DECEMBER. Boris Yeltsin occupies Gorbachev's office in the Kremlin.

1992

WINTER–SPRING. Yeltsin and Gaidar make a start with economic reform; prices soar and galloping inflation is the result. Conflicts between Russia and Ukraine erupt over control over nuclear arms, the Black Sea Fleet, the status of Crimea and various other military matters; conflict between Russia and Moldova over the Fourteenth Army in Dniester Moldavian Republic; conflict between the president of the Russian Federation, his vice president, and the RCPD.

13–31 MARCH. President Yeltsin and representatives of all territorial and national regions of the RF except Tatarstan and Checheno-Ingushetia sign federation treaties on dilimitation of powers between the federal center and the regions.

20 MARCH. In Kiev, heads of state of ten of the eleven CIS member states sign an agreement on "Groups of military observers and collective peacekeeping forces in the CIS": Armenia, Belarus, Kazakhstan, Kyrgyzstan, Moldova, RF, Tajikistan, Uzbekistan, and (conditionally) Azerbaijan and Ukraine.

6–21 APRIL. Sixth session of the RCPD changes the RF Constitution (21 April).

7 MAY. President Yeltsin decrees the creation of the armed forces of the Russian Federation and appoints himself commander-in-chief.

15 MAY. In Tashkent the heads of state of six CIS member states sign a collective security treaty: Armenia, Kazakhstan, Kyrgyzstan, RF, Tajikistan, and Uzbekistan.

20 MAY. First session of the RF Security Council.

23 MAY. Foreign ministers of U.S. and four CIS nuclear weapons states sign "Lisbon Protocol" to the START-1 treaty.

JUNE. Popularly elected Moscow mayor Popov resigns. War in Dniester Moldavian Republic.

21 JUNE. Democratic Party of Russia (DPR, Travkin), People's Party of Free Russia (NPSR, Rutskoi), Russian Union of Industrialists and Entrepreneurs (RSPP, Volskii), parliamentary fraction "Smena" and twelve smaller organizations form the centrist Civic Union (Grazhdanskii Soiuz) alliance.

6 JULY. Constitutional Court begins proceedings in CPSU case.

7 JULY. Ceasefire in Dniester Moldavian Republic.

21 JULY. President Yeltsin signs the "Protocol on temporary procedures for the formation and functioning of groups of military observers and collective peacekeeping troups." Other signatories of the 20 March agreement follow. On 14 and 29 July, peacekeeping forces arrive in South Ossetia and the Dniester Moldavian Republic.

9 SEPTEMBER. After a meeting of the Russian Security Council, President Yeltsin cancels his visit to Japan and South Korea, planned for 13–16 September, citing "domestic problems."

8 OCTOBER. Yeltsin decrees the creation of an Interdepartmental Commission for Fighting Crime and Corruption, to be headed by Vice President Rutskoi.

16 OCTOBER. The newspaper *Izvestia* reports on a private security company said to be controlled by parliamentary chairman Khasbulatov. The company is said to guard seventy government buildings. President Yeltsin suggests to postpone the next session of the RCPD from 1 December to the spring of 1993; four high government officials sound the alarm for a "constitutional coup."

29–30 NOVEMBER. Founding congress of Democratic Choice alliance.

30 NOVEMBER. Constitutional Court ends proceedings in CPSU case.

1–14 DECEMBER. Tumultuous seventh session of the RCPD. On the initiative of Constitutional Court chairman Zorkin, Yeltsin and Khasbulatov on 12 December reach a compromise: the basic principles of a new Constitution will be the subject of a nationwide referendum, to take place on 11 April 1993. The constitutional changes, adopted by the RCPD on 9–10 December and unacceptable to Yeltsin, will enter into force only after the referendum. In consultation with the Congress, Yeltsin will appoint a new prime minister; on 14 December, president and parliament agree on the centrist Victor Chernomyrdin for the post.

19–20 DECEMBER. Third congress of Democratic Russia.

21 DECEMBER. At a meeting with representatives of the CIS states, Marshal Shaposhnikov says that the collective security treaty and the agreement on peacekeeping forces are not yet operative.

1993

9 FEBRUARY. Under pressure from Constitutional Court chairman Zorkin, parliamentary speaker Khasbulatov, and the leaders of republics and provinces, President Yeltsin declares it will be better not to have a referendum in April.

10–13 MARCH. Extraordinary session of the RCPD is to decide on constitutional impasse; on 12 March, it annuls 11 April referendum and limits the powers of the president. In a deal between the RCPD, Constitutional Court chairman Zorkin, and Prime Minister Chernomyrdin, parliament can now suspend presidential decrees and nullify them upon a conclusion by the Constitutional Court. Chernomyrdin's government can introduce draft laws independent of the president. President Yeltsin angrily leaves the meeting on 12 March, saying that he will not return in this Congress. Chernomyrdin expresses his thanks to the Congress for its trust in him.

20 MARCH. In a televised address, Yeltsin announces a "special regime of government" and a "vote of confidence" to take place on 25 April.

24 MARCH. Yeltsin decree of 20 March published, its text changed.

26–29 MARCH. Ninth session of the RCPD; motion to impeach Yeltsin voted down.

25 APRIL. In a nationwide referendum, the public is asked to express its confidence in either President Yeltsin and his team or in parliament. A majority of 53 to 58 percent of the voters express their confidence in Yeltsin and his economic policy.

MAY. Parliament's Constitutional Commission rejects President Yeltsin's constitutional draft; so do the chairmen of eleven republican parliaments. Yeltsin decrees that the draft Constitution is to be ready by 10 June and calls for the convening of a constitutional assembly. Continuing disputes on the contents and procedure for adoption of the Constitution. Yeltsin suggests three alternatives for adopting the Constitution: a constituent assembly, a referendum, or adoption by a newly elected parliament.

5 JUNE. Constitutional Conference (Konstitutsionnoe Soveshchanie) starts its work with about seven hundred members, representing all subjects of the federation and the most important forces of the country. Its tasks are to prepare and agree on a text for a new Constitution and to propose a procedure for its adoption.

15 JUNE. Marshal Shaposhnikov accepts appointment as secretary of the RF Security Council.

17 JUNE. Yeltsin and Ukrainian president Kravchuk sign agreement on division of Black Sea Fleet.

26 JUNE. Deputies in the Supreme Soviet call on their colleagues to support a no-confidence motion on Chairman Khasbulatov; by early July, eighty deputies have supported the call.

1 JULY. Fifty-seven percent of small businesses have been privatized.

3 JULY. Political movement "Russia's Choice," led by Yegor Gaidar, starts preparations for possible early parliamentary elections.

JULY–AUGUST. Several regions of the Russian Federation move unilaterally to adopt the status of republic; some of the republics have ceased to transfer tax money to Moscow.

9 JULY. RSS decides to award city and environs of Sebastopol (Crimea, Ukraine) Russian federal status; strong condemnations by Russian president, foreign ministry, and Ukrainian authorities. Cheliabinsk provincial soviet decides to start process for becoming Republic of Southern Urals.

12 JULY. Constitutional Conference accepts text of draft Constitution, 433 votes (74 percent) for, 62 (10.6 percent) against, 63 (10.7 percent) abstaining.

16 JULY. RSS resolution on the procedure for the adoption of a new Constitution.

20 JULY. UN Security Council adopts by consensus a statement by its president in which it expresses "deep concern" over the Russian parliament's decision on Sebastopol, condemning it as "incompatible" with the 1990 Ukraine-Russian treaty.

23 JULY. RSS allows General Prosecutor Stepankov to start criminal proceedings against First Deputy Prime Minister Shumeiko.

24 JULY. Conflict between the Central Bank of Russia, the president, Finance Minister Boris Fedorov, and parliament when CBR and Council of Ministers (excluding Fedorov and Shakhrai) invalidate all pre-1993 ruble notes and announce scheme for citizens to exchange old notes for new (to maximum of 35,000) within two weeks. On 26 July, Yeltsin by decree softens the measure; Fedorov, Vice President Rutskoi, and parliament protest it. The measure is partly motivated by trying to force other CIS states that use the ruble to choose for or against it. On 27 July, CBR deputy head Khandurev says that intergovernmental and interbank agreements must be signed between Russia and those states that want to remain in the ruble zone; such agreements must provide for the opportunity for the national banks of these states to reject "a number of functions in monetary and credit policy" and their transfer to the CBR.

27 JULY. President Yeltsin fires Security Minister Victor Barannikov.

AUGUST. Vice prime ministers of Belarus, Russia, and Ukraine continue talks on economic integration of three states—an economic community; legislative war between president and parliament on furthering privatization.

10 AUGUST. Marshal Shaposhnikov resigns from post of secretary of Security Council.

13 AUGUST. Council of the Heads of Russian Republics and representatives of regional associations approve in Petrozavodsk the draft of the principles of legislation to implement the federative treaties. Yeltsin vows that he will not allow the Russian state to fall apart.

18–24 AUGUST. Vice President Rutskoi implicated in corruption by the president's Anti-Crime and Corruption Committee.

1 SEPTEMBER. By decree, President Yeltsin suspends both First Deputy Prime Minister Vladimir Shumeiko and Vice President Alexander Rutskoi from office, pending corruption charges. On 7 September, Rutskoi is denied entry to his office. President Yeltsin visits army units in a bid for their support.

3 SEPTEMBER. RSS suspends President Yeltsin's decree of 1 September on the suspension of Shumeiko and Rutskoi. Moscow's Public Prosecutor's office finds corruption accusations against Rutskoi justified. Yeltsin and Ukrainian president Kravchuk agree to a deal in which the Ukrainian half of the Black Sea Fleet will be ceded to Russia in exchange for settlement of Ukraine's two-billion dollar debt for energy supplies from Russia; and Ukrainian nuclear warheads (not the rockets) will go to Russia in exchange for uranium for Ukraine's nuclear power plants. The Ukrainian parliament is furious; leaders announce it will not ratify the agreement.

17 SEPTEMBER. President Yeltsin visits internal security troops division in the Moscow area. Vice President Rutskoi and parliamentary speaker Khasbulatov warn on 17–18 September that direct presidential rule and dictatorship by Yeltsin are at hand.

18 SEPTEMBER. Yegor Gaidar appointed first deputy prime minister, replacing Oleg Lobov; Lobov appointed secretary of the Security Council. Nikolai Golushko appointed security minister, replacing Barannikov (fired 27 July).

20 SEPTEMBER. Parliament of Azerbaijan decides to accede to CIS.

21 SEPTEMBER. Yeltsin decrees breakup of parliament and election of new State Duma for 11–12 December. In the meantime, all government bodies, including the Central Bank, will be under direct Cabinet and presidential control. The consultative Council

of the Federation (regional leaders) will temporarily act as a Federal Assembly. After Yeltsin's televised address, parliament goes into emergency session, declaring that by his move, Yeltsin has on the basis of Articles 121-6 and 121-11 of the Constitution lost his powers as president; the Constitutional Court finds Yeltsin's decree unconstitutional in a nine to four ruling. Alexander Rutskoi takes oath as "new" president at 00:25 on 22 September. RSS votes to dismiss Ministers Grachev (Defense) and Golushko (Security) and to appoint general Vladislav Achalov (Defense) and Victor Barannikov (Security).

23 SEPTEMBER. Yeltsin decrees early presidential elections for 12 June 1994.

24–28 SEPTEMBER. Parliament (about one hundred remaining legislators) and Alexander Rutskoi isolated in Belyi Dom, electricity and telephones cut off, and building surrounded by police. Periodic sessions of RCPD and RSS. Yeltsin announces visit to Japan for 12 October. Meeting of CIS states in Moscow and agreement among nine for economic union.

27 SEPTEMBER. Sukhumi in hands of Abkhaz forces while Georgian president Shevardnadze remains in the town. After armistice was reached in July under Russian mediation, Abkhaz forces resumed fighting in mid-September, while armed supporters of former president Zviad Gamsakhurdia stepped up their action in western Georgia. Later in the week Shevardnadze returns to Tbilisi, accusing Russia of helping Abkhaz forces take Sukhumi.

28 SEPTEMBER. Clashes between pro-parliament crowd and police; one militiaman killed.

29 SEPTEMBER. Ultimatum: Russian government demands that White House be vacated by 4 October. There are said to be over one thousand illegally armed supporters in the parliamentary building. Citizens in and around parliament must surrender their arms.

30 SEPTEMBER. Representatives of sixty-two regional units (fifty-six representing legislatures; of the republics, fifteen present, only five of whom represent their executives) meet in Moscow and demand lifting of the "siege" of the White House, and call for simultaneous parliamentary and presidential elections. In letters to the leaders of France, Germany, the U.S., and Britain, Yeltsin warns them against expanding NATO to admit former communist Central and Eastern European states. Instead, he proposes that NATO and the RF jointly guarantee the security of Eastern Europe.

1 OCTOBER. President changes number of Duma seats by decree to 450, fixes date of elections for 12 December only, and promulgates changed electoral Rules.

3 OCTOBER. Irregular armed groups and forces loyal to Rutskoi and Khasbulatov storm and try to take the building of Ostankino television and the Moscow mayor's office, incited to do so by Rutskoi speaking from the White House balcony. Yeltsin returns to Moscow from his country residence, and at 16:00 hours declares state of emergency in the city until 10 October, and calls in troops.

4 OCTOBER. Troops loyal to President Yeltsin take the White House. Rutskoi and Khasbulatov surrender at 18:00. Publication of *Pravda, Sovetskaia Rossiia, Den, Glasnost, Narodnaia Gazeta,* and other papers suspended by Russian Press and information minister; some editorial offices occupied. Press, radio, and television censorship instituted. National Salvation Front, Russian Communist Workers Party, Officers Union,

United Front of Russian Working People, "Shield," and other movements suspended by justice minister. Khasbulatov, Rutskoi, Barannikov, Dunaev, Achalov, Makashov, and some twenty-four other persons from the White House taken into custody to Lefortovo prison. Pockets of sniper resistance are put down by 20:00. Curfew imposed as of 23:00 hrs to 05:00 A.M. More than 125 reported dead in the disturbances of 3–4 October.

5 OCTOBER. President Yeltsin replaces Procurator-General Stepankov with Aleksei Kazannik.

6 OCTOBER. Chairman Zorkin of Constitutional Court resigns. President Yeltsin lifts press censorship and demands local and regional soviets to dissolve and be newly elected on December 12. Yeltsin removes honor guard at Lenin Mausoleum. Baltic states crack down on Communist Party organizations and on press as well.

7 OCTOBER. Funeral of 189 victims in Moscow. President Yeltsin decrees Moscow city soviet and city regional soviets disbanded. By decree, Yeltsin establishes temporary legislative order. In a sharp decree on the Constitutional Court, Yeltsin "establishes" that it cannot function now that a number of judges have declared that they refuse to take part in its sessions.

8 OCTOBER. Georgian president Shevardnadze announces that his country will become a member of the CIS in the hope of averting total destruction of the state.

9 OCTOBER. Yeltsin extends state of emergency in Moscow until 18 October.

11 OCTOBER. President Yeltsin decrees elections for the Federation Council of the Federal Assembly for 12 December. Upon departure for Tokyo, Yeltsin says he hopes that Japan will not touch on the Northern Territories issue.

13 OCTOBER. Yeltsin signs "Tokyo Declaration," implicitly reaffirming 1956 Joint Communiqué on Northern Territories issue, and returns to Moscow. General Albert Makashov charged for his part in the October 3 events.

15 OCTOBER. President Yeltsin signs decree for referendum on the draft Constitution, to be held on 12 December.

16–17 OCTOBER. Founding conventions of electoral bloc "Vybor Rossii" (Russia's Choice, Yegor Gaidar) and of PRES, the "Party of Russian Unity and Harmony" (Sergei Shakhrai).

17 OCTOBER. Russian navy tanker dumps nine hundred tons of liquid radioactive waste into the Sea of Japan, 550 kilometers west of Hokkaido.

18 OCTOBER. State of emergency lifted in Moscow.

19 OCTOBER. By decree, President Yeltsin bans a number of parties and movements from participation in the Federal Assembly elections.

20 OCTOBER. President Yeltsin changes the composition of the RF Security Council; its members are: Gaidar, Golushko, Grachev, Danilov-Danilan, Yerin, Kalmykov, Kozyrev, Nechaev, Primakov, Fedorov, and Shakhrai.

22 OCTOBER. Yeltsin decrees new elections for regional legislatures in all "subjects" of the federation except republics, between December 1993 and March 1994, and advises republics to reorganize their administrative organs as well.

23 OCTOBER. Georgian president Shevardnadze signs decree on Georgian entry into CIS; the CIS now consists of all former Soviet republics except Moldova and the three Baltic states.

26 OCTOBER. Yeltsin decrees elections for local councils (districts and towns) between December 1993 and June 1994 and advises authorities in the federation's "subjects" to reorganize local government in accordance with his Rules.

27 OCTOBER. Yeltsin signs decree on land ownership, removing sale and purchase restrictions.

28 OCTOBER. Sverdlovsk provincial soviet adopts constitution, thereby transforming the province into the "Ural Republic."

2 NOVEMBER. Basic outline of new Russian military doctrine approved by the RF Security Council; published 18 November in *Izvestia*.

6 NOVEMBER. President Yeltsin signs draft Constitution; changes electoral rules; says he will reconsider his decision of 23 September on early presidential elections planned for 12 June 1994.

26 NOVEMBER. President Yeltsin threatens to deny parties free television time if they criticize each other or the draft Constitution.

30 NOVEMBER. Allegations concerning the use of American tax money for the electoral campaign of "Vybor Rossii."

4–6 DECEMBER. Miners' strikes in Vorkuta and other regions; President Yeltsin raises the minimum monthly wage for government workers from 7,740 to 14,620 rubles.

12 DECEMBER. General elections and plebiscite.

1994

23 FEBRUARY. State Duma grants "amnesty" to imprisoned suspects of August 1991 coup and October 1993 events; they are released from prison on 26 February by Procurator-general Kazannik against Yeltsin's strict orders. Kazannik resigns.

24 FEBRUARY. Yeltsin presents "state of the nation" address to parliament.

28 APRIL. "Social Accord" Agreement signed.

27 MAY. Alexander Solzhenitsyn returns to Russia twenty years after he had been exiled. He had been invited to return in 1990. His first stop after leaving the U.S. is in Magadan.

12 JUNE. Presidential elections, decreed by Yeltsin on 23 September 1993, do not take place.

NOTES

INTRODUCTION

1   "Post-Communist Eastern Europe: A Survey of Opinion," 195.
2   *Izv*, 30 November 1992.
3   Yel'tsin, *Zapiski prezidenta*, 165.
4   O'Donnell and Schmitter, *Transitions from Authoritarian Rule: Tentative Conclusions*, 72.
5   Holmes uses the concept of "double rejective revolution" to characterize the two aspects of the legacy of communist rule; see Holmes, *The End of Communist Power*, xi. For a similar approach, see Motyl, *Dilemmas of Independence*.
6   See Löwenhardt, *Het Sovjetsyndroom*.
7   Jon Elster, in Greenberg et al., *Constitutionalism and Democracy*, 267–274.
8   See, for example, Holmes, *The End of Communist Power*, 308.
9   Michel Korzec, "Op weg naar de Tweede Koude Oorlog?" *Intermediair*, 12 November 1993. This fear was particularly strong among Central European observers. For a contrary view, see "Not So Big and Bad After All," *Newsweek*, 15 November 1993.
10 O'Donnell and Schmitter, *Transitions from Authoritarian Rule: Tentative Conclusions*, 65, 78 n. "Stern Principle" refers to Fritz Stern, who was the first to invoke the principle in its inverse sense in differentiating between the fall of the Weimar Republic and the advent of National Socialism.
11 Garton Ash quoted in Oriol Pi-Sungar, "The Spanish Route to Democracy: A Model for Eastern Europe in Transition?" in Hermine G. DeSoto and David G. Anderson, eds., *The Curtain Rises: Rethinking Culture, Ideology, and the State in Eastern Europe* (Atlantic Heights, N.J.: Humanities Press, 1992), 305. I am grateful to Sabrina Petra Ramet for this reference. Another deceiving voice was that of Leszek Kolakowski, who denounced "the army of Sovietologists who for years and years . . . kept repeating that the communist system was getting better and better every day," "tried to convince us that the system was becoming more

and more democratic, more and more pluralistic, and more and more rational with every passing night," and "kept explaining to us—until quite recently—that there were not the slightest symptoms of instability, let alone of crisis or disintegration, in the Soviet Union" (Leszek Kolakowski, "The Postrevolutionary Hangover," in Diamond and Plattner, *The Global Resurgence of Democracy,* 272. Marcin Krol of *Res Publica* in Warsaw spoke of "Sovietologists and other pseudo-scholars" in "Post-Communist Eastern Europe: A Survey of Opinion," 159. For a response to Shlapentokh's charges at the profession, see Joseph S. Berliner, "The Voice of American Sovietology," *NewsNet* (Newsletter of the AAASS) 34, no. 1 (January 1994): 11.

12   Talcott Parsons, "Communism and the West: The Sociology of the Conflict," in Amitai and Eva Etzioni, eds., *Social Change: Sources, Patterns, and Consequences* (New York: Basic Books, 1964), 397, as quoted by Gibson et al., "Democratic Values and Transformation of the Soviet Union," 361.

13   Andrei Amal'rik, *Prosushchestvuet-li Sovetskii Soiuz do 1984 goda?* (Amsterdam: Alexander Herzen Foundation, 1969). The manuscript found its way to the Netherlands through Professor Karel van het Reve and was subsequently published in many languages (American edition: New York: Harper, 1970). Andrei Amal'rik was born in 1938 and died in 1980 in a car accident in Spain.

14   For the actual predictions and references (excluding Yanov), see Ramet, *Social Currents in Eastern Europe,* chap. 1. In his book *The Russian New Right,* Alexander Yanov in 1978 predicted the overturn of communism to nationalism.

15   See Teresa Rakowska-Harmstone, "Ethnicity in the Soviet Union," *Annals of the American Academy of Political and Social Science,* no. 433 (1977): 73–87; Hélène Carrère d'Encausse, *L'Empire eclaté: La revolte des nations en URSS* (Paris, 1978); L. M. Drobizheva, *Dukhovnaia obshchnost' narodov SSSR: Istoriko-sotsiologicheskii ocherk mezhnatsional'nykh otnoshenii* (Moscow: Mysl', 1981); Victor Zaslavsky and Robert J. Brym, *Soviet-Jewish Emigration and Soviet Nationality Policy* (New York: St. Martin's Press, 1983); Rasma Karklins, *Ethnic Relations in the USSR: The Perspective from Below* (Boston: Allen and Unwin, 1986); by the same author, "Nationality Policy and Ethnic Relations in the USSR," in Millar, *Politics, Work, and Daily Life in the USSR* (Cambridge: Cambridge UP, 1987), 301–331; Gerhard Simon, *Nationalismus und Nationalitätenpolitik in der Sowjetunion* (Baden-Baden: Nomos, 1986).

1. TOWARD DEMOCRACY?

1   Alexander Tsipko, "Restavratsiia ili polnaia i okonchatel'naia sovetizatsiia?" 161.

2   Paul G. Lewis, "Democracy and its Future in Eastern Europe," in Held, *Prospects for Democracy,* 296.

3   The term is Leslie Holmes's, in *The End of Communist Power,* xi. See also Motyl, *Dilemmas of Independence.*

4   The discussion in this chapter excludes direct democracy where intermediates between citizens and government are absent.

5   John Miller, *Mikhail Gorbachev,* 203. On the rise of the professional middle class, see also Lewin, *The Gorbachev Phenomenon.*

6   Samuel P. Huntington, "Democracy's Third Wave," in Diamond and Plattner, *The*

Global Resurgence of Democracy, 3–25. On the underlying forces, see also Pye, "Political Science and the Crisis of Authoritarianism," 3–19.

7   David Held, "Democracy: From City-States to a Cosmopolitan Order?" in Held, *Prospects for Democracy*, 13.

8   Larry Diamond and Marc F. Plattner, "Introduction," in Diamond and Plattner, *The Global Resurgence of Democracy*, ix.

9   Of course, Stalin had used the same trick in 1936, but it had been aimed primarily at the outside world.

10 Ken Jowitt, "The New World Disorder," in Diamond and Plattner, *The Global Resurgence of Democracy*, 251.

11 O'Donnell and Schmitter, *Transitions from Authoritarian Rule: Tentative Conclusions*, 3.

12 Ibid., 6.

13 Ibid., 66.

14 Diamond et al., *Democracy in Developing Countries*.

15 Hadenius, *Democracy and Development*.

16 O'Donnell and Schmitter, *Transitions from Authoritarian Rule: Tentative Conclusions*, 6.

17 Adam Przeworski, "Some Problems in the Study of the Transition to Democracy," in O'Donnell et al., *Transitions from Authoritarian Rule: Comparative Perspectives*, 7.

18 On the role of discourse, particularly during the opening phase of the Gorbachev transition, see Urban, *More Power to the Soviets*.

19 O'Donnell and Schmitter, *Transitions from Authoritarian Rule: Tentative Conclusions*, 8.

20 See in particular John Miller, *Mikhail Gorbachev*, and Holmes, *The End of Communist Power*.

21 Giuseppe Di Palma, "Why Democracy Can Work in Eastern Europe," in Diamond and Plattner, *The Global Resurgence of Democracy*, 261.

22 Ibid., 262.

23 Ibid., 263.

24 Ibid., 264.

25 Ibid.

26 Ibid., 266.

27 Ibid., 267.

28 O'Donnell and Schmitter, *Transitions from Authoritarian Rule: Tentative Conclusions*, 72.

29 Philippe C. Schmitter and Terry Lynn Karl, "What Democracy Is . . . and Is Not," in Diamond and Plattner, *The Global Resurgence of Democracy*, 40.

30 See Hadenius, *Democracy and Development*, 61–62. In his empirical study, Hadenius ranked (on a scale of 0 to 10) 132 states in the Third World by their level of democracy in 1988 in an effort to find explanations for the differences.

31 Schmitter and Karl, "What Democracy Is . . . and Is Not," in Diamond and Plattner, *The Global Resurgence of Democracy*, 45.

32 Ibid., 43.

33 Larry Diamond, "Three Paradoxes of Democracy," in Diamond and Plattner, *The Global Resurgence of Democracy*, 97. Sabrina Ramet, however, believes that "no

society would freely say 'Let us be oppressed.'" See Ramet, *Social Currents in Eastern Europe*, chap. 1.

34 Huntington, "Democracy's Third Wave," in Diamond and Plattner, *The Global Resurgence of Democracy*, 10.

35 With thanks to Harry Rigby, from whom I borrowed the example. See Rigby, "Yeltsin's Presidency," 16–17.

36 Holmes, *The End of Communist Power*, 13–18.

37 Schmitter and Karl, "What Democracy Is . . . and Is Not," in Diamond and Plattner, *The Global Resurgence of Democracy*, 41.

38 Danilo Zolo, "Democratic Citizenship in a Post-communist Era," in Held, *Prospects for Democracy*, 259–260.

39 Diamond, "Three Paradoxes of Democracy," in Diamond and Plattner, *The Global Resurgence of Democracy*, 103.

40 O'Donnell and Schmitter, *Transitions from Authoritarian Rule: Tentative Conclusions*, 7–8.

41 See Zolo, "Democratic Citizenship in a Post-communist Era," in Held, *Prospects for Democracy*, 255.

42 Thus the conclusion of Hadenius from his statistical analysis of 132 countries in the Third World (Hadenius, *Democracy and Development*, 154).

43 In his study of the level of democracy in 132 Third World countries, Hadenius has indeed found "a strong association between political freedoms and capitalism" (Hadenius, *Democracy and Development*, 151).

44 Di Palma, "Why Democracy Can Work," in Diamond and Plattner, *The Global Resurgence of Democracy*, 265.

45 Elster, "The Necessity and Impossibility of Simultaneous Economic and Political Reform," in Greenberg et al., *Constitutionalism and Democracy*, 267–274.

46 Diamond, "Three Paradoxes of Democracy," in Diamond and Plattner, *The Global Resurgence of Democracy*, 106.

47 Julio Maria Sanguinetti, "Present at the Transition," in Diamond and Plattner, *The Global Resurgence of Democracy*, 55–56.

48 Di Palma, "Why Democracy Can Work," in Diamond and Plattner, *The Global Resurgence of Democracy*, 265.

49 O'Donnell and Schmitter, *Transitions from Authoritarian Rule: Tentative Conclusions*, 38.

50 Ibid.

51 Dankwart Rustow, "Transitions to Democracy: Towards a Dynamic Model," *Comparative Politics* 2, no. 3 (April 1970): 337–363, as referred to by O'Donnell and Schmitter, *Transitions from Authoritarian Rule: Tentative Conclusions*, 38.

52 O'Donnell and Schmitter, *Transitions from Authoritarian Rule: Tentative Conclusions*, 59.

53 Robert Axelrod, *The Evolution of Cooperation* (New York: Basic Books, 1984), as quoted in Breslauer, "The Roots of Polarization: A Comment," 228.

54 O'Donnell and Schmitter, *Transitions from Authoritarian Rule: Tentative Conclusions*, 69.

55 A slightly different version of this section was included in my "Institutional Choices in the Transition to Democracy," 1–24.

56 The articles were reproduced in Diamond and Plattner, *The Global Resurgence of Democracy*, 108–177.

57   The exceptions being France, Ireland, Japan, and Switzerland (Lijphart, "Constitutional Choices for New Democracies," in Diamond and Plattner, *The Global Resurgence of Democracy*, 149).

58   The point was made in 1959 by Douglas Verney, in *The Analysis of Political Systems*; see Lijphart, "Constitutional Choices for New Democracies," in Diamond and Plattner, *The Global Resurgence of Democracy*, 149.

59   Juan Linz being the most outspoken opponent; see his contributions in Diamond and Plattner, *The Global Resurgence of Democracy*, 108–126 and 138–145.

60   Ibid., 118.

61   Ibid., 144.

62   W. Arthur Lewis, *Politics in West Africa* (London: Allen and Unwin, 1965), 71, as quoted by Lijphart, "Constitutional Choices for New Democracies," in Diamond and Plattner, *The Global Resurgence of Democracy*, 175–176.

63   Quoted by Lijphart, "Constitutional Choices for New Democracies," in Diamond and Plattner, *The Global Resurgence of Democracy*, 147.

64   Ibid., 177.

65   Donald Horowitz, in Diamond and Plattner, *The Global Resurgence of Democracy*, 130–131.

66   The fourteen countries he selected are: nine parliamentary-PR (Austria, Belgium, Denmark, Finland, Germany, Italy, the Netherlands, Norway, and Sweden), four parliamentary-plurality (Australia, Canada, New Zealand, and the United Kingdom), and one presidential-plurality (United States). See Lijphart, "Constitutional Choices for New Democracies," in Diamond and Plattner, *The Global Resurgence of Democracy*, 150–157.

67   Quentin L. Quade, in Diamond and Plattner, *The Global Resurgence of Democracy*, 168.

68   Seymour Martin Lipset, in Diamond and Plattner, *The Global Resurgence of Democracy*, 137.

69   Cappelli, "The Short Parliament 1989–91," 112.

70   Pye, "Political Science and the Crisis of Authoritarianism," 3–19.

71   O'Donnell and Schmitter, *Transitions from Authoritarian Rule: Tentative Conclusions*, 68.

72   For an encyclopedic treatise on constitutions, see Walter F. Murphy, "Constitutions, Constitutionalism, and Democracy," in Greenberg et al., *Constitutionalism and Democracy*, 3–25.

73   On this subject, see O'Donnell and Schmitter, *Transitions from Authoritarian Rule: Tentative Conclusions*, 11–14.

74   Ramet, *Social Currents in Eastern Europe*, chap. 1, p. 21–22.

2. THE SOVIET BEQUEST TO RUSSIA

1   Quoted in *Newsweek*, 4 October 1993, 13.

2   Quoted in *Japan Times*, 24 November 1993.

3   Kliamkin, "Postkommunisticheskaia demokratiia i ee istoricheskie osobennosti v Rossii," 9–10.

4   See, for example, my article "The tale of the Torch," 113–121. See further the extensive "village prose" literature.

5   "Undesirable" literature (both scientific and fiction) was either not published, de-

stroyed, or kept in the closed sections of libraries; all contemporary literature was heavily censored. The only way to learn about the past was through *samizdat* (unauthorized literature) or from foreign radio stations such as Radio Liberty.

6 See my article on "Soviet-Russian Federalism in Comparative Perspective," in Takayuki Ito and Shinichiro Tabata, eds., *Between Disintegration and Reintegration*, 91–125.

7 Richard Pipes, paraphrased by Karen Dawisha and Bruce Parrott, in *Russia and the New States of Eurasia: The Politics of Upheaval* (Cambridge, New York, and Melbourne: Cambridge UP, 1994), 26.

8 T. H. Rigby, "Yeltsin's Presidency," 5–21; on the Boiar Duma, see V. O. Kliuchevskii, *Boiarskaia Duma Drevnei Rusi* (Petrograd, 1919); on the Zemskii Sobor, see Hellie, "Zemskii Sobor," 226–234.

9 Hellie, "Zemskii Sobor," 233 (capitals added).

10 There is extensive literature on the Duma. For a survey article, see Malloy and Good, "Duma."

11 Rigby, "Yeltsin's Presidency," 10.

12 See my *Decision Making in Soviet Politics*.

13 Urban, *More Power to the Soviets*; see also Rigby, *The Changing Soviet System*, and his "Yeltsin's Presidency."

14 Lewin, *The Gorbachev Phenomenon*. For earlier sociological works, see D. S. Lane, *The Socialist Industrial State: Towards a Political Sociology of State Socialism* (London, 1976); David Lane and Felicity O'Dell, *The Soviet Industrial Worker: Social Class, Education and Control* (Oxford: Martin Robertson, 1978); David Lane, *Soviet Economy and Society* (Oxford: Blackwell, 1985); Starr, "The Changing Nature of Change in the USSR"; and by the same author "The USSR: A Civil Society," *Foreign Policy* 70 (1989): 26–41.

15 Pye, "Political Science and the Crisis of Authoritarianism," 9–10. See also Seweryn Bialer, "Gorbachev's Program of Change: Sources, Significance, Prospects," *Political Science Quarterly* 103 (1988): 403–460.

16 John Miller, *Mikhail Gorbachev*.

17 On this subject, see Remington, "Regime Transition," and Holmes, *The End of Communist Power*, 304–327. Holmes also deals extensively with postcommunism and *post*-modernity.

18 Remington, "Regime Transition," 166.

19 John Miller, *Mikhail Gorbachev*, 203.

20 Blansaer-Van Reesch, *De Russische bevolking*, 6.

21 John Miller, *Mikhail Gorbachev*, 202.

22 Ibid., 107.

23 "Doklad predsedatelia Mandatnoi kommissii G. P. Viatkina," *SR*, 18 May 1990.

24 I will not go into the reliability of these projects. Suffice it to say that in all of them questions of reliability and bias were dealt with extensively.

25 Inkeles and Bauer, *The Soviet Citizen*.

26 Zvi Gitelman, "Soviet Political Culture."

27 On the SIP, see James R. Millar, "History, Method, and the Problem of Bias," in Millar, *Politics, Work, and Daily Life in the USSR*, 3–30.

28 The results were published in Gibson et al., "Democratic Values and Transformation of the Soviet Union."

29 A professional center for opinion research was finally set up under the leadership

of Tatiana Zaslavskaia in 1987: VTSIOM, the All-Union Center for Public Opinion Research. On its history and the shortcomings of its work during the first years, see White et al., *The Politics of Transition,* 180–183.

30 James Millar in Millar, *Politics, Work, and Daily Life in the USSR,* 26; and Donna Bahry in the same volume, 91–94.

31 Donna Bahry, "Politics, Generations, and Change in the USSR," in Millar, *Politics, Work, and Daily Life in the USSR,* 61–99.

32 With due apologies to senior citizens in the West!

33 Silver, "Political Beliefs of the Soviet Citizen," 127, 131–133. The concept "Big Deal," borrowed from Vera Dunham, is used for the post-World War II promise to the educated class of a comfortable material life and a modicum of freedom in private life in exchange for hard work and support for the regime (Silver, 102).

34 John Miller, *Mikhail Gorbachev,* 203.

35 The concept of civic culture originated with Gabriel A. Almond and Sidney Verba; see *The Civic Culture.*

36 Bahry and Silver, "Soviet Citizen Participation on the Eve of Democratization," 831–832.

37 Ibid., 837.

38 Gibson et al., "Democratic Values and Transformation of the Soviet Union."

39 Ibid., 351.

40 Ibid., 342, 344.

41 Ibid., 340–341.

42 Colton, "The Politics of Democratization," 336–337.

43 However, preliminary analyses of a survey of the entire European part of the Soviet Union, conducted by the same authors, have, in their words, revealed a remarkable degree of similarity in the answers to the same questions as posed in Moscow *oblast'* (Gibson et al., "Democratic Values and Transformation of the Soviet Union," 361).

44 Ibid., 359.

45 Ibid., 361.

46 Two Russians among the few realists were Igor Kliamkin and Andranik Migranian. See "Nuzhna 'Zheleznaia Ruka'?" *Litgazeta,* 16 August 1989.

47 Results of an opinion poll conducted by VTSIOM on 23 September 1993, two days after Yel'tsin's televised speech and decree, as reported in *Izv,* 25 September 1993. In a representative sample of 1,187 Muscovites, 25 percent were reported to be ready to take to the streets in support of Yel'tsin, 10 percent in support of the Supreme Soviet. Asked whether they believed that the struggle would be solved in a peaceful way or would result in civil war (with no alternative in between), 72 percent said they believed in a peaceful solution, and 19 percent feared civil war.

48 Samuel P. Huntington, *The Third Wave: Democratization in the Late Twentieth Century* (Norman and London: University of Oklahoma Press, 1991), 263, as quoted by Timothy J. Colton in Colton and Legvold, *After the Soviet Union,* 42.

49 Jeffrey Hahn, "Attitudes toward Reform," 84. The provinces were: Belgorod, Ivanovo, Kostroma, Saratov, and Iaroslavl'.

50 For the August 1992 poll, see *Izv,* 21 September 1992, as reported by White et al., in *The Politics of Transition,* 189; on the referendum, see *RG,* 19 May 1993.

51 Survey commissioned by the RFE/RL Research Institute and carried out by the Russian Public Opinion and Market Research (ROMIR) organization, among a

sample of 2,060 respondents representative of the population of European Russia, from 14 April to 12 May 1993. Twenty-one percent thought their economic situation had improved over the previous year. See Amy Corning, "Public Opinion and the Russian Parliamentary Elections," *RFE/RL* 2, no. 48 (3 December 1993): 16–23.

52 Gibson et al., "Democratic Values and Transformation of the Soviet Union," 363. The article's final manuscript was received by the journal's editors in September 1991.

53 Paul G. Lewis, "Democracy and Its Future in Eastern Europe," in Held, *Prospects for Democracy*, 302.

54 The metaphor is John Keane's, as quoted by Paul Lewis, in ibid., 302.

3. BETWEEN SOVEREIGNTY AND INDEPENDENCE

1 At a conference in Bremen, Germany, quoted in John B. Dunlop, "Moscow at a Turning Point," *RUSSR*, 15 June 1990, 8.

2 I. M. Kliamkin, "Postkommunisticheskaia demokratiia i ee istoricheskie osobennosti v Rossii," 12.

3 On "village prose," see Carter, *Russian Nationalism*, 89–101.

4 See Alexander Yanov's summary of Mikhail Lobanov's article on "Educated Shopkeepers" (*Molodaia Gvardia*, 1968, no 4), in Yanov, *The Russian Challenge and the Year 2000*, 109.

5 For a polemic summary, see Yanov, *The Russian Challenge and the Year 2000*.

6 Yanov, *The Russian New Right*. See also his *The Russian Challenge and the Year 2000*.

7 Solzhenitsyn finally returned on 27 May 1994.

8 Dobrokhotov, *Gorbachev-El'tsin*, 221–222.

9 I. M. Kliamkin, "Postkommunisticheskaia demokratiia i ee istoricheskie osobennosti v Rossi," 7.

10 "Deklaratsiia o gosudarstvennom suverenitete Rossiiskoi Sovetskoi Federativnoi Sotsialisticheskoi Respubliki," *SR*, 14 June 1990.

11 Article 1 of "Zakon sssr O razgranichenii polnomochii mezhdu Soiuzom SSR i sub"ektami federatsii" (26 April 1990), *VedSSSR* 1990, no. 19: 429–433.

12 For a list of the precise dates, see Ann Sheehy, "Fact Sheet on Declarations of Sovereignty," *RUSSR*, 9 November 1990, 23–25.

13 White et al., *The Politics of Transition*, 84.

14 Rabochaia gruppa, obrazovannaia sovmestnym resheniem M. S. Gorbacheva i B. N. El'tsina, *Perekhod k rynku*, 'chast' 1, *Kontseptsiia i Programma*; chast' 2, *Proekty zakonodatel'nykh aktov* (Moscow: Arkhangel'skoe, August 1990). The plan had been prepared in twenty-nine days (2–31 August). For the history and for comparisons of the different plans, see Hewett, "The New Soviet Plan"; "500 Days: Shatalin At Columbia"; Desai, "Soviet Economic Reform"; Schroeder, "*Perestroyka* in the Aftermath of 1990"; and Morrison, *Boris Yeltsin*, 164–178.

15 Shatalin, in "500 Days: Shatalin At Columbia," 20, on blood types; Desai, "Soviet Economic Reform," 2, on Yel'tsin's metaphor.

16 Hewett, "The New Soviet Plan," 150.

17 "Zakon rsfsr Ob obespechenii ekonomicheskoi osnovy suvereniteta RSFSR" (31 October 1990), *VedRSFSR*, 1990, no. 22 (1 November): 305–307.

18 On 8 October; "Weekly Record of Events," *RUSSR* 2, no. 42 (19 October 1990): 38.

19 Published in *SR*, 24 November 1990.

20 "Kak nam obustroit' Rossiiu" was published on 18 September 1990 in *KomsPr* and *Literaturnaia Gazeta*.

21 Quoted by John B. Dunlop, in "Russian Reactions to Solzhenitsyn's Brochure," *RUSSR* 2, no. 50 (14 December 1990): 5.

22 On the negative attitude of the military toward Gorbachev, see Ivashov, *Marshal Yazov*.

23 According to the official registration of parliamentary factions as reported in *Izv*, 27 December 1990. The parliament's total membership was 2,250. See Elizabeth Teague's profile of "The 'Soyuz' Group," *RUSSR* 3, no. 20 (17 May 1991): 17.

24 "Ukaz Prezidenta SSSR O nekotorykh aktakh po voprosam oborony, priniatykh v soiuznykh respublikakh" (1 December 1990), *VedSSSR*, 1990, no. 49 (5 December): 1303–1304.

25 *Izv*, 20 December 1990.

26 Tolz and Newton, *The USSR in 1991*, 11.

27 Alksnis interview, "Moskva nas brosila," *AiF*, 1991, no 4 (January): 2.

28 Morrison, *Boris Yeltsin*, 214.

29 Tolz and Newton, *The USSR in 1991*, 46.

30 Ivashov, *Marshal Yazov (Rokovoi Avgust 91–go)*, 62–64.

31 Yet, in these six republics polling stations were set up here and there, guarded by the Soviet military, and over two million voters expressed their support for the USSR. See "Postanovlenie Verkhovnogo Soveta SSSR 'Ob itogakh referenduma SSSR 17 marta 1991 goda'" (21 March 1991), in A. P. Nenarokov, sost., *Nesostoiavshiisia yubilei*, 435–438. See also Tolz and Newton, *The USSR in 1991*, 199–200.

32 Morrison, *Boris Yeltsin*, 242.

33 "Rasporiazhenie Predsedatelia Verkhovnogo Soveta RSFSR Ob izmenenii uslovii khoziaistvovaniia predpriatii ugol'noi i drugikh bazovykh otraslei promyshlennosti na territorii RSFSR" (1 May 1991), *VedRSFSR*, 1991, no. 18: 571–574.

34 "Sovmestnoe zaiavlenie o bezotlogatel'nykh merakh po stabilizatsii obstanovki v strane i preodoleniiu krizisa" (23 April 1991), *Pravda*, 24 April 1991.

35 Roman Solchanyk, "The Draft Union Treaty and the 'Big Five,'" *RUSSR* 3, no. 18 (3 May 1991): 18.

36 *SR*, 19 January 1991.

37 *Moscow News*, 1991, no. 8, as quoted by Vera Tolz, in "The Democratic Opposition in Crisis," *RUSSR* 3, no. 18 (3 May 1991): 3.

38 Quoted from *Los Angeles Times*, 20 June 1991, by Dawn Mann, "An Abortive Constitutional Coup d'Etat?" *RUSSR* 3, no. 27 (5 July 1991): 2.

39 Dawn Mann, "An Abortive Constitutional Coup d'Etat?" *RUSSR* 3, no. 27 (5 July 1991): 5.

40 *SR*, 24 May 1991.

41 Ibid.

42 Julia Wishnevsky, "Multiparty System, Soviet Style," *RUSSR* 2, no. 47 (23 November 1990): 5.

43 Tolz and Newton, *The USSR in 1991*, 400. For a history of Russian fascist ideology, see Alexander Yanov, *The Russian Challenge and the Year 2000*.

44 "Ukaz Prezidenta RSFSR O prekrashchenii deiatel'nosti organizatsionnykh struk-

tur politicheskikh partii i massovykh obshchestvennykh dvizhenii v gosudarstvennykh organakh, uchrezhdeniiakh i organizatsiiakh RSFSR" (20 July 1991),
VedRSFSR, 1991, no. 31: 1321–1322.

45 *SR*, 23 July 1991.

46 Luk'ianov, *Perevorot Mnimyi i Nastoiashchii*, 40–41.

47 Yel'tsin, *Zapiski prezidenta*, 56.

48 Ivashov, *Marshal Yazov (Rokovoi Avgust 91–go)*, 72.

49 Videotaped recordings of the interrogations of Yazov, Kriuchkov, and Pavlov were
leaked to the German weekly *Der Spiegel* (7 October 1991) and subsequently re-
translated and published in *Izv*, 10 October 1991. The translation of this quote
was taken from John Miller, *Mikhail Gorbachev*, 177.

50 See Ivashov, *Marshal Yazov (Rokovoi Avgust 91–go)*; Aleksandr Lebed', *Spek-
takl' Nazyvalsia Putch*; Anatolii Luk'ianov, *Perevorot Mnimyi i Nastoiashchii*;
A. V. Nikol'skii, *Avgust-91* (Moscow, 1991); Pavlov, *Avgust Iznutri*; Varennikov,
Sud'ba i Sovest'; Yel'tsin, *Zapiski prezidenta*; E. Rassivalova and N. Seregin, eds.,
Putch: Khronika trevozhnykh dnei (Moscow, 1991); Dobrokhotov et al., *Kras-
noe ili beloe! Drama Avgusta-91*; Morrison, *Boris Yeltsin*; Roxburgh, *De tweede
Russische revolutie*.

51 Members of the GKCHP were, in addition to Yanaev: first deputy chairman of
the USSR Defense Council Oleg Baklanov; USSR KGB chairman Vladimir Kriuchkov; Cabinet Chief Pavlov; USSR defense minister Yazov; USSR internal affairs minister Boris Pugo; chairman of the Peasants' Union Vasilii Starodubtsev;
and president of the USSR Association of State Owned Industries, Construction,
Transport, and Communications Enterprises Alexander Tiziakov. The delegation
that went to Foros on 18 August consisted of Baklanov, Gorbachev's chief of staff
Valerii Boldin, CPSU secretary Oleg Shenin, General Varennikov, and KGB general
Yurii Plekhanov.

52 "Ukaz Prezidenta RSFSR" (no. 59; 19 August 1991), *VedRSFSR*, 1991, no. 34:
1412–1413; "Ukaz Prezidenta RSFSR O Predsedatele Gosudarstvennogo komiteta
RSFSR po oboronnym voprosam" (19 August 1991), *VedRSFSR*, 1991, no. 34: 1413.

53 Hersh, "The Wild East," 84–86. As of 18 August, the NSA allegedly provided
the Russian president "in real time" with a steady stream of transcripts of de-
crypted conversations between Kriuchkov and Yazov. According to Hersh, in
early spring the intelligence service had warned the Bush administration of the
plotting against Gorbachev, and during Yel'tsin's visit in June, Deputy National
Security Adviser Robert M. Gates asked "a ranking senator" to discuss the matter
with Yel'tsin. "Are we being overwrought about the coup?" asked the senator.
Yel'tsin's response: "Absolutely not! There will be a coup before the end of the
calendar year. Gorbachev doesn't believe it, but I'm preparing for it."

54 According to the results of a study of the Control Department of Yel'tsin's office,
made public in late October 1991. See Tolz and Newton, *The USSR in 1991*,
757–758.

55 Tolz and Newton, *The USSR in 1991*, 561, 594.

56 Pomerants, "The Irrational in Politics," *Russian Social Science Review* 34, no. 6
(November–December 1993): 42–43.

57 *Economist* (20 October 1990) estimates; see Ben Slay, "On the Economics of
Interrepublican Trade," *RUSSR* 3, no. 48 (29 November 1991): 1–2. See also the
diagrams in *Perekhod k rynku*, chast' 1, 18–19.

58   Andorra (464 square kilometers, 21,000 inhabitants) adopted its constitution by referendum on 14 March 1993 and had its first parliamentary elections on 12 December (*Europa Archiv* 48, no. 7 (1993): Z79, and 49, no. 1 [1994]: Z1). Its economy is based on tourism, international commerce, shepherding, and the sale of postage stamps.

59   *Perekhod k rynku*, chast' 1, 15. For a balanced analysis of the economic prospects of one of the republics, see John Tedstrom, "The Economic Costs and Benefits of Independence for Ukraine," *RUSSR* 2, no. 49 (7 December 1990): 11–16.

60   The *Economist* estimated the RSFSR's subsidies to the other republics at sixty-four billion rubles in 1988. See Ben Slay, "On the Economics of Interrepublican Trade" (note 57 above).

61   The percentage of CPSU members in the 1984 Supreme Soviet had been 72; in the 1989 USSR Congress of People's Deputies it was 87 (John Miller, *Mikhail Gorbachev*, 116).

62   "Postanovlenie S"ezda narodnykh deputatov SSSR O merakh, vytekaiushchikh iz sovmestnogo Zaiavleniia Prezidenta SSSR i vysshikh rukovoditelei soiuznykh respublik i reshenii vneocherednoi sessii Verkhovnogo Soveta SSSR" (5 September 1991), *VedSSSR*, 1991, no. 37 (11 September 1991): 1485–1486.

63   "Postanovlenie Gosudarstvennogo Soveta SSSR O priznanii nezavisimosti Litovskoi Respubliki" (6 September 1991), *VedSSSR*, 1991, no. 37 (11 September 1991): 1497.

64   "Zakon SSSR Ob organov gosudarstvennoi vlasti i upravleniia Soiuza SSR v perekhodnyi period" (5 September 1991), *VedSSSR*, 1991, no. 37 (11 September 1991): 1487–1488.

65   "Postanovlenie S"ezda narodnykh deputatov SSSR O merakh."

66   Keith Bush, "El'tsin's Economic Reform Program," *RUSSR* 3, no. 46 (15 November 1991): 5.

67   "Ukaz Prezidenta Rossiiskoi Sovetskoi Federativnoi Sotsialisticheskoi Respubliki O deiatel'nosti KPSS i KP RSFSR" (6 November 1991), *VedRSFSR*, 1991, no. 45: 1799–1800.

68   "Zakon RSFSR O Konstitutsionnom Sude RSFSR," (6 May 1991), *VedRSFSR*, 1991, no. 19: 579–620, art. 1–3. The proceedings in the CPSU case began on 6 July 1992 and ended, after fifty-two court sessions, on 30 November. On the history of the case, see Feofanov, "The Establishment of the Constitutional Court," 623–637.

69   "Weekly Record of Events," *RUSSR* 3, no. 50 (13 December 1991): 27.

70   "Zaiavlenie Soveta Respublik Verkhovnogo Soveta SSSR" (3 December 1991), *Vedomosti Verkhovnogo Soveta SSSR*, 1991, no. 50 (11 December 1991): 1886–1888.

71   "Weekly Record of Events," *RUSSR* 3, no. 50 (13 December 1991): 34.

72   The CIS documents signed in Minsk (8 December) and Almaty (21 December) were published in *Diplomaticheskii Vestnik*, 1992, no. 1 (15 January): 3–10. The only other signatory to the 1922 treaty had been the Transcaucasian federative republic.

73   "Weekly Record of Events," *RUSSR* 3, nos. 51/52 (20 December 1991): 36.

74   N. Ziat'kov, "Sud'ba Prezidenta," *AiF*, 1991, no. 50 (December): 1; Dobrokhotov et al., *Krasnoe ili beloe! Drama Avgusta-91*, 424; Gorbachev, *Dekabr'-91: Moia pozitsiia*, 67.

75   "Weekly Record of Events," *RUSSR* 3, nos. 51/52 (20 December 1991): 30.

76 Roman Glebov, "Sovetskaia Armiia: Odna na vsekh, my za tsenoi ne postoim?" *Kom*, 1991, no. 19 (6–19 December): 19; see also A. Krainii, in *KomsPr*, 14 December 1991.

77 For reports on the 10–11 December meetings at the Ministry of Defense, see *Izv*, 11 December 1991; *KomsPr* and *SR*, 12 December 1991.

78 *Izv*, 12 December 1991.

79 Tolz and Newton, *The USSR in 1991*, 895–896.

80 "Ukaz Prezidenta Soiuza Sovetskikh Sotsialisticheskikh Respublik O slozhenii Prezidentom SSSR polnomochii Verkhovnogo Glavnokomanduiushchego Vooruzhennymi Silami SSSR i uprazdnenii Soveta oborony pri Prezidente SSSR" (25 December 1991), *Vedomosti Verkhovnogo Soveta SSSR*, 1991, no. 52 (25 December 1991): 2060.

81 "Deklaratsiia Soveta Respublik Verkhovnogo Soveta SSSR v sviazi s sozdaniem Sodruzhestva Nezavisimykh Gosudarstv" (26 December 1991), *Vedomosti Verkhovnogo Soveta SSSR*, 1991, no. 52 (25 December 1991): 2058–2059.

82 The quote refers to the first line of the Soviet national anthem. The definition of the "near abroad" in Russian post-1991 discourse has remained vague. The term can be taken to refer to either the CIS countries or all of the former Soviet republics.

4. THE UNREMITTING CRISIS

1 Interview in *AiF*, 1992, no. 42 (October); Televised speech of 6 October 1993, *RG*, 7 October 1993; Speech in Spanish parliament, *RFE/RL DR*, no. 70 (13 April 1994).

2 Interview, 23 July 1990, in Harrogate, England: Roman Solchanyk, "Ukraine, Russia, and the National Question: An Interview with Aleksandr Tsipko," *RUSSR* 2, no. 33 (17 August 1990): 23.

3 Zhirinovskii, *Poslednii brosok na Iug*, 99.

4 Defense Minister Pavel Grachev interview, *Izv*, 1 June 1992.

5 Stephen Foye, "The CIS Armed Forces," *RFE/RL* 2, no. 1 (1 January 1993): 42–43.

6 On these and related issues, see the solid article by John W. R. Lepingwell, "Ukraine, Russia, and the Control of Nuclear Weapons," *RFE/RL* 2, no. 8 (19 February 1993): 7.

7 Ibid., 14.

8 *Izv*, 15 January 1994.

9 *Washington Post*, 24 May 1992, as referred to by Lepingwell, in "Ukraine, Russia, and the Control of Nuclear Weapons" (note 6 above).

10 On the formative period of Russian foreign policy, see my article "The Foreign Policy of the Russian Federation."

11 Kozyrev, "Russia and Human Rights," 290.

12 *RG*, 20 April 1991.

13 *RG*, 23 April 1991; *Izv*, 16–18 April 1991.

14 Andrei V. Kozyrev, "Russia and Human Rights," 291. "Nearly abroad" was the heading of an article in the *Economist*, 5 February 1994. In Russian sources, instead of "Russians," the term "Russian-speaking" is used; not all Russian-speaking people are necessarily "ethnic Russians," i.e., people with "Russian" as their nationality in their passport. The numerical strength of the "Russian dias-

pora" is usually given as twenty-five million, but this number is thought to exclude the military. An internal Ministry of Foreign Affairs (MID) document dating from 1992–1993 refers to 3.3 million being "almost 10 percent of the total number of Russians in the near abroad," bringing the total number to over thirty million people ("O zashchite russkoiazychnogo naseleniia v strankah Srednei Azii," Internal document, Russian Ministry of Foreign Affairs, Moscow 1992). In 1989 the 25.3 million Russians outside the borders of the RSFSR were 17.4 percent of the total Russian population in the Soviet Union. The number of military personnel in 1959 was 3.6 million (Ellen Blansaer-Van Reesch, *De Russische bevolking*, 3).

15 On the operation of the Security Council during its first months, see the Filatov interview in *RV*, 13 August 1992.

16 *KomsPr*, 9 June 1992, as quoted by Jan S. Adams, in "Legislature Asserts Its Role in Russian Foreign Policy," *RFE/RL* 2, no. 4 (22 January 1993): 33.

17 A comprehensive study of the conflict was written by Pål Kolstø et al., "The Dniester Conflict," 980.

18 Ibid., 992–993.

19 Within three months after the USSR had ceased to exist, peacekeeping in Russia's "near abroad" had become one of its foreign policy instruments. In March, the heads of ten of the CIS's eleven member states had signed an agreement on groups of military observers and collective peacekeeping forces in the CIS.

20 Reported by Stephen Foye, "The CIS Armed Forces," 44 (note 5 above).

21 *Izv*, 1 June 1992.

22 Yevgenii Ambartsumov, "Rekomendatsii (po itogam zakrytykh slushanii ministra inostrannykh del Rossii A. V. Kozyreva na Komitete po mezhdunarodnym delam o vneshnepoliticheskoi kontseptsii MID RF 30 iiunia 1992 g.)," as quoted by Konstantin Eggert in *Izv*, 7 August 1992.

23 "Rasporiazhenie Prezidenta Rossiiskoi Federatsii O voprosakh zashchity prav i interesov rossiiskikh grazhdan za predelami Rossiiskoi Federatsii" (30 November 1992), *Diplomaticheskii Vestnik*, 1993, nos. 1–2: 8.

24 Blansaer-Van Reesch, *De Russische bevolking*, 44.

25 "K voprosu o zashchite prav russkoiazychnogo naseleniia v strankah SNG, Baltiki i Gruzii," Internal document, Russian Ministry of Foreign Affairs (Moscow, 1992).

26 Quoted by Suzanne Crow, in "Russia Asserts Its Strategic Agenda," *RFE/RL* 2, no. 50 (17 December 1993): 4.

27 Roman Solchanyk, "Ukraine: A Year of Transition," *RFE/RL* 2, no. 1 (1 January 1993): 62.

28 See the article by four deputies including Sergei Baburin, "Agents of Influence," *SR*, 21 November 1992.

29 Jan Adams, "Legislature Asserts Its Role," 35 (note 16 above).

30 Stanislav Kondrashov in *Izv*, 30 November 1992.

31 The main principles of the doctrine were published in *Izv*, 18 November 1993. The relieved Western leaders responded with NATO's "Partnership for Peace" program, of which Ukraine became a member in February 1994, and Russia on 22 June 1994.

32 Crow, "Russia Asserts Its Strategic Agenda," 7 (note 26 above).

33 *ITAR-TASS*, 8 December 1993, as quoted by Crow, in "Russia Asserts Its Strategic Agenda," 2.

34 Vitalii Portnikov in *Nezavisimaia Gazeta*, 1 December 1993.

35 *Russian Federation*, IMF Economic Reviews 1993, no. 8, 5. Except when otherwise indicated, all data in this economic section are taken from this source.

36 Tabata, "Inflation in Russia," 1.

37 Schröder, "Eine Armee in der Krise," 40.

38 Ann Sheehy, "The CIS: A Shaky Edifice," *RFE/RL* 2, no. 1 (1 January 1993): 38.

39 Fomin, "The Economic Developments in Ukraine," 11–12. The internal crude oil price in the Soviet Union was 103 rubles per ton in 1989, 2,200 rubles in May 1992, 4,000 rubles in September.

40 Banknotes were printed in Russia exclusively; see Smith, *International Trade and Payments in the Former Soviet/CMEA Area*, 61.

41 *Russian Federation*, IMF Economic Reviews 1993, 29. Cash rubles were 17 percent of "broad ruble money" at the end of 1991, 23 percent at the end of June 1992, and 26 percent at the end of the year.

42 Fomin, "The Economic Developments in Ukraine," 10. The 1993 inflation rate in Ukraine was 38,000 percent (*Interfax Business Report*, 26 January 1994).

43 Tabata, "Inflation in Russia," 2.

44 White, *After Gorbachev*, 277.

45 *Interfax Statistical Report*, 4 March 1994, 3; *RFE/RL Daily Report*, 10 June 1994.

46 Valeri I. Rybin, Russian financier, at a seminar in Sapporo (Slavic Research Center), 28 January 1994.

47 *Russian Federation*, IMF Economic Reviews 1993, 23; White, *After Gorbachev*, 273. The percentage mentioned most often from mid-1992 was 50.

48 Olga Glezer, in Poljan, "Die Bevölkerung Rußlands."

49 Data of the Institute of Social and Political Research, Russian Academy of Sciences. See *RFE/RL DR*, no. 74 (19 April 1994).

50 *Japan Times*, 17 August 1993.

51 According to Guy Standing, head of ILO's Central and East European Team at a news conference in Geneva, reported in *Japan Times*, 9 February 1994. The total Russian workforce was approximately seventy million.

52 *Russian Federation*, IMF Economic Reviews 1993, 2.

53 Interview in *Der Spiegel*, 1994, no. 4 (24 January): 115–116.

54 On 14 January 1994, at the press conference at the end of President Clinton's visit to Moscow, Yel'tsin said "I do not think it will be long before the G-7 becomes the G-8" (*FBIS-SOV-94-011*, 6).

55 Ito, "Regionalism in Russian Politics," 25–57.

56 Tolz and Newton, *The USSR in 1991*, 549.

57 Sergej Saizew, "Separatismus in Rußland," *BiOS*, 1992, no. 42 (14 October): 12–13.

58 For their text, and that of the agreement with Tatarstan, see Berg, *Comments to the Constitution of the Russian Federation*, 80–87.

59 Theen, "Russia at the Grassroots," 85.

60 Ito, "Regionalism in Russian Politics," 41.

61 *Interfax Business Report*, 9 July 1993.

62 Ito, "Regionalism in Russian Politics," 29–33.

63 Tolz and Newton, *The USSR in 1991*, 706, 769. In June 1990, the Congress had (over strong opposition) elected him first deputy chairman. Since Yel'tsin had been president, Khasbulatov had been acting chairman. In July 1991, Congress had voted on the chair six times in five days with no results. Yel'tsin failed

to convince many of his supporters in the Congress, who feared Khasbulatov's "authoritarian methods of leadership."

64 "Postanovlenie Prezidiuma Verkhovnogo Soveta RSFSR Ob organizatsii Upravleniia Delami Prezidiuma Verkhovnogo Soveta RSFSR" (30 July 1991), *VedRSFSR*, 1991, no. 31: 1341.

65 On the Moscow elections, see Colton, "The Politics of Democratization," 285–344; on the subsequent troubles of the new *Mossovet*, see Boyce, "Local Government Reform and the New Moscow City Soviet," 245–271. Boyce (248, 250) claims 291 DR-deputies out of a total of 498 in the *Mossovet*.

66 Brudny, "The Dynamics of 'Democratic Russia,' 1990–1993," 161–162.

67 A thorough study of Civic Union has been written by Michael McFaul: "Russian Centrism and Revolutionary Transitions." See also Lohr, "Arkadii Volsky's Political Base."

68 McFaul, "Russian Centrism," 204.

69 Ibid., 207.

70 Foster, "Izvestiia as a Mirror of Russian Legal Reform," 737.

71 *AiF*, 1992, no. 42 (October). Yel'tsin said ". . . mne by podpisat' ukaz o zemle," which can be translated as "I should have" / "should perhaps have" / "ought to have" / "could have." Considering his next sentence, the last version was chosen. I am grateful to Professor Tetsuo Mochizuki for our long discussion on this translation problem.

72 Ibid.

73 And punished the minister with an official reprimand for his lack of control (*Izv*, 28 October 1992).

74 For a history of the battle, see Foster, "Izvestiia as a Mirror of Russian Legal Reform," 675–747.

75 Brudny, "The Dynamics of 'Democratic Russia,' 1990–1993," 164.

76 The constitutional amendments concerned Articles 109–19, 110, and 121[6].

77 On the "Russia" television channel, 21:40 GMT, 20 March; see *BBC SWB SU/1643* C1/5–6.

78 For the translated text of Yel'tsin's televised speech of 20 March, see *BBC SWB SU/1643* C1/1–4 (22 March 1993). A decree, of which the text differed in several respects from what Yel'tsin had said on 20 March, was finally published on 24 March: "Ukaz Prezidenta Rossiiskoi Federatsii O deiatel'nosti ispolnitel'nykh organov do preodoleniia krizisa vlasti" (no. 379; 20 March 1993), *RV*, 25 March 1993.

79 Quoted by Lipitskii in *RG*, 3 April 1993.

80 Löwenhardt, "The New Political Map of Russia." Regional referendum results were published in *RG*, 19 May 1993.

81 "Ukaz Prezidenta Rossiiskoi Federatsii O poetapnoi konstitutsionnoi reforme v Rossiiskoi Federatsii" (no. 1400; 21 September 1993, 20:00 hrs.), *RG* 23 September 1993; and in *SAPP*, no. 39. In his reminiscences Yel'tsin later claimed that he had signed the decree one week earlier (Yel'tsin, *Zapiski prezidenta*, 364).

82 Ito, "Regionalism in Russian Politics," 46.

83 *RG*, 7 October 1993.

84 Yel'tsin, *Zapiski prezidenta*, 176–177, 347–387. In an interview, broadcast 12 November on German television, Yel'tsin claimed that he had written ("with my

own hand, with my own pen") Decree 1400 one month before it was announced, had "told nobody anything about it and kept it in my safe. . . . It was top secret" (*RFE/RL News Briefs* 2, no. 47 [15–19 November 1993]: 1). In his book he told a completely different story.

85 For an analysis of the rules, see my article "General Elections in Russia: Yel'tsin's Rules for the Election of the Federal Assembly and for the Plebiscite," in Löwenhardt, *Cutting the Gordian Knot*, 23–42; and my article "Institutional Choices in the Transition to Democracy," 7–24.

86 *Preliminary Staff Report, North Atlantic Assembly Mission to Monitor Russian Elections, 8–13 December 1993.* On PRES, see Ito, "Regionalism in Russian Politics," 40.

87 Article 14–1 in "Polozhenie o vsenarodnom golosovanii po proektu Konstitutsii Rossiiskoi Federatsii 12 dekabria 1993 goda," *SAPP*, no. 42, 18 October 1993.

88 "Postanovlenie Tsentral'noi izbiratel'noi komissii Rossiiskoi Federatsii O rezul'tatakh vsenarodnogo golosovaniia po proektu Konstitutsii Rossiiskoi Federatsii," *RG*, 25 December 1993.

89 The percentage of invalid votes was 1.7; see "Election Results," in Löwenhardt, *Cutting the Gordian Knot*, 43–47.

90 *Preliminary Staff Report*, 2.

91 *Izv*, 4 May 1994; Lyubarsky, "Election Rigging," 6–13.

92 For the translated text of the Yeltsin constitution and a detailed commentary, see Berg, *Comments to the Constitution of the Russian Federation.*

93 *RG*, 7 October 1993.

5. TRANSITION *À LA RUSSE*

1 From *Perepiska s druz'iami*, as quoted by Nove, in *The Soviet System in Retrospect*, 10.

2 Morrison, *Boris Yeltsin*, 154.

3 John Löwenhardt, *Heb geduld, kameraad: Michail Gorbatsjov en het einde van de Sovjetunie (Be Patient, Comrade: Mikhail Gorbachev and the End of the Soviet Union)* (Amsterdam: Jan Mets, 1992), 81.

4 TASS, 8 May 1991, as quoted by Alexander Rahr, in "The Presidential Race in the RSFSR," *RUSSR* 3, no. 23 (7 June 1991): 28.

5 *RG*, 28 December 1993.

6 *Japan Times*, 22 December 1993.

7 Kolstø et al., "The Dniester Conflict," 993.

8 Umov, "Rossiiskii srednii klass," 26.

9 O'Donnell and Schmitter, *Transitions from Authoritarian Rule: Tentative Conclusions*, 65.

10 Ramet, *Social Currents in Eastern Europe*, chap. 1, p. 4.

11 Dawisha and Parrott, *Russia and the New States of Eurasia*, 134.

12 Paul G. Lewis, "Democracy and Its Future in Eastern Europe," in Held, *Prospects for Democracy*, 296.

13 Pomerants, "The Irrational in Politics," 50.

14 Holmes, *The End of Communist Power*, 305.

15 Ibid.

16 In a conversation with Dutch journalists, May 1990, as reported in Löwenhardt, *Heb geduld, kameraad*, 58 (see note 3 above).

17 Pomerants, "The Irrational in Politics," 50, 49.

18 Simon Dixon, "The Russians: The Dominant Nationality," in Graham Smith, *The Nationalities Question in the Soviet Union*, 22. Among postcommunist nations, Russians were not unique in this destructive feeling—the nationalist ideologies in Gamsakhurdia's Georgia and Milošević's Serbia were strikingly similar; on the Serbs, see Ramet, " 'Triple Chauvinism' in the New Eastern Europe."

19 Weigle and Butterfield, "Civil Society in Reforming Communist Regimes," 3. See also Paul G. Lewis, "Democracy and Its Future in Eastern Europe," in Held, *Prospects for Democracy*.

20 Andrei Amal'rik, in *Involuntary Journey to Siberia* (1970), as restated by Weigle and Butterfield, "Civil Society in Reforming Communist Regimes," 8.

21 Weigle and Butterfield, "Civil Society in Reforming Communist Regimes," 9. See also John Miller, *Mikhail Gorbachev*, 102–103. Biographies of the 3,400 dissidents who were active in the twenty years between 1956 and 1975 can be found in Boer, et al., *Biographical Dictionary of Dissidents in the Soviet Union, 1956–1975*.

22 In particular the USSR law on social organizations (including political parties) of 9 October 1990, and the RSFSR law on the press of 25 December 1991.

23 Kagarlitsky and Clarke, "Russia's Trade Union Movement."

24 Ibid.

25 Ibid.

26 *Russian Federation*, IMF Economic Reviews 1993, [no.] 8, [p.] 18. Workers paid by way of a 5.4 percent payroll tax; in 1992 the revenues amounted to 215 billion rubles as a result of rising wages.

27 See Berg, "The Right to Work and Politically Motivated Discrimination in Soviet Labor Law," and Livshits, *Trudovoe zakonodatel'stvo*, 49–69.

28 A few small, independent trade unions had existed during the Brezhnev period, such as the Free Trade Unions in Donetsk (1977) and the Free Interprofessional Association of Workers (SMOT, 1978). They suffered suppression, but their day came in the Gorbachev period. See White et al., *The Politics of Transition*, 145.

29 Kagarlitsky and Clarke, "Russia's Trade Union Movement."

30 Ibid.

31 See "Ukaz Prezidenta Rossiiskoi Federatsii Ob upravlenii gosudarstvennym sotsial'nym strakhovaniem v Rossiiskoi Federatsii" (no. 1503; 28 September 1993), SAPP, no. 40; "Postanovlenie Soveta Ministrov—Pravitel'stva Rossiiskoi Federatsii: Voprosy Fonda sotsial'nogo strakhovaniia Rossiiskoi Federatsii" (no. 1094; 26 October 1993), SAPP, no. 44; and the interview with Deputy Minister of Labor Shatyrenko in *RG*, 15 October 1993.

32 Umov, "Rossiiskii srednii klass," 27.

33 Ibid., 29.

34 Ibid., 34.

35 Two useful studies on Civic Union are McFaul, "Russian Centrism and Revolutionary Transitions," and Lohr, "Arkadii Volsky's Political Base."

36 McFaul, "Russian Centrism and Revolutionary Transitions," 198.

37 Umov, "Rossiiskii srednii klass," 38.

38 Timothy J. Colton, "Politics," in Colton and Legvold, *After the Soviet Union,* 21.

39 *Izv,* 17 December 1991, as quoted in Boyce, "Local Government Reform and the New Moscow City Soviet," 268.

40 Yel'tsin's draft "Covenant (*Soglashenie*) on Reaching Civic Accord in Russia" was published in *RG,* 7 April 1994; the final "Agreement on Social Accord" (*Dogovor ob obshchestvennom soglasii*), with several significant changes if compared to the Covenant, was in *RG,* 29 April 1994.

41 Yel'tsin, *Zapiski prezidenta,* 310.

42 Yel'tsin interview in *AiF,* 1992, no. 42 (October).

43 *Izv,* 25 October 1989.

44 On 15 March 1990, Mikhail Gorbachev received 1,329 votes of 1,878 voting members of the USSR Congress of People's Deputies. He ran unopposed.

45 For a summary and analysis of the new constitutional structure and electoral procedure, see my "Institutional Choices in the Transition to Democracy."

46 Even more amazing was that one of the deputies elected on the list of Zhirinovskii's Liberal Democratic Party (Victor Vishniakov) was a member of the Communist Party of Russia, one of the other parties competing in the elections. See "Election Results," in Löwenhardt, *Cutting the Gordian Knot,* 43–47.

47 In 1990, 205 Russian deputies (roughly 20 percent) claimed to belong to DR; in 1993 their number had dwindled to sixty-seven (Brudny, "The Dynamics of 'Democratic Russia,' 1990–1993," 146).

48 Ibid., 147–148.

49 "Zakon RSFSR O Prezidente RSFSR" (24 April 1991), *VedRSFSR,* 1991, no. 17: 463–466. A few weeks after the law had been adopted, Vladimir Zhirinovskii told the legislators to consider the provision an "unnecessary limitation" of the rights of the president. He would work for it to be scrapped in the event he was elected president (*SR,* 24 May 1991).

50 Yel'tsin, *Zapiski prezidenta,* 14–15.

51 "Ukaz Prezidenta SSSR O roli Soveta Ministrov RSFSR v sisteme ispolnitel'noi vlasti Rossiiskoi Federatsii" (11 September 1991), *VedRSFSR,* 1991, no. 37: 1462–1464.

52 Yel'tsin, *Zapiski prezidenta,* 237. Literally, Yel'tsin wrote: ". . . allowed the accumulation of a number of wholesome tendencies."

53 Hersh, "The Wild East," 62.

54 See Vaksberg, *The Soviet Mafia;* Simis, *USSR: The Corrupt Society;* Rigby, *Political Elites in the USSR;* and Willerton, *Patronage and Politics in the USSR.*

55 Zemtsov, *Partiia ili mafiia.*

56 Data for 1993 and percentages for 1992–1993 are from *AiF,* 1994, no. 15 (April), 1; all other data in this paragraph are taken from Van den Berg, *Strafrecht van de Russische Federatie,* 24–41. The data published on 1993 may have been somewhat inflated by the police and public prosecutor's office for maximum political effect.

57 In computing the figure for the Russian Federation, the number of attempts included in the absolute number of 29,213 has been assumed to be 15 percent, and has been substracted.

58 For extensive documentation, see Hersh, "The Wild East."

59 Pomerants, "The Irrational in Politics," 47.

60 As stated by Gennadii Burbulis during a conversation at the Slavic Research Center, Hokkaido University (Japan), 6 September 1993. When asked about the strategy after August 1991, Burbulis, who in 1991 was one of Yel'tsin's main advisors, responded as follows: The main strategic goal was to find a painless road for the breakup of the Soviet Union. We understood that Russia would have to find a new social order. We decided not to limit pluralism and deliberately excluded a repetition of Bolshevik methods—i.e., no purge of the security organs or the bureaucracy. Overall, this strategy has been successful, for we have been able to prevent social earthquakes or a civil war. Moreover, the relations between countries of the Commonwealth of Independent States are getting stronger; in the economy irreversible changes have taken place. As to the political battle "at the top," it has no influence on the population. The population has already decided for the new, democratic order —Thus Burbulis, who at the time of the conversation headed the "Strategy Center" (Tsentr 'Strategiia'), a consultancy organization in Moscow.

61 'Ukaz Prezidenta Rossiiskoi Sovetskoi Federativnoi Sotsialisticheskoi Respubliki O deiatel'nosti KPSS i KP RSFSR' (6 November 1991), *Vedomosti S"ezda narodnykh deputatov RSFSR i Verkhovnogo Soveta RSFSR*, 1991, no. 45: 1799–1800.

62 Morrison, *Boris Yeltsin*, 10.

63 Karen Dawisha and Bruce Parrott, *Russia and the New States of Eurasia*, 27.

CONCLUSION

1 Pomerants, "The Irrational in Politics," 51.
2 "Agenty Vliianiia," *SR*, 21 November 1992.
3 Excerpts in *Izv*, 15 December 1992.
4 Baturin interview, *Der Spiegel*, 1994, no. 6 (7 February): 123–124.
5 See Kuiper, "Keeping the Peace."
6 *Izv*, 7 August 1992.
7 Quoted in *Japan Times*, 23 February 1994. On his geopolitical appetites, see also his *Poslednii brosok na Iug*.
8 Quoted (and italics) by Oversloot, "Ruslands keuze?" 145.
9 From the unofficial translation of the "Tokyo Declaration," signed by President Yel'tsin and Japan's Prime Minister Morihiro Hosokawa on 13 October 1993 (*Japan Times*, 14 October 1993).
10 Organski and Kugler, "The Costs of Major Wars." I am grateful to Hiroshi Kimura for drawing my attention to this study.
11 Ibid., 1364–1365.
12 Hadenius, *Democracy and Development*, 152–154.
13 Halperin, "Guaranteeing Democracy." In 1993, President Clinton nominated Halperin assistant secretary of defense for democracy and peacekeeping, but the Senate did not act on the nomination. Halperin withdrew, and Defense Secretary Inman voiced doubts on this new position.
14 The Al Capone comparison was made by an anonymous former national security official of the Reagan and Bush administrations; see Hersh, "The Wild East," 81.

BIBLIOGRAPHY

Abbreviations in notes and bibliography for newspapers, weeklies and journals:

AiF	Argumenty i Fakty
APSR	American Political Science Review.
BiOS	Berichte des Bundesinstituts für ostwissenschaftliche und internatio- nale Studien (Köln)
EAS	Europe-Asia Studies (continues *SovSt*)
Izv	Izvestia
JCS	The Journal of Communist Studies
Kom	Kommersant"
KomsPr	Komsomol'skaia Pravda
Polis	Polis: Politicheskie Issledovaniia
PSA	Post-Soviet Affairs (continues *SE*)
RevCEEL	Review of Central and East European Law (continues *RevSL*)
RevSL	Review of Socialist Law (continued by *RevCEEL*)
RFE/RL	*RFE/RL* Research Report (continues *RUSSR*)
RFE/RL DR	*RFE/RL* Daily Report
RG	Rossiiskaia gazeta
RUSSR	Report on the USSR (continued by *RFE/RL*)
RV	Rossiiskie vesti
SAPP	Sobranie aktov Prezidenta i Pravitel'stva Rossiiskoi Federatsii
SE	Soviet Economy (continued by *PSA*)
SovSt	Soviet Studies (continued by *EAS*)
SR	Sovetskaia Rossiia
BBC SWB	BBC Summary of World Broadcasts Third Series, Former USSR
VedRSFSR	Vedomosti S"ezda narodnykh deputatov RSFSR i Verkhovnogo Soveta RSFSR.
VedSSSR	Vedomosti S"ezda narodnykh deputatov SSSR i Verkhovnogo Soveta SSSR.

1. GENERAL

Ágh, Attila. "The Transition to Democracy in Central Europe: A Comparative View." *Journal of Public Policy* 11, no. 2 (1991): 133–151.

Aivazian, M. S., V. A. Levanskii, V. I. Lysenko, and T. V. Novikova. "Obnovlenie izbiratel'nogo zakonodatel'stva v Rossii." *Gosudarstvo i Pravo*, 1993, no. 8: 32–42.

Alexandrova, Olga. "Perzeptionen der auswärtigen Sicherheit in der Ukraine." *BiOS*, 1993, no. 40.

Almond, Gabriel A., and Sidney Verba. *The Civic Culture: Political Attitudes and Democracy in Five Nations.* Princeton: Princeton UP, 1963.

Alter, Peter. *Nationalism.* London: Edward Arnold, 1989.

Åslund, Anders. *Gorbachev's Struggle for Economic Reform: The Soviet Reform Process, 1985–88.* Ithaca, N.Y.: Cornell UP, 1989.

Bahry, Donna, and Brian D. Silver. "Soviet Citizen Participation on the Eve of Democratization." *APSR* 84, no. 3 (September 1990): 821–847.

Bakatin, Vadim. *Osvobozhdenie ot illiuzii.* Kemerovo: Kemerovskoe Knizhnoe Izdatel'stvo, 1992.

Berezovskii, V. N., and N. I. Krotov. *Neformal'naia Rossiia.* Moscow: Molodaia Gvardiia, 1990.

Berg, Ger P. van den. "The Right to Work and Politically Motivated Discrimination in Soviet Labor Law." *RevSL* 5, no. 3 (1979): 251–313.

——— . *Comments to the Constitution of the Russian Federation: With the Text of the Constitution of 12 December 1993.* Leiden: Institute of East European Law and Russian Studies, 1994.

——— . *Strafrecht van de Russische Federatie.* Leiden: Institute of East European Law and Russian Studies, 1994.

Bezemer, J. W. *Het einde van de Sovjetunie.* Amsterdam: Van Oorschot, 1992.

Blansaer–Van Reesch, Ellen. *De Russische bevolking van Centraal-Azië en het Balticum: Politieke, juridische en demografische problemen voor Rusland en de niet-Russische voormalige sovjetrepublieken.* Masters Thesis, Program of Russian Studies. Leiden, 1994.

Boer, S. P. de, E. J. Driessen, and H. L. Verhaar, eds. *Biographical Dictionary of Dissidents in the Soviet Union, 1956–1975.* The Hague, Boston, and London: Martinus Nijhoff, 1982.

Boyce, J. H. "Local Government Reform and the New Moscow City Soviet." *JCS* 9, no. 3 (September 1993): 245–271.

Bremmer, Ian, and Ray Taras, eds. *Nations and Politics in the Soviet Successor States.* Cambridge: Cambridge UP, 1993.

Breslauer, George W. "The Roots of Polarization: A Comment." *PSA* 9, no. 3 (July–September 1993): 223–230.

Brown, A. H. *Soviet Politics and Political Science.* London and Basingstoke: Macmillan, 1974.

Brown, Archie, "Ideology and Political Culture." In Seweryn Bialer, ed., *Politics, Society, and Nationality inside Gorbachev's Russia.* Boulder, Colo.: Westview, 1989.

——— . "The October Crisis of 1993: Context and Implications." *PSA* 9, no. 3 (July–September): 183–195.

Brudny, Yitzhak M. "The Dynamics of 'Democratic Russia,' 1990–1993." *PSA* 9, no. 2 (1993): 141–170.

Brunner, Georg. *Politische Soziologie der UdSSR*. Teil II. Wiesbaden, 1977.

Buckley, Mary. "Political Groups and Crisis." *JCS* 9, no. 1 (March 1993): 173–191.

Cappelli, Ottorino. "The Short Parliament 1989–91: Political Elites, Societal Cleavages and the Weakness of Party Politics." *JCS* 9, no. 1 (March 1993): 109–130.

Carrère d'Encausse, Hélène. *L'Empire eclaté: La revolte des nations en URSS*. Paris, 1978.

———. *Victorieuse Russie*. Paris: Fayard, 1992.

Carstairs, Andrew McLaren. *A Short History of Electoral Systems in Western Europe*. London: Allen and Unwin, 1980.

Carter, Stephen K. *Russian Nationalism: Yesterday, Today, Tomorrow*. London: Pinter, 1990.

Cherniaev, A. S. *Shest' let s Gorbachevym: Po dnevnikovym zapisam*. Moscow: Progress/Kultura, 1993.

Chiesa, Giulietto. *Transition to Democracy in the USSR: Ending the Monopoly of Power and the Evolution of New Political Forces*. Kennan Institute Occasional Paper 237. Washington, D.C.: Kennan Institute, 1990.

Colton, Timothy J. "The Politics of Democratization: The Moscow Election of 1990." *SE* 6, no. 4 (October–December 1990): 285–344.

Colton, Timothy J., and Robert Legvold, eds. *After the Soviet Union: From Empire to Nations*. New York and London: Norton, 1992.

Dadashev, Alikhan. "Regional'naia politika v Rossiiskoi Federatsii": Tezisy doklada. Sapporo: Slavic Research Center, 1994.

Dahl, Robert A. *Modern Political Analysis*. 5th ed. Englewood Cliffs, N.J.: Prentice Hall, 1991.

Dahrendorf, Ralf. *Reflections on the Revolution in Europe: In a Letter Intended to Have Been Sent to a Gentleman in Warsaw, 1990*. London: Chatto and Windus, 1990.

Dawisha, Karen, and Bruce Parrott. *Russia and the New States of Eurasia: The Politics of Upheaval*. Cambridge, New York, and Melbourne: Cambridge UP, 1994.

Desai, Padma. "Soviet Economic Reform: A Tale of Two Plans." *The Harriman Institute Forum* 3, no. 12 (December 1990): 1–12.

Diamond, Larry, Juan J. Linz, and Seymour Martin Lipset, eds. *Democracy in Developing Countries*. Vol. 2, *Africa*; vol. 3, *Asia*; vol. 4, *Latin America*. Boulder, Colo.: Lynne Rienner, 1988–1989.

Diamond, Larry, and Marc F. Plattner, eds. *The Global Resurgence of Democracy*. Baltimore and London: The Johns Hopkins UP, 1993.

Dmitriev, Iu. A., and A. A. Zlatopol'skii. *Grazhdanin i Vlast'*. Moscow: Manuskript, 1994.

Dobrokhotov, L. N., sost. *Gorbachev-El'tsin: 1500 dnei politicheskogo protivosostoianiia*. Moscow: Terra, 1992.

Dobrokhotov, L. N., V. N. Kolodezhnyi, A. I. Kozhokina, and A. D. Kotykhov, sost. *Krasnoe ili beloe? Drama Avgusta-91: Fakty, gipotezy, stolknovenie mnenii*. Moscow: Terra, 1992.

Embree, Gregory J. "RSFSR Election Results and Roll Call Votes." *SovSt* 43, no. 6 (1991): 1065–1085.

Erickson, John. "Fallen from Grace: The New Russian Military." *World Policy Journal* 10, no. 2 (Summer 1993): 19–24.

Evans, Alfred B., Jr. "Problems of Conflict Management in Russian Politics." *JCS* 9, no. 2 (June 1993): 1–19.

Fainsod, Merle. *How RUSSIA is Ruled.* Rev. ed. Cambridge, Mass.: Harvard UP, 1967.

Feldbrugge, F.J.M. *Russian Law: The End of the Soviet System and the Role of Law.* Law in Eastern Europe, no. 45. Dordrecht, Boston, and London: Nijhoff, 1993.

Feofanov, Yuri. "The Establishment of the Constitutional Court in Russia and the Communist Party Case." *RevCEEL* 19, no. 6 (December 1993): 623–637.

"500 Days: Shatalin at Columbia." *The Harriman Institute Forum* 3, no. 12 (December 1990): 1–12.

Fomin, S. "The Economic Developments in Ukraine: Some Causes of the Crisis." Paper presented at the 1994 Annual National Conference of the Slavic Research Center, Sapporo (Japan), 27 January 1994.

Foster, Frances H. "Izvestiia as a Mirror of Russian Legal Reform: Press, Law, and Crisis in the Post-Soviet Era." *Vanderbilt Journal of Transnational Law* 26, no. 4 (November 1993): 675–747.

Friedgut, Theodore H. *Political Participation in the USSR.* Princeton: Princeton UP, 1979.

Friedrich, Carl Joachim. *Man and His Government: An Empirical Theory of Politics.* New York: McGraw-Hill, 1963.

Fuchs, Marina. "Die russischen Nationalidee als Faktor im politischen Kampf für Reformen." *Osteuropa* 43, no. 4 (April 1993): 328–340 (I); no. 5 (May 1993): 461–472 (II).

Gestwa, Klaus. "Die Wiedergeburt des Kosakentums." *Osteuropa* 43, no. 5 (May 1993): 452–460.

Gibson, James L., and Raymond M. Duch. "Emerging Democratic Values in Soviet Political Culture." In Arthur Miller, William Reisinger, and Vicki Heslie, *The New Soviet Citizen: Public Opinion and Political Transformations in the Gorbachev Era.* Boulder, Colo.: Westview, 1992.

Gibson, James L., Raymond M. Duch, and Kent L. Tedlin. "Democratic Values and Transformation of the Soviet Union." *Journal of Politics* 54, no. 2 (May 1992): 329–371.

Gitelman, Zvi. "Soviet Political Culture: Insights from Jewish Emigres." *SovSt* 29 (1977): 543–564.

Gleason, Gregory. *Federalism and Nationalism: The Struggle for Republican Rights in the USSR.* Boulder, Colo.: Westview Press, 1990.

Gorbachev, M. S. *Dekabr'-91: Moia pozitsiia.* Moscow: Novosti, 1992.

Götz, Roland, and Uwe Halbach. "Daten zur Geographie, Bevölkerung, Politik und Wirtschaft der Staaten der GUS." *BiOS* (Sonderveröffentlichung), July 1992.

Grachev, Andrei. *Dal'she bez menia . . . Ukhod prezidenta.* Moscow: Progress/Kultura, 1994.

Greenberg, Douglas, Stanley N. Katz, Melanie Beth Oliviero, and Steven C. Wheatley, eds. *Constitutionalism and Democracy: Transitions in the Contemporary World.* New York and Oxford: Oxford UP, 1993.

Hadenius, Axel. *Democracy and Development.* Cambridge: Cambridge UP, 1992.

Hahn, Jeffrey W. "Local Politics and Political Power in Russia: The Case of Yaroslavl'." *SE* 7, no. 4 (October–December 1991): 322–341.

———. "Continuity and Change in Russian Political Culture." *British Journal of Political Science* 21, no. 4 (November 1991): 393–421.

———. "Attitudes toward Reform among Provincial Russian Politicians." *PSA* 9, no. 1 (1993): 66–85.

Halperin, Morton H. "Guaranteeing Democracy." *Foreign Policy*, no. 91 (Summer 1993): 105–122.

Held, David, ed. *Prospects for Democracy: North, South, East, West.* Cambridge: Polity Press, 1993.

Helf, Gavin, and Jeffrey W. Hahn. "Old Dogs and New Tricks: Party Elites in the Russian Regional Elections of 1990." *Slavic Review* 51, no. 3 (Fall 1992): 511–530.

Hellie, Richard, "Zemskii Sobor." In Joseph L. Wiecsynski, ed., *The Modern Encyclopedia of Russian and Soviet History*, 45: 226–234. Gulf Breeze, Fla.: Academic International Press, 1987.

Hendrikse, Huib. *Gorbatsjov en de neergang van het communisme.* Clingendael Cahier 17. 's-Gravenhage: Nederlands Instituut voor Internationale Betrekkingen "Clingendael," 1991.

———. "De politieke neergang van Boris Jeltsin." *Internationale Spectator* 47, no. 12 (December 1993): 685–692.

Hersh, Seymour M. "The Wild East." *Atlantic Monthly*, June 1994, 61–86.

Hewett, Ed A. "The New Soviet Plan." *Foreign Affairs* 69, no. 5 (1990–1991): 146–167.

Holmes, Leslie. *The End of Communist Power: Anti-Corruption Campaigns and Legitimation Crisis.* Cambridge: Polity Press, 1993.

Hosking, Geoffrey A., Jonathan Aves, and Peter J. S. Duncan. *The Road to Post-Communism: Independent Political Movements in the Soviet Union, 1985–1991.* London and New York: Pinter, 1992.

Hughes, Michael. "The Never-Ending Story: Russian Nationalism, National Communism and Opposition to Reform in the USSR and Russia." *JCS* 9, no. 2 (June 1993): 41–61.

Huntington, Samuel P. *The Third Wave: Democratization in the Late Twentieth Century.* Norman and London: University of Oklahoma Press, 1991.

Inkeles, Alex, and Raymond Bauer. *The Soviet Citizen: Daily Life in a Totalitarian Society.* New York: Atheneum, 1968.

International Association "For Collaboration of the Scientists of the World." Brochure. Moscow: Nedra, n.d.

Ito, Takayuki. "Political Fragmentation in Russia: Is the Multi-Party System Bound to Fail in a Post-Communist Country?" Paper presented to the 4th Russo-Japanese Conference of Political Scientists, Moscow 25–26 May 1993.

———. "Regionalism in Russian Politics." In *Realignment of Russian Politics*, 25–57. Slavic Research Center Occasional Paper, no. 50. Sapporo: Slavic Research Center, Hokkaido University, 1994.

Ivashov, L. G. *Marshal Yazov (Rokovoi Avgust 91-go).* Vel'sk: MP Vel'ti, 1993.

Jarygina, T., and G. Martschenko. "Regionale Prozesse in der ehemaligen UdSSR und im neuen Rußland." *Osteuropa* 43, no. 3 (March 1993): 211–228.

Jeltsin, Boris. *Getuigenis van een opposant.* Baarn: Anthos/Iannoo, 1990.

———. *Het alternatief: Onze weg naar de democratie.* Met een voorwoord van Huib Hendrikse. Amsterdam: Jan Mets, n.d. (1992).

See also Yel'tsin, Boris.

Jukes, Geoffrey J. "Russia's Problems and the Russian Military." In *Suravu-Yurajia ni okeru hendō-to shin chitsujo no mosaku* (Transformations in Slavic Eurasia and the search for a new order), 136–146. Slavic Research Center Occasional Paper, no. 45. Sapporo: Slavic Research Center, Hokkaido University, 1993.

"K voprosu o zashchite prav russkoiazychnogo naseleniia v stranakh SNG, Baltiki i Gruzii." Internal document, Russian Ministry of Foreign Affairs. Moscow, 1992/1993.

Kagarlitsky, Boris, and Renfrey Clarke. "Russia's Trade Union Movement: Bureaucrats and Militants in the Epoch of Capitalist Restoration." Distributed by e-mail, 3 January 1994.

Karklins, Rasma. "Explaining Regime Change in the Soviet Union." *EAS* 46, no. 1 (1994): 29–45.

Khasbulatov, Ruslan. *The Struggle for Russia: Power and Change in the Democratic Revolution.* Edited by Richard Sakwa. London and New York: Routledge, 1993.

Kliamkin, I. M. "Postkommunisticheskaia demokratiia i ee istoricheskie osobennosti v Rossii." *Polis*, 1993, no. 2: 6–24.

———. "Politicheskaia sotsiologiia perekhodnogo obshchestva." *Polis*, 1993, no. 4: 41–64.

Kliamkin, I., E. Petrenko, and D. Chubukov. *Vlast', Oppozitsiia i Russkoe Obshchestvo.* Moscow: Fond Obshchestvennoe Mnenie, 1992.

Kolstø, Pål, and Andrei Edemsky, with Natalya Kalashnikova. "The Dniester Conflict: Between Irredentism and Separatism." *EAS* 45, no. 6 (1993): 973–1000.

Komarovskii, V. S. "Politicheskii vybor izbiratelia." *Sotsiologicheskie issledovaniia*, 1992, no. 3: 23–34. Translation: "The Political Choice of the Voter." *Russian Social Science Review* 34, no. 3 (May–June 1993): 3– .

Kooijmans, P. H. *Maintaining the Peace in the Shadowland between the Old and the New International Order.* Tenth Uhlenbeck Lecture. Wassenaar: NIAS, 1992.

Kornhauser, William. *The Politics of Mass Society.* Glencoe, Ill.: The Free Press, 1959.

Kovacs, Dezsö, and Sally Ward Maggard. "The Human Face of Political, Economic, and Social Change in Eastern Europe." *East European Quarterly* 27, no. 3 (September 1993): 317–345.

Kozyrev, Andrei V. "Russia and Human Rights." *Slavic Review* 51, no. 2 (Summer 1992): 287–293.

Kuiper, Marcus A. "Keeping the Peace: Reflections on the Rules of the Game for International Intervention in the 1990s." *The Journal of Slavic Military Studies* 6, no. 4 (December 1993): 562–575.

Kunaev, Dinmukhamed. *O moem vremeni.* Alma-Ata: RGZhI Deuir, 1992.

Kutsyllo, Veronika. *Zapiski iz Belogo Doma: 21 sentiabria–4 oktiabria 1993g.* Moscow: Izdatel'skii Dom Kommersant," 1993.

Lamont, Neil V. "Territorial Dimensions of Ethnic Conflict: The Moldovan Case, 1991–March 1993." *Journal of Slavic Military Studies* 6, no. 4 (December 1993): 576–612.

Laqueur, Walter, ed. *Fascism: A Reader's Guide: Analyses, Interpretations, Bibliography.* Berkeley and Los Angeles: University of California Press, 1976.

Lebed', Aleksandr. *Spektakl' Nazyvalsia Putch: Neizvestnoe ob izvestnom: Vospominaniia generala vozdushno-desantnykh voisk.* Tiraspol': Rekliz-EOLIS/Lada, 1993.

Legvold, Robert. "Russia and the Major Powers of East Asia." Paper prepared for the third RIPS Japan/US Conference on the Former Soviet Union, Honolulu, November 17–18, 1993.

Lepenies, Wolf. *Toleration in the New Europe: Three Tales.* Eleventh Uhlenbeck Lecture. Wassenaar: NIAS, 1993.

Lewin, Moshe. *The Gorbachev Phenomenon: A Historical Interpretation.* London: Hutchinson Radius, 1988.

Ligachev, Yegor. *Inside Gorbachev's Kremlin: The Memoirs of Yegor Ligachev.* Introduction by Stephen F. Cohen. Translated from the Russian by Catherine A. Fitzpatrick, Michele A. Berdy, and Dobrochna Dyrcz-Freeman. New York: Pantheon Books, 1993.

Lijphart, Arend, and Bernard Grofman, eds. *Choosing an Electoral System: Issues and Alternatives.* New York: Praeger, 1984.

Litvinova, G. I. *Svet i teni progressa.* Moscow, 1989.

Livshits, R. Z. *Trudovoe zakonodatel'stvo: Nastoiashchee i budushchee.* Moscow: Nauka, 1989.

Lohr, Eric. "Arkadii Volsky's Political Base." *EAS* 45, no. 5 (1993): 811–829.

Löwenhardt, John. "The Tale of the Torch: Scientists-entrepreneurs in the Soviet Union." *Survey,* 1974, vol. 4 [no. 93]: 113–121.

———. *Decision Making in Soviet Politics.* London: Macmillan; New York: St. Martin's Press, 1981.

———. "The Foreign Policy of the Russian Federation." *Internationale Spectator* 45, no. 12 (December 1991): 734–741.

———. *Het Sovjetsyndroom: Over de politieke nalatenschap van de Sovjetunie* (The Soviet syndrome: On the political legacy of the Soviet Union). Leiden: Stichting Oosteuropees Recht, 1993.

———. "The New Political Map of Russia: Regional Variations in the 25 April 1993 referendum." Research paper, Slavic Research Center, Hokkaido University. August 1993.

———. "Soviet-Russian Federalism in Comparative Perspective." In Takayuki Ito and Shinichiro Tabata, eds., *Between Disintegration and Reintegration: Former Socialist Countries and the World since 1989.* Sapporo: Slavic Research Center, 1994: 91–125.

———. "Institutional Choices in the Transition to Democracy: Russia between Parliamentarianism and Presidentialism." In *Realignment of Russian Politics,* 1–24. Slavic Research Center Occasional Paper, no. 50. Sapporo: Slavic Research Center, Hokkaido University, 1994.

———, ed. *Cutting the Gordian Knot: Responsible Government and Elections in Russia.* Slavic Research Center Occasional Paper, no. 49. Sapporo: Slavic Research Center, Hokkaido University, 1994.

Luchterhandt, Galina. "Ruzkoj im Aufwind: Rußlands Vizepräsident und seine 'Volkspartei Freies Rußland.'" *Osteuropa* 43, no. 1 (January 1993): 3–20.

Luk'ianov, Anatolii. *Perevorot Mnimyi i Nastoiashchii: Otvety na voprosy iz "Matroskoi tishiny."* Moscow: Paleia, 1993.

Lyubarsky, Kronid. "Election Rigging." *New Times International,* 1994, no. 7: 6–13.

Malek, Martin. "Die Krim im russisch-ukrainischen Spannungsfeld." *Osteuropa* 43, no. 6 (June 1993): 551–562.

Malloy, James A., Jr., and Jane E. Good. "Duma." In Joseph L. Wiecsynski, ed., *The*

Modern Encyclopedia of Russian and Soviet History, 10:39–51. Gulf Breeze, Fla.: Academic International Press, 1979.

Markov, Sergei, and Michael McFaul. *The Troubled Birth of Russian Democracy: Parties, Personalities and Programs.* Stanford: Hoover Institution Press, 1993.

McAuley, Mary. "Politics, Economics, and Elite Realignment in Russia: A Regional Perspective." *SE* 8, no. 1 (January–March 1992): 46–88.

McFaul, Michael. "Russian Centrism and Revolutionary Transitions." *PSA* 9, no. 3 (July–September 1993): 196–222.

Migranian, A. M. "The End of Perestroika's Euphoric Stage." In Shugo Minagawa, ed., *Thorny Path to the Post-Perestroika World: Problems of Institutionalization,* 99–126. Sapporo: Slavic Research Center, Hokkaido University, 1992.

Mikhaleva, N. A., and V. A. Rakhlevskii. *Gosudarstvennoe ustroistvo Rossii.* Moscow: Nezavisimoe Izdatel'stvo Manuskript, 1994.

Millar, James R., ed. *Politics, Work, and Daily Life in the USSR: A Survey of Former Soviet Citizens.* Cambridge: Cambridge UP, 1987.

Miller, John. *Mikhail Gorbachev and the End of Soviet Power.* New York: St. Martin's Press, 1993.

Miller, Robert F., ed. *The Development of Civil Society in Communist Systems.* Sydney: Allen and Unwin, 1992.

Morrison, John. *Boris Yeltsin: From Bolshevik to Democrat.* Harmondsworth: Penguin, 1991.

Moses, Joel. "Soviet Provincial Politics in an Era of Transition and Revolution, 1989–1991." *SovSt* 44, no. 3 (1992): 479–509.

Motyl, Alexander J. *Dilemmas of Independence: Ukraine after Totalitarianism.* New York: Council of Foreign Relations Press, 1993.

Nadais, A. "Vybor izbiratel'nykh sistem." *Polis,* 1993, no. 3: 70–78.

Nahaylo, Bohdan, and Victor Swoboda. *Soviet Disunion: A History of the Nationalities Problem in the USSR.* New York: The Free Press, 1989.

Nenarokov, A. P., sost. *Nesostoiavshiisia iubilei: Pochemu SSSR ne otprazdnoval svoego 70-letiia!* Moscow: Terra, 1992.

Nove, Alec. *The Soviet System in Retrospect: An Obituary Notice.* The Forth Annual W. Averell Harriman Lecture, 17 February 1993. New York: The Harriman Institute, Columbia University, 1993.

"O problemakh russkoiazychnogo naseleniia v Uzbekistane." Internal document, Russian Ministry of Foreign Affairs. Moscow, 1992/1993.

"O territorial'nykh pretenziiakh Estonii k Rossii." Internal document, Russian Ministry of Foreign Affairs. Moscow, 1993.

"O zashchite russkoiazychnogo naseleniia v stranakh Srednei Azii." Internal document, Russian Ministry of Foreign Affairs. Moscow, 1992/1993.

O'Donnell, Guillermo, and Philippe C. Schmitter, eds. *Transitions from Authoritarian Rule: Tentative Conclusions about Uncertain Democracies.* Baltimore and London: The Johns Hopkins UP, 1986.

O'Donnell, Guillermo, Philippe C. Schmitter, and Laurence Whitehead, eds. *Transitions from Authoritarian Rule: Comparative Perspectives.* Baltimore and London: The Johns Hopkins UP, 1986.

———. *Transitions from Authoritarian Rule: Latin America.* Baltimore and London: The Johns Hopkins UP, 1986.

———. *Transitions from Authoritarian Rule: Southern Europe.* Baltimore and London: The Johns Hopkins UP, 1986.

Organski, A.F.K., and Jacek Kugler. "The Costs of Major Wars: The Phoenix Factor." *APSR* 71 (1977): 1347–1366.

Oversloot, Hans. "Ruslands keuze?" *Socialisme en Democratie* 51, no. 3 (March 1994): 142–147.

Pavlov, Valentin. *Avgust Iznutri: Gorbachev-Putch.* Moscow: Delovoi Mir/Business World, 1993.

Pipes, Richard. *Survival Is Not Enough: Soviet Realities and America's Future.* New York: Simon and Schuster, 1984.

Pivovarov, Jurij, and Andrej Fursov. "Die KPdSU und das kommunistische System: Zum Prozeß über das Verbot der KPdSU vor dem russischen Verfassungsgericht." *BiOS*, 1993, no. 30.

Poljan, Pawel, hg. "Die Bevölkerung Rußlands: Neue Tendenzen und Veränderungen." *BiOS* (Sonderveröffentlichung), May 1993.

Pomerants, G. S. "The Irrational in Politics." *Russian Social Science Review* 34, no. 6 (November–December 1993): 42–51. Translation of "Irratsional'noe v politike." *Voprosy Filosofii*, 1992, no. 4: 16–21.

Popov, N. A. "Agrarnaia reforma i fermerstvo v Rossii." Tezisy doklada v Universitete Khokkaido, August 1993.

"Post-Communist Eastern Europe: A Survey of Opinion," *East European Politics and Societies* 4, no. 2 (Spring 1990): 153–207.

Preliminary Staff Report, North Atlantic Assembly Mission to Monitor Russian Elections, 8–13 December 1993. Brussels: North Atlantic Assembly, December 1993.

Pye, Lucian W. "Political Science and the Crisis of Authoritarianism." APSA presidential address, 2 September 1989. *APSR* 84, no. 1 (March 1990): 3–19.

———, ed. *Political Science and Area Studies: Rivals or Partners?* Bloomington and London: Indiana UP, 1975.

Rabochaia gruppa, obrazovannaia sovmestnym resheniem M. S. Gorbacheva i B. N. El'tsina. *Perekhod k rynku.* Chast' 1, *Kontseptsiia i Programma;* Chast' 2, *Proekty zakonodatel'nykh aktov.* Moscow: Arkhangel'skoe, August 1990.

Ramet, Sabrina P. "'Triple Chauvinism' in the New Eastern Europe." *Acta Slavica Iaponica* 12 (1994): 121–49.

———. *Social Currents in Eastern Europe: The Sources and Consequences of the Great Transformation.* 2d ed. Durham, N.C.: Duke UP, 1995.

Remington, Thomas F. "Regime Transition in Communist Systems: The Soviet Case." *SE* 6, no. 2 (April–June 1990): 160–190.

Rigby, T. H. *The Changing Soviet System: Mono-Organizational Socialism from its Origins to Gorbachev's Restructuring.* Aldershot: Edward Elgar, 1990.

———. *Political Elites in the USSR: Central Leaders and Local Cadres from Lenin to Gorbachev.* Aldershot: Edward Elgar, 1990.

———. "The USSR: End of a long, dark night?" In Robert F. Miller, ed., *The Development of Civil Society in Communist Systems,* 11–23. Sydney: Allen and Unwin, 1992.

———. "The Troubled Path to a New Socio-political Order in Russia." Paper for the International Symposium, Tokyo, 24 November 1993.

———. "Yeltsin's Presidency and the Evolution of Representative and Responsible

Government in Russia." In John Löwenhardt, ed., *Cutting the Gordian Knot: Responsible Government and Elections in Russia*, 5–21. Slavic Research Center Occasional Papers, no. 49. Sapporo: Slavic Research Center, Hokkaido University, 1994.

Roxburgh, Angus. *De tweede Russische revolutie: De strijd om de macht in het Kremlin*. Vertaald door Ton Stauttener. Amsterdam: Bert Bakker, 1992.

Rubinstein, Alvin Z. *Soviet Foreign Policy Since World War II: Imperial and Global*. 2d ed. Boston and Toronto: Little, Brown and Co., 1985.

Russian Federation. IMF Economic Reviews 1993, [no.] 8. Washington, D.C.: International Monetary Fund, June 1993.

Saizew, Sergej. "Separatismus in Rußland." *BiOS*, 1992, no. 42 (14 October).

Sakwa, Richard. *Gorbachev and His Reforms, 1985–1990*. New York: Philip Allan, 1990.

Salmin, Aleksei M. "From the Union to the Commonwealth: The Problem of the New Federalism." *JCS* 9, no. 1 (March 1993): 33–53.

Savitsky, Valery. "Will There Be a New Judicial Power in the New Russia?" *RevCEEL* 19, no. 6 (December 1993): 639–660.

Schröder, Hans-Hennig. "Kameradenschinderei und Nationalitätenkonflikte: Ein Rückblick auf die inneren Probleme der sowjetischen Streitkräfte in den Jahren 1987–1991." *BiOS*, 1992, no. 39 (September).

———. "Eine Armee in der Krise: Die russischen Streitkräfte 1992–93: Risikofaktor oder Garant politischer Stabilität?" *BiOS*, 1993, no. 45.

Schroeder, Gertrude E. "*Perestroyka* in the Aftermath of 1990." *SE* 7, no. 1 (1991): 3–13.

Shiokawa, Nobuaki. "Russia's Fourth *Smuta*: What Was, Is, and Will Be Russia?" In Osamu Ieda, ed. *New Order in Post-Communist Eurasia*, 201–221. Sapporo: Slavic Research Center, Hokkaido University, 1993.

Shlapentokh, Vladimir. *Public and Private Life of the Soviet People: Changing Values in Post-Stalin Russia*. New York and Oxford: Oxford UP, 1989.

Shmelev, G. I. "Agrarnyi sektor v usloviiakh provedeniia agrarnoi reformy." Doklad dlia vystupleniia v Universitete Khokkaido, August 1993.

Silver, Brian D. "Political Beliefs of the Soviet Citizen: Sources of Support for Regime Norms." In James R. Millar, ed., *Politics, Work, and Daily Life in the USSR: A Survey of Former Soviet Citizens*, 100–141. Cambridge: Cambridge UP, 1987.

Simis, Konstantin. *USSR: The Corrupt Society: The Secret World of Soviet Capitalism*. New York: Simon and Schuster; London: Dent, 1982.

Skilling, H. Gordon, and Franklyn Griffiths, eds. *Interest Groups in Soviet Politics*. Princeton, NJ: Princeton UP, 1971.

Smith, Alan. *International Trade and Payments in the Former Soviet/CMEA Area*. Post-Soviet Business Forum. London: Royal Institute of International Affairs, 1994.

Smith, Graham, ed. *The Nationalities Question in the Soviet Union*. London and New York: Longman, 1990.

Speckhard, Michael. *The Awakening Bear: The Development of a Competitive Party System in Russia*. Ph.D. dissertation, University of Houston, 1991. Ann Arbor: UMI Dissertation Information Service, 1992.

Starr, S. Frederick. "The Changing Nature of Change in the USSR." In Seweryn

Bialer and Michael Mandelbaum, eds., *Gorbachev's Russia and American Foreign Policy*. Boulder and London: Westview, 1988.

———. "The USSR: A Civil Society." *Foreign Policy* 70 (1989): 26–41.

Strashun, B. A., and V. L. Sheinis. "Politicheskaia situatsiia v Rossii i novyi izbiratel'nyi zakon." *Polis*, 1993, no. 3: 65–69.

A Study of the Soviet Economy. Vol. 1. Paris: IMF, The World Bank, OECD, EBRD, 1991.

Szamuely, Tibor. *The Russian Tradition*. Edited with an introduction by Robert Conquest. London: Secker and Warburg, 1974.

Szporluk, Roman. "The Soviet West—Or Far Eastern Europe?" *East European Politics and Societies* 5, no. 3 (Fall 1991): 466–482.

Tabata, Shinichiro. "Inflation in Russia." Paper prepared for the Symposium (3–4 March 1994) organized by the Economic Planning Agency, Tokyo, Japan.

Theen, Rolf H. W. "Political Reform in the Soviet Union." In Ilpyong J. Kim and Jane Shapiro Zacek, eds., *Reform and Transformation in Communist Systems: Comparative Perspectives*, 15–53. New York: Paragon House, 1991.

———. "'Habits of the Heart' and the Empire Mentality in Russia: From Homo Etaticus to Citizen?" Unpublished manuscript, 1992.

———. "Russia at the Grassroots: Reform at the Local and Regional Levels." *In Depth*, Winter 1993: 53–90.

Titma, Mikk, and Nancy B. Tuma. "Migration in the Former Soviet Union." *BiOS*, 1992, no. 22 (April).

Tolz, Vera, and Melanie Newton, eds. *The USSR in 1991: A Record of Events*. Boulder, Colo.: Westview Press, 1993.

Tsipko, Alexander S. "Dialectics of the Ascent of a New Russian Statehood." In Osamu Ieda, ed., *New Order in Post-Communist Eurasia*. 187–201. Sapporo: Slavic Research Center, Hokkaido University, 1993.

———. "Restavratsiia ili polnaia i okonchatel'naia sovetizatsiia? Nepreryvnost' i preryvnost' v Rossiiskoi istorii XX veka," in *Suravu-Yurajia ni okeru hendō to shin chitsujo no mosaku* (Transformations in Slavic Eurasia and the search for a new order), 155–190. Slavic Research Center Occasional Paper, no. 45. Sapporo: Slavic Research Center, Hokkaido University, 1993.

Umov, V. I. "Rossiiskii srednii klass: Sotsial'naia real'nost' i politicheskii fantom." *Polis*, 1993, no. 4: 26–40.

Urban, Michael E. *More Power to the Soviets: The Democratic Revolution in the USSR*. Aldershot: Edward Elgar, 1990.

Vaksberg, Arkady. *The Soviet Mafia*. London: Weidenfeld and Nicolson, 1991.

Varennikov, Valentin. *Sud'ba i Sovest'*. Moscow: Paleia, 1993.

Weigle, Marcia A., and Jim Butterfield. "Civil Society in Reforming Communist Regimes: The Logic of Emergence." *Comparative Politics* 25, no. 1 (October 1992): 1–23.

Wettig, Gerhard, hg. "Sicherheits- und Bedrohungsperzeptionen in Ost- und Mitteleuropa." *BiOS*, 1993, no. 43.

White, Stephen. *Political Culture and Soviet Politics*. London and Basingstoke: Macmillan, 1979.

———. *After Gorbachev*. Cambridge: Cambridge University Press, 1993.

———. "Post-Communist Politics: Towards Democratic Pluralism?" *JCS* 9, no. 1 (March 1993): 18–32.

White, Stephen, Graeme Gill, and Darrell Slider. *The Politics of Transition: Shaping a Post-Soviet Future.* Cambridge and New York: Cambridge UP, 1993.
Willerton, John P. *Patronage and Politics in the USSR.* Cambridge: Cambridge UP, 1992.
Yanov, Alexander. *The Russian New Right: Right-wing Ideologies in the Contemporary USSR.* Berkeley: University of California, Institute of International Studies, 1978.
———. *The Russian Challenge and the Year 2000.* Translated by Iden J. Rosenthal. Oxford: Basil Blackwell, 1987.
Yel'tsin, Boris. *Zapiski prezidenta.* Moscow: Ogonek, 1994. *See also Jeltsin, Boris.*
Zaslavskaya, Tatyana. "The Novosibirsk Report." In Murray Yanovitch, ed., *A Voice of Reform: Essays by Tat'iana I. Zaslavskaia.* 158–183. Armonk, N.Y., and London: M. E. Sharpe, 1989.
———. *The Second Socialist Revolution: An Alternative Soviet Strategy.* Translated by Susan M. Davies with Jenny Warren. London: I. B. Tauris, 1990.
Zemtsov, Ilia. *Partiia ili mafiia: Razvorovannaia respublika.* Paris: Les Editeurs Reunis, 1976.
Zhirinovskii, Vladimir. *Obrashchenie k chlenam LDPR i sochuvstvuiushchim: Programma Liberal'no-Demokraticheskoi partii Rossii: Ustav LDPR.* N.p.: N.d. [1993].
———. *Poslednii brosok na Iug.* Moscow: Pisatel'/Bukvitsa, 1993.
Ziuganov, Gennadii. *Drama Vlasti: Stranitsy Politicheskoi Avtobiografii.* Moscow: Paleia, 1993.

2. SELECTED RUSSIAN LEGISLATION AND OTHER LEGISLATIVE DOCUMENTS IN CHRONOLOGICAL ORDER:

"Zakon SSSR O razgranichenii polnomochii mezhdu Soiuzom SSR i sub"ektami federatsii" (26 April 1990). *VedSSSR*, 1990, no. 19: 429–433.
"Doklad predsedatelia Mandatnoi kommissii G. P. Viatkina." *SR*, 18 May 1990.
"Deklaratsiia o gosudarstvennom suverenitete Rossiiskoi Sovetskoi Federativnoi Sotsialisticheskoi Respubliki" (12 June 1990). *SR*, 14 June 1990.
"Zakon RSFSR Ob obespechenii ekonomicheskoi osnovy suvereniteta RSFSR" (31 October 1990). *VedRSFSR*, 1990, no. 22: 305–307.
"Ukaz Prezidenta SSSR O nekotorykh aktakh po voprosam oborony, priniatykh v soiuznykh respublikakh" (1 December 1990). *VedSSSR*, 1990, no. 49: 1303–1304.
"Zaiavlenie Prezidiuma Verkhovnogo Soveta RSFSR v sviazi s situatsiei, slozhivsheisia v respublikakh Pribaltiki" (12 January 1991). *VedRSFSR*, 1991, no. 2: 11.
"Postanovlenie Verkhovnogo Soveta SSSR 'Ob itogakh referenduma SSSR 17 marta 1991 goda'" (21 March 1991). In A. P. Nenarokov, sost., *Nesostoiavshiisia iubilei: Pochemu SSSR ne otprazdnoval svoego 70-letiia?* 435–438. Moscow: Terra, 1992.
"Sovmestnoe zaiavlenie o bezotlagatel'nykh merakh po stabilizatsii obstanovki v strane i preodoleniiu krizisa" (23 April 1991). *Pravda*, 24 April 1991.
"Zakon RSFSR O vyborakh Prezidenta RSFSR" (24 April 1991). *VedRSFSR*, 1991, no. 17: 455–463.
"Zakon RSFSR O Prezidente RSFSR" (24 April 1991). *VedRSFSR*, 1991, no. 17: 463–466.

"Rasporiazhenie Predsedatelia Verkhovnogo Soveta RSFSR Ob izmenenii uslovii khoziaistvovaniia predpriatii ugol'noi i drugikh bazovykh otraslei promyshlennosti na territorii RSFSR" (1 May 1991). *VedRSFSR*, 1991, no. 18: 571–574.

"Zakon RSFSR O Konstitutsionnom Sude RSFSR" (6 May 1991). *VedRSFSR*, 1991, no. 19: 579–620.

"Postanovlenie Prezidiuma Verkhovnogo Soveta RSFSR O poriadke ucheta izbiratel'nykh biulletenei po vyboram Prezidenta RSFSR 12 iiunia 1991 goda" (20 May 1991). *VedRSFSR*, 1991, no. 21: 714.

"Postanovlenie Prezidiuma Verkhovnogo Soveta RSFSR O vvedenii instituta nabliudatelei Prezidiuma Verkhovnogo Soveta RSFSR za provedeniem vyborov Prezidenta RSFSR" (20 May 1991). *VedRSFSR*, 1991, no. 21: 715.

"Ukaz Prezidenta RSFSR O prekrashchenii deiatel'nosti organizatsionnykh struktur politicheskikh partii i massovykh obshchestvennykh dvizhenii v gosudarstvennykh organakh, uchrezhdeniiakh i organizatsiiakh RSFSR" (20 July 1991). *VedRSFSR*, 1991, no. 31: 1321–1322.

"Postanovlenie Prezidiuma Verkhovnogo Soveta RSFSR Ob organizatsii Upravleniia Delami Prezidiuma Verkhovnogo Soveta RSFSR" (30 July 1991). *VedRSFSR*, 1991, no. 31: 1341.

"Ukaz Prezidenta RSFSR" (no. 59; 19 August 1991). *VedRSFSR*, 1991, no. 34: 1412–1413.

"Ukaz Prezidenta RSFSR O Predsedatele Gosudarstvennogo komiteta RSFSR po oboronnym voprosam" (19 August 1991). *VedRSFSR*, 1991, no. 34: 1413.

"Ukaz Prezidenta RSFSR" (no. 61; 19 August 1991). *VedRSFSR* 1991, no. 34: 1413–1414.

"Ukaz Prezidenta RSFSR" (no. 63; 19 August 1991). *VedRSFSR*, 1991, no. 34: 1414–1415.

"Ukaz Prezidenta RSFSR Ob upravlenii Vooruzhennymi Silami Soiuza SSR na territorii RSFSR v uslaviiakh chrezvychainoi situatsii" (20 August 1991). *VedRSFSR*, 1991, no. 34: 1416–1417.

"Ukaz Prezidenta RSFSR O naznachenii Ministra oborony RSFSR" (20 August 1991). *VedRSFSR*, 1991, no. 34: 1419.

"Postanovlenie Verkhovnogo Soveta RSFSR O politicheskoi situatsii v respublike, slozhivsheisia v rezultate antikonstitutsionnogo gosudarstvennogo perevorota v SSSR" (22 August 1991). *VedRSFSR*, 1991, no. 34: 1404–1405.

"Postanovlenie S"ezda narodnykh deputatov SSSR O merakh, vytekaiushchikh iz sovmestnogo Zaiavleniia Prezidenta SSSR i vysshikh rukovoditelei soiuznykh respublik i reshenii vneocherednoi sessii Verkhovnogo Soveta SSSR" (5 September 1991). *VedSSSR*, 1991, no. 37: 1485–1486.

"Zakon SSSR Ob organov gosudarstvennoi vlasti i upravleniia Soiuza SSSR v perekhodnyi period" (5 September 1991). *VedSSSR*, 1991, no. 37: 1487–1488.

"Deklaratsiia prav i svobod cheloveka' (5 September 1991). *VedSSSR*, 1991, no. 37: 1489–1492.

"Postanovlenie Gosudarstvennogo Soveta SSSR O priznanii nezavisimosti Litovskoi Respubliki" (6 September 1991). *VedSSSR*, 1991, no. 37: 1497.

"Ukaz Prezidenta RSFSR O roli Soveta Ministrov RSFSR v sisteme ispolnitel'noi vlasti Rossiiskoi Federatsii" (11 September 1991). *VedRSFSR*, 1991, no. 37: 1462–1464.

"Ukaz Prezidenta Rossiiskoi Sovetskoi Federativnoi Sotsialisticheskoi Respubliki O deiatel'nosti KPSS i KP RSFSR" (6 November 1991). *VedRSFSR*, 1991, no. 45: 1799–1800.

"Ukaz Prezidenta Rossiiskoi Sovetskoi Federativnoi Sotsialisticheskoi Respubliki O reorganizatsii pravitel'stva RSFSR" (6 November 1991). *Kom*, 1991, no. 43: 24.

"Ukaz Prezidenta Rossiiskoi Sovetskoi Federativnoi Sotsialisticheskoi Respubliki Ob organizatsii raboty Pravitel'stva RSFSR v usloviiakh ekonomicheskoi reformy" (6 November 1991). *VedRSFSR*, 1991, no. 45: 1800–1803.

"Obrashchenie Soveta Respublik Verkhovnogo Soveta SSSR K Verkhovnym Sovetam suverennykh gosudarstv" (3 December 1991). *Vedomosti Verkhovnogo Soveta SSSR*, 1991, no. 50: 1885.

"Zaiavlenie Soveta Respublik Verkhovnogo Soveta SSSR" (3 December 1991). *Vedomosti Verkhovnogo Soveta SSSR*, 1991, no. 50: 1886–1888.

"Postanovlenie Soveta Soiuza Verkhovnogo Soveta SSSR O proekte Dogovora o Soiuze Suverennykh Gosudarstv" (4 December 1991). *Vedomosti Verkhovnogo Soveta SSSR*, 1991, no. 50: 1891.

"Zaiavlenie narodnykh deputatov SSSR" (17 December 1991). *Vedomosti Verkhovnogo Soveta SSSR*, 1991, no. 52, 1972–1973.

"Zaiavlenie Soveta Respublik Verkhovnogo Soveta SSSR." *Vedomosti Verkhovnogo Soveta SSSR*, 1991, no. 52 (25 December 1991): 1973.

"Postanovlenie Soveta Respublik Verkhvnogo Soveta SSSR Ob osvobozhdenii narodnykh deputatov SSSR i narodnykh deputatov respublik, rabotaiushchikh na postoiannoi osnove v Sovete Respublik Verkhovnogo Soveta SSSR i organakh palaty, a takzhe rabotnikov Sekretariata Verkhovnogo Soveta SSSR ot vypolneniia sluzhebnykh obiazannostei" (24 December 1991). *Vedomosti Verkhovnogo Soveta SSSR*, 1991, no. 52: 1974.

"Ukaz Prezidenta Soiuza Sovetskikh Sotsialisticheskikh Respublik O slozhenii Prezidentom SSSR polnomochii Verkhovnogo Glavnokomanduiushchego Vooruzhennymi Silami SSSR i uprazdnenii Soveta oborony pri Prezidente SSSR" (25 December 1991). *Vedomosti Verkhovnogo Soveta SSSR*, 1991, no. 52: 2060.

"Deklaratsiia Soveta Respublik Verkhovnogo Soveta SSSR v sviazi s sozdaniem Sodruzhestva Nezavisimykh Gosudarstv" (26 December 1991). *Vedomosti Verkhovnogo Soveta SSSR*, 1991, no. 52: 2058–2059.

"O mezhdunarodno-pravovom statuse Rossii i drugikh gosudarstv-uchastnikov SNG kak pravopreemnikov SSSR." *Diplomaticheskii Vestnik*, 1992, no. 3: 18–19.

"Ukaz Prezidenta Rossiiskoi Federatsii O merakh po zashchite denezhnoi sistemy Rossiiskoi Federatsii" (no. 636; 21 June 1992). *SAPP*, 1992, no. 26: 1825–1826.

"Rasporiazhenie Prezidenta Rossiiskoi Federatsii" (Disbanding "Khasbulatov guard," 27 October 1992). *Izv*, 28 October 1992.

"Rasporiazhenie Prezidenta Rossiiskoi Federatsii O voprosakh zashchity prav i interesov rossiiskikh grazhdan za predelami Rossiiskoi Federatsii" (30 November 1992). *Diplomaticheskii Vestnik*, 1993, no. 1–2: 8.

"Ukaz Prezidenta Rossiiskoi Federatsii O deiatel'nosti ispolnitel'nykh organov do preodoleniia krizisa vlasti" (no. 379; 20 March 1993). *RV*, 25 March 1993.

"Ukaz Prezidenta Rossiiskoi Federatsii Ob osushchestvlenii Vitse-prezidentom Rossiiskoi Federatsii otdel'nykh polnomochii Prezidenta Rossiiskoi Federatsii" (no. 1398; 18 September 1993). *SAPP*, no. 38 (20 September 1993).

"Ukaz Prezidenta Rossiiskoi Federatsii O poetapnoi konstitutsionnoi reforme v Rossiiskoi Federatsii" (no. 1400; 21 September 1993, 20:00 hrs.). *RG*, 23 September 1993; *SAPP*, no. 39.

"Polozhenie o federal'nykh organakh vlasti na perekhodnyi period." *Izv,* 24 September 1993; *SAPP,* no. 39.

"Polozhenie o vyborakh deputatov gosudarstvennoi dumy." *Izv,* 24 September 1993; *SAPP,* no. 39.

"Ukaz Prezidenta Rossiiskoi Federatsii O dosrochnykh vyborakh Prezidenta Rossiiskoi Federatsii" (no. 1434; 23 September 1993). *SAPP,* no. 39.

"Ukaz Prezidenta Rossiiskoi Federatsii Ob upravlenii gosudarstvennym sotsial'nym strakhovaniem v Rossiiskoi Federatsii" (no. 1503; 28 September 1993). *SAPP,* no. 40.

"Polozhenie o Tsentral'noi izbiratel'noi komissii po vyboram v Gosudarstvennuiu Dumu Federal'nogo Sobraniia Rossiiskoi Federatsii v 1993 godu" (29 September 1993). *SAPP,* no. 40.

"Ukaz Prezidenta Rossiiskoi Federatsii Ob utverzhdenii utochnennoi redaktsii Polozheniia o vyborakh deputatov Gosudarstvennoi dumy v 1993 godu i vnesenii izmenenii i dopolnenii v Polozhenie o federal'nykh organakh vlasti na perekhodnyi period" (no. 1557; 1 October 1993). *RV,* no. 197 (366); *SAPP,* no. 41.

"Polozhenie o vyborakh deputatov gosudarstvennoi dumy v 1993 godu." *RV,* no. 197 (366); *SAPP,* no. 41.

"Ukaz Prezidenta Rossiiskoi Federatsii O vvedenii chrezvychainogo polozheniia v gorode Moskve" (no. 1575; 3 October 1993). *RV,* 5 October 1993; *SAPP,* no. 40.

"Ukaz Prezidenta Rossiiskoi Federatsii Ob osvobozhdenii Rutskogo A. V. ot dolzhnosti vitse-prezidenta Rossiiskoi Federatsii." *SAPP,* no. 40.

"Ukaz Prezidenta Rossiiskoi Federatsii O prekrashchenii polnomochii Moskovskogo gorodskogo Soveta narodnykh deputatov, Zelenogradskogo gorodskogo Soveta narodnykh deputatov, raionnykh Sovetov narodnykh deputatov, poselkovykh i sel'skogo Sovetov narodnykh deputatov v g. Moskve" (no. 1594; 7 October 1993). *SAPP,* no. 41.

"Ukaz Prezidenta Rossiiskoi Federatsii O poriadke naznacheniia i osvodozhdeniia ot dolzhnosti glav administratsii kraev, oblastei, avtonomnoi oblasti avtonomnykh okrugov, gorodov federal'nogo znacheniia" (no. 1597; 7 October 1993). *RG,* 9 October 1993; *SAPP,* no. 41.

"Ukaz Prezidenta Rossiiskoi Federatsii O pravovom regulirovanii v period poetapnoi konstitutsionnoi reformy v Rossiiskoi Federatsii" (no. 1598; 7 October 1993). *RG,* 9 October 1993; *SAPP,* no. 41.

"Ukaz Prezidenta Rossiiskoi Federatsii O Konstitutsionnom sude Rossiiskoi Federatsii" (no. 1612; 7 October 1993). *RG,* 9 October 1993.

"Ukaz Prezidenta Rossiiskoi Federatsii O reforme predstavitel'nykh organov vlasti i organov mestnogo samoupravleniia v Rossiiskoi Federatsii" (no. 1617; 9 October 1993). *SAPP,* no. 41.

"Postanovlenie Tsentral'noi Izbiratel'noi Kommissii po vyboram v Gosudarstvennuiu Dumu Federal'nogo Sobraniia Rossiiskoi Federatsii Ob utverzhdenii skhemy odnomandatnykh izbiratel'nykh okrugov po vyboram v Gosudarstvennuiu Dumu i ee opublikovanii v pechati" (no. 7; 10 October 1993); and "Skhema odnomandatnykh izbiratel'nykh okrugov po vyboram v Gosudarstvennuiu Dumu v 1993 godu." *RG,* 13 October 1993.

"Ukaz Prezidenta Rossiiskoi Federatsii O vyborakh v Sovet Federatsii Federal'nogo Sobraniia Rossiiskoi Federatsii" (no. 1626; 11 October 1993). *RG,* 12 October 1993; *RV,* 21 October 1993; *SAPP,* no. 42.

"Polozhenie o vyborakh deputatov Soveta Federatsii Federal'nogo sobraniia Rossiiskoi Federatsii v 1993 godu." *RV*, 21 October 1993; *SAPP*, no. 42.

"Ukaz Prezidenta Rossiiskoi Federatsii O vnesenii izmenenii i dopolnenii v Polozhenie o federal'nykh organakh vlasti na perekhodnyi period" (no. 1625; 11 October 1993). *RG*, 13 October 1993; *RV*, 21 October 1993; *SAPP*, no. 42.

"Rasporiazhenie Prezidenta Rossiiskoi Federatsii Ob obrazovanii Gosudarstvennoi palaty Konstitutsionnogo soveshchaniia," "Polozhenie o Gosudarstvennoi palate Konstitutsionnogo soveshchaniia," "Rasporiazhenie Prezidenta Rossiiskoi Federatsii Ob utverzhdenii Polozheniia ob Obshchestvennoi palate Konstitutsionnogo soveshchaniia," "Polozhenie ob Obshchestvennoi palate Konstitutsionnogo soveshchaniia" (11 October 1993). *SAPP*, no. 42.

"Ukaz Prezidenta Rossiiskoi Federatsii O provedenii vsenarodnogo golosovaniia po proektu Konstitutsii Rossiiskoi Federatsii" (no. 1633; 15 October 1993). *RV*, 21 October 1993; *SAPP*, no. 42.

"Polozhenie o vsenarodnom golosovanii po proektu Konstitutsii Rossiiskoi Federatsii 12 dekabria 1993 goda." *RV*, 21 October 1993; *SAPP*, no. 42.

"Ukaz Prezidenta Rossiiskoi Federatsii O nekotorykh merakh po obespecheniiu gosudarstvennoi i obshchestvennoi bezopasnosti v period provedeniia izbiratel'noi kampanii 1993 goda" (no. 1661; 19 October 1993). *SAPP*, no. 43.

"Ukaz Prezidenta Rossiiskoi Federatsii O sovershenstvovanii deiatel'nosti mezhvedomstvennykh komissii Soveta bezopasnosti Rossiiskoi Federatsii" (no. 1686; 20 October 1993). *SAPP*, no. 43.

"Ukaz Prezidenta Rossiiskoi Federatsii O chlenakh Soveta bezopasnosti Rossiiskoi Federatsii" (no. 1688; 20 October 1993). *SAPP*, no. 43.

"Ukaz Prezidenta Rossiiskoi Federatsii Ob osnovnykh nachalakh organizatsii gosudarstvennoi vlasti v sub"ektakh Rossiiskoi Federatsii" (no. 1723; 22 October 1993). *RV*, 26 October 1993.

"Polozhenie ob osnovnykh nachalakh organizatsii i deiatel'nosti organov gosudarstvennoi vlasti kraev, oblastei, gorodov federal'nogo znacheniia, avtonomnoi oblasti, avtonomnykh okrugov Rossiiskoi Federatsii na period poetapnoi konstitutsionnoi reformy." *RV*, 26 October 1993.

"Postanovlenie Soveta Ministrov—Pravitel'stva Rossiiskoi Federatsii: Voprosy Fonda sotsial'nogo strakhovaniia Rossiiskoi Federatsii" (no. 1094; 26 October 1993). *SAPP*, no. 44.

"Ukaz Prezidenta Rossiiskoi Federatsii O reforme mestnogo samoupravleniia v Rossiiskoi Federatsii" (no. 1760; 26 October 1993). *RV*, 29 October 1993.

"Polozhenie ob osnovakh organizatsii mestnogo samoupravleniia v Rossiiskoi Federatsii na period poetapnoi konstitutsionnoi reformy." *RV*, 29 October 1993.

"Ukaz Prezidenta Rossiiskoi Federatsii O proekte Konstitutsii Rossiiskoi Federatsii, predstavliaemom na vsenarodnoe golosovanie" (no. 1845; 6 November 1993). *RV*, 10 November 1993.

"Konstitutsiia Rossiiskoi Federatsii (Proekt)." *RV*, 10 November 1993.

"Ukaz Prezidenta Rossiiskoi Federatsii Ob utochnenii Polozheniia o vyborakh deputatov Gosudarstvennoi dumy v 1993 godu i Polozheniia o vyborakh deputatov Soveta Federatsii Federal'nogo sobraniia Rossiiskoi Federatsii v 1993 godu" (no. 1846; 6 November 1993). *RV*, 10 November 1993.

"Postanovlenie Tsentral'noi izbiratel'noi komissii Rossiiskoi Federatsii O rezul'tatakh vsenarodnogo golosovaniia po proektu Konstitutsii Rossiiskoi Federatsii." *RG*, 25 December 1993.

"Postanovlenie Tsentral'noi izbiratel'noi komissii Rossiiskoi Federatsii Ob ustanovlenii obshchikh itogov vyborov deputatov Gosudarstvennoi Dumy Federal'nogo Sobraniia Rossiiskoi Federatsii." *RG*, 28 December 1993.

"Postanovlenie Tsentral'noi izbiratel'noi komissii Rossiiskoi Federatsii O dopolnitel'nom vydvizhenii kandidatov v deputaty Soveta Federatsii i Gosudarstvennoi Dumy Federal'nogo Sobraniia Rossiiskoi Federatsii i o naznachenii povtornykh vyborov deputatov Gosudarstvennoi Dumy Federal'nogo Sobraniia Rossiiskoi Federatsii v Respublike Tatarstan." *RG*, 31 December 1993.

INDEX

John Löwenhardt is Senior Lecturer in Politics and
Coordinator of the Russian Studies Program at the
Institute of East European Law and Russian Studies,
Leiden University. Among his many books are *The
Russian Politburo: History, Profile and Mode of
Operation*, and *Decision Making in Soviet Politics*.
He is coauthor of *The Rise and Fall of the Soviet
Politburo*.

Library of Congress Cataloging-in-Publication Data
Löwenhardt, John.
The reincarnation of Russia : struggling with the
legacy of communism, 1990–1994 / by John
Löwenhardt.
Includes bibliographical references (p.   ) and index.
ISBN 0-8223-1606-4. — ISBN 0-8223-1623-4 (pbk.)
1. Russia (Federation)—Politics and government—
1991– 2. Post-communism—Russia (Federation)
3. Russia (Federation)—Social conditions.   I. Title.
JN6692.L69   1995
947.086—dc20   94-38510   CIP